AMERICA'S NIGHT

No
COLORS

100 Ways to
STOP GANGS
from Taking Away
Our Communities

NCPCV

National Center for the Prevention of Community Violence

BOBBY KIPPER
& BUD RAMEY

NEW YORK

AMERICA'S NIGHTMARE
No colors

100 Ways to **STOP GANGS** *from Taking Away Our Communities*

by BOBBY KIPPER & BUD RAMEY

© 2012 BOBBY KIPPER & BUD RAMEY. All rights reserved.

No part of this publication may be reproduced or transmitted in any form or by any means, mechanical or electronic, including photocopying and recording, or by any information storage and retrieval system, without permission in writing from author or publisher (except by a reviewer, who may quote brief passages and/or show brief video clips in a review).

Disclaimer: The Publisher and the Author make no representations or warranties with respect to the accuracy or completeness of the contents of this work and specifically disclaim all warranties, including without limitation warranties of fitness for a particular purpose. No warranty may be created or extended by sales or promotional materials. The advice and strategies contained herein may not be suitable for every situation. This work is sold with the understanding that the Publisher is not engaged in rendering legal, accounting, or other professional services. If professional assistance is required, the services of a competent professional person should be sought. Neither the Publisher nor the Author shall be liable for damages arising herefrom. The fact that an organization or website is referred to in this work as a citation and/or a potential source of further information does not mean that the Author or the Publisher endorses the information the organization or website may provide or recommendations it may make. Further, readers should be aware that internet websites listed in this work may have changed or disappeared between when this work was written and when it is read.

ISBN 978-1-61448-099-0 (paperback)
ISBN 978-1-61448-100-3 (eBook)
Library of Congress Control Number: 2011934903

Published by:
MORGAN JAMES PUBLISHING
The Entrepreneurial Publisher
5 Penn Plaza, 23rd Floor
New York City, New York 10001
(212) 655-5470 Office
(516) 908-4496 Fax
www.MorganJamesPublishing.com

Cover Design by:
Rachel Lopez
rachel@r2cdesign.com

Interior Design by:
Bonnie Bushman
bbushman@bresnan.net

In an effort to support local communities, raise awareness and funds, Morgan James Publishing donates one percent of all book sales for the life of each book to Habitat for Humanity.
Get involved today, visit
www.HelpHabitatForHumanity.org.

Dedication

Father Gregory Boyle

"It is when we can move ourselves 'from judgment —
to awe,' that we should begin."

As we were preparing this compilation for publication, we were listening to the *NPR* radio program *On Point*, with a live audience out of *KCLU* studio in Santa Barbara. Host Tom Ashbrook had an amazing guest in his studio, Father Gregory Boyle.

Father Boyle, or "Father G" as they call him on the street, is a Jesuit priest and director and founder of *Homeboy Industries,* which assists at-risk, recently released and formerly gang involved youth to become contributing members of their communities.

Listening to this interview, we were absolutely inspired by his views on gangs.

Father G. believes that jobs "do about 85% of what needs to happen to reclaim a life of someone who has joined a gang."

He dispels the myth that there are severe penalties for dropping out of a gang. "It's a myth that somehow people will hunt you down simply because you have stepped away…"

In fact, he views the gang as a kid thing and chides older gang members for "still doing" that as an adult.

A reformed gang member on the program described her life experience as having never matured after joining the gang as part of her family as a little kid. Gang members have a kid mentality and many never grow up.

And he notes that gangs are the places kids go when their lives have encountered misery. And misery loves company.

"They have had to carry a lot more than I have had to carry," Father G notes. "I stand in awe of what they have had to carry."

And it is when we can move ourselves "from judgment — to awe," that we should begin. We must stop believing that there are lives out there that are less valuable than ours. We need to stand with those who are demonized so that the demonizing will stop. It's an illusion, he says, when "we talk about *them*. It's just… *us*."

It is to the spirit that Father Gregory Boyle brings to the national gang crisis that we dedicate *No COLORS*.

Hector Verdugo, associate executive director of Homeboy Industries, said at the 2011 Orlando gang summit, "Our biggest problem is the funding." The lack of funding has produced a three-month waiting list among the 8,000 gang members who come to Homeboy Industries in LA annually to build a new life.

Contents

Foreword

What we learn in this life of sending and receiving messages is that some of them appeal primarily to the intellect while others go straight to the heart. The best manage to span the distance between.

No COLORS is one of those bridges that connect our minds and emotions, yet it also strikes something else that lies deep within all of us. It touches our notion of community and our primal sense of home, because at its core, *No COLORS* is about the places we live, collectively and individually. More specifically, it's about the devastating changes that can and have occurred in those places as the result of gang-related youth violence.

It touches our notion of community and our primal sense of home...

The intense and unwavering light that Bud Ramey and Bobby Kipper shine on this subject illuminates a world that many of us thought existed only in the news and other media. In reading through the pages of *No COLORS*, we are reminded again and again that this world now surrounds us whether we live in the densest urban setting, the most orderly suburb or even a bucolic rural haven. And when I say "reminded" I am speaking with a gentleness unrelated to the issue at hand because *No COLORS* grabs us by the collar, turns our head around and holds our face to a passing scene that ranges from inconvenient and troublesome to dangerous and even lethal. But the hope, and equally important, the practical tools that the book provides, let us know that the view need not be permanent.

Part of defining where *No COLORS* fits into the growing canon of gang and youth violence literature can be best accomplished by describing what it isn't. And what it isn't includes an academic tome, a list of government statistics and an ex-gang member's memoir. It isn't the latest news on behavioral development, law enforcement or public health, nor is it the final word on the subject from the perspectives of education or criminal justice.

What *No COLORS* is falls more closely into the area of a direction finder and a guide. It gives community and business leaders, elected and appointed officials, educators, clergy, opinion leaders and everyone else who has a stake in the future, clear instructions for constructing a Strategic Plan. Just as essential, it provides the building materials needed, in the form of tactics, best practices and specific interventions, to help municipalities across America and Canada stand against gang-generated crime.

Ultimately, this book, and the significant research and effort on which it is based, represents the many voices and experiences, including their own, that Ramey and Kipper have brought together to share with you. I hope you will read it carefully. At the very least it will inform you. At best it will enlighten you. And if you are open to its compelling message, my hope for you and for your community is that it will move you to action. ***Tom Emswiller*** *San Jose, California*

• PART ONE •

AMERICA'S NIGHTMARE

---

*"Gangs don't just show
up in a community.
They are allowed to grow there."*

The Problem

On summer nights under the lights of the South Morrison field in Newport News, the sound of gunshots punctuated almost every adult league softball game.

From time to time, gang members as young as ten would race past the field, running from something, or someone, unseen. Later, an ambulance siren would cast a flashing red light on the field as the EMTs worked expertly, but sometimes futilely, over another kid who took a bullet.

Both of us spent a quarter century living in the same town, watching gangs slowly take over our city — a problem unacknowledged by the community for years.

It takes a while.

In consulting across the country, we continue to see a strong element of denial almost everywhere. The biggest struggle initially in communities is in countering the disbelief that gangs are a clear and present threat.

So two people who played softball, and who happened to be a seasoned cop and a public affairs specialist respectively, began collaborating, beginning with the compilation of the tactics, approaches and best practices being deployed to combat gangs and youth violence both at home and internationally.

Our hope is that the good and well-intended people who see this book will arrive at the conclusion that, yes, we must deal with the crisis in our community, and yes, in doing so we can be effective and creative and can even find the experience itself rewarding.

At first, creating anti-gang strategies seems intimidating, one of those things best left up to the police and other authorities. But few if any problems experienced in a community can be solved without a broader-based, as well as a personal, involvement. And the stakes are high. At its basis, this effort is focused on saving a generation of youth from the streets, for a nation that needs their involvement desperately. So make the decision to act an easy one. Make it about those kids. That's our hope for them and we know it's your hope, also.

It's about re-claiming and strengthening your community's original legacy.

And in the simplest of terms, hope is what this book is about. It's about re-claiming and strengthening your community's original legacy.

We offer a clear, well-lit pathway for making significant headway against the youth violence crisis in our communities. We also offer the reminder that while the loss of potential represented by young people in gangs is tragic, there are other critical issues to consider.

This is much more than a melancholy episode in the growth of your hometown. It's all on the line here. The presence of gang activity affects the value of homes in a violence-plagued environment resulting in subsequent flight that affects everything from the diversity and viability of neighborhoods to who goes to public schools.

This is much more than a melancholy episode in the growth of your hometown. It's all on the line here.

Similarly, violence and the threat of violence impacts businesses and can result in the loss of jobs. Gangs erode our school system, which feeds into the continuum of neighborhood dissolution.

Youth violence and gangs also add significantly to the unsustainable cost of incarcerating so many young people.

And of course, the direct relationship between gangs and drugs helps create an economy that yields no taxes. So beyond the loss of life and potential there is damage to our collective and individual quality of life. And returning full cycle, it's increasingly clear that the local police can't solve the problem alone.

We believe the "deer in headlights" reaction by most disinterested adults is closely related to the lack of community leadership with regard to acknowledging the problem, and then articulating clear strategies to deal with it.

We continue to be mystified by this phenomenon of why a responsible city leader or official would stick his or her head in the sand and allow the community to implode around them.

We were always taught to name our problem and to wrestle power from it. Give it a name and you begin to take away its power: Bullying, Global Warming, White Flight, the Achievement Gap, Racial Profiling, Youth Violence.

In the past, youth violence was perceived almost exclusively as an inner city problem. We called it a "gang problem" and limited to the projects. Not anymore. Ask any Californian. Just as California has historically proven to be bell weather for a wide range of cultural issues, the state began to recognize the problem two decades ago and many areas have made significant progress.

Now, it's "youth violence" they are tackling and it has few if any geographic boundaries.

If you hold to the "misery loves company" school of thought there may be some comfort in noting that this phenomenon is happening all over the world - in Canada, South America, Central America, Mexico, Great Britain, in Europe, in Australia, in Asia. But, when it's happening in your neighborhood, that's small comfort, indeed.

Rising gang crime is threatening democratic development and slowing economic growth across Central America and Mexico. Increasingly sophisticated gang networks are taking over. Whereas gang activity used to be territorially confined to local neighborhoods, globalization, sophisticated communications technologies and travel patterns have facilitated the expansion of gang activity across neighborhoods, cities and countries.

The monikers of *MS-13* and other international gangs now appear in communities throughout the United States, Central America and Mexico.

When we examine the common denominator of severe gang problems, it's the big money in drugs. We would like to repeat that for emphasis. It's the big money in drugs, especially as many gangs branch out from retail sales into the wholesale area.

One can look at de-criminalization efforts such as in Holland and conclude that taking the money out of the equation has definitely softened the gang problem in terms of violent behavior. But not completely, as the gangs still get their share, preying on those who produce the product.

It takes a while.

The Denial

If you think that "it can't happen here" keep in mind that "here" is now almost every community in America. Shocked residents of previous havens of peaceful living are now being forced to admit that we have an issue with youth violence and gangs, while many law enforcement experts are describing the wave as growing larger than they can handle.

The National Gang Center reports approximately 27,900 gangs. Other surveys estimate that we have over 1,000,000 gang members in the United States.

While gang problems are most widespread in the largest cities in the United States, the National Gang Center also identifies the frightening growth of gangs in suburban and rural areas.

... "here" is now almost every community in America.

And in case the ongoing nature of the violence lulls us into a numb acceptance, the spikes of brutality continue to grab our attention:

- In Chicago last year, according to *NPR*, almost 700 children were hit by gunfire. Recent reports place the gang membership in Chicago at over 100,000.

- In Richmond, VA, an entire family was found murdered in their home on New Year's Day 2006. This violent and senseless event caused the entire community to wake up to the fact that Richmond had become one of America's top five cities for murder per capita. A community-wide Strategic Plan was drawn up.

- In California, Governor Arnold Schwarzenegger, shortly after taking office, summarized the violence crisis in his state.

"A growing number of Californians are living a nightmare. Trapped inside their homes, afraid to come out unless they absolutely have to. That's because in many of our cities, whole neighborhoods are

terrorized and intimidated by street gangs. Kids are scared to go to school and parents are terrified for their safety."

Community-wide Strategic Plans became commonplace in municipalities throughout California.

- In New London, CT, in late fall 2010, six bored teenage gang members stabbed a helpless 25-year-old citizen to death because, as they later claimed, they had nothing to do. A community-wide Strategic Plan resulted.

- In Minneapolis, the business community moved into action when an article in the *New York Times* nicknamed their city *Murderapolis*. An effective Strategic Plan was put into place.

- In Newport News, VA, we now have gang members whose parents and grandparents were members of the same gang. One gang members' initiation requires the recruit to shoot someone. Another gang requires the prospect to have served time in jail. After three years of slow community acceptance that there was a problem, or if it mattered, this Virginia city is finally developing a Strategic Plan to address the 188 identified gang sets and more than 2,400 gang members who are taking over their neighborhoods.

- In Denver, diligent community leaders worked for four years to gather the united community consensus and strength to attract federal assistance and combat the 8,800 gang members in the city. A focused Strategic Plan evolved.

These and many other communities are crying out – emergency sessions, committees forming, proposals surfacing on what to do. What is the root cause of this? How can we fix this problem?

When this subject is discussed, it will be emotional. The discourse will reveal all the frailties and faults and flaws of the community. There will be consensus and there will be quarrels. This is very predictable as you begin to protect future generations from our mistakes.

You can deal with the youth violence that is taking over your community now, or deal with it later — after the coming tragedy gets your attention.

Finally we will awaken.

It takes a while.

Former Justice Department Official Robert Flores summed it up.

"Gangs are a sign of community dysfunction… gangs don't just show up one day in a community. They are allowed to grow there."

We are quickly becoming victim to a homegrown insurgency that shows no signs of stopping. Many have labeled the rapid growth of terrorism "a silent insurgency."

The sad reality is that most gang-related crime and violence traditionally did not go beyond the boundaries of many of our inner cities. So when it first appears, we always assign it as a law enforcement issue.

We are being repetitive for the reason that it bears repeating: this is not a police problem. It's not a City Council problem. It is not a school problem. It is not a problem you can leave alone since it does not affect your neighborhood.

It's a community problem and if we leave it unaddressed it will slowly collapse our community.

The traditional gang role of spray-painting buildings has evolved into spraying bullets into all parts of our communities.

More affluent neighborhoods all over the planet are now feeling the rapid movement of drug and gang-related crime and violence. We now have achieved the realization that gang wars have no boundaries. Many of the upscale neighborhoods have awakened as drive-by shootings, home invasions and other forms of gang-related crime and violence hit close to home. Exasperation has arrived.

Urban flight to avoid violent crime is no longer a sure bet to escape the rapid spread of senseless violence that follows the intense new level of gang involvement.

Why Now?

Many wonder why the gang insurgency has grown so rapidly. Others argue that gangs have always been a problem — so why is there is so much attention to it now?

America is a nation where it is estimated that 7.3 million children have a parent in prison, jail, on probation or on parole. Things do finally sink in.

It takes a while.

Sheriff Gabe Morgan, the outspoken elected Sheriff in Newport News, VA often testifies before Congressional panels. He said in a presentation to the Mayor's Task Force on the Prevention of Youth Violence in early 2011 that most of the people he has in his jail — will be coming home.

"And, most of the people in state penitentiaries will be coming home. Most of the people in federal prisons will be coming home. Only life sentences and death penalty felons will not be coming home. And the invisible penal system comes with them," Morgan said.

"They get $25 and a bus ticket," Morgan said.

He explained that because of their record, they cannot get a job. In most cases, they cannot vote. What can we expect them to do? And they are flowing back into our communities every day. Naturally, they will have little choice but to find their way back onto the streets – most likely in a predatory way.

Morgan explained his view on incarceration in terms everyone can understand.

"We have to decide as a society, once we find someone guilty of a societal offense, whether we're "just mad at that person" or whether we're "afraid of that person," Morgan said.

> *We have to decide as a society… whether we're "just mad at that person", or whether we're "afraid of that person."*

Morgan noted that we should then provide an alternative to incarceration for those we are just mad at, and jail the ones we are afraid of. That sounds simple, but it's the core direction we must take.

Youth violence is not occurring in just a few communities. It is an epidemic that is spreading across America, Canada and, in fact, the world. We are rapidly gaining speed, inexorably racing to an end that is both uncertain and frightening.

We have watched with apparent disinterest as three generations of youth grow up on the streets –kids from poverty with broken family structures and no positive alternative to the pull of drugs, gangs, guns and eventually, prison.

The mentors, the role models available to these kids, are a steady flow of released professional criminals coming home from Gladiator School.

The criminal college we call the U.S. prison system continues to crank out professional gang members every day. With well over 2 million men currently incarcerated, America has the highest total prison and jail population in the world. And as we punish our offenders by sending them into this system, they inevitably return with "a record," un-employability and renewed street life skills.

The level of denial and the glacial movement toward remedy is reminiscent of the 1940s and 1950's, a time when our fighting forces in World War II received cigarettes in their C-rations, athletes endorsed cigarettes and doctors, who were often smokers themselves, recommended that their patients smoke as a way of relaxing.

Then, curiously, we spent a decade arguing whether or not smoking resulted in lung cancer. The Surgeon General had his say, the millions of premature deaths got the attention of the public and we figured it out.

It takes a while.

That is exactly where we are in America today – beginning to figure it out – as we experience a few million young people in gangs, gunshots ringing out in all parts of thousands of communities and the emergency rooms treating a steady flow of gunshot victims.

All this, and your kid is sitting next to a Blood in math class.

All this, and your kid is sitting next to a Blood in math class. So you begin to understand. The dictates of conscience will reveal your role in re-shaping this idea of community.

Warning Signs That Your Child or Student May Be Involved with a Gang

- Admits to "hanging out" with kids in gangs
- Shows an unusual interest in one or two particular colors of clothing or a particular logo
- Has an unusual interest in gangster-influenced music, videos, movies or websites
- Uses unusual hand signals to communicate with friends
- Has specific drawings or gang symbols on school books, clothing, walls or display tattoos
- Comes home with unexplained physical injuries (fighting-related bruises, injuries to hand/knuckles)
- Has unexplained cash or goods such as clothing or jewelry
- Carries a weapon
- Has trouble with the police
- Exhibits negative changes in behavior such as:
  - Withdrawing from family
  - Declining school attendance or performance
  - Staying out late without a reason
  - Displaying an unusual desire for secrecy
  - Exhibiting signs of drug use
  - Breaking rules consistently
  - Speaking in gang-style slang

Source: U.S. Department of Justice, COPS Office, and
National Center for the Prevention of Community Violence

NCPCV
National Center for the Prevention of Community Violence

Just How Bad Can This Get?

Home of the Free, But You Better Be Brave

As Tom Emswiller says in the Foreword to **No COLORS**, this book is about the places we live, collectively and individually. More specifically, it's about the devastating changes that can and have occurred in those places as the result of gang-related youth violence.

We now illuminate a world that many of us thought existed only in the news and other media.

In reading through the pages of **No COLORS**, we are reminded again and again that this world now surrounds us whether we live in the densest urban setting, the most orderly suburb or even a bucolic rural haven.

> *We now illuminate a world that many of us thought existed only in the news and other media.*

We seek to grab you by the collar turn your head around and holds your face to a passing scene that ranges from inconvenient and troublesome to dangerous and even lethal.

But the hope, and equally important, the practical tools that this book provides, let us know that the view need not be permanent.

Herman McCloud has not totally lost that hope. Not yet.

Herman has always looked forward to these days in his life. The former U.S. Marine, professional athlete, and small business owner envisioned the "good life" after he retired from owning two health clubs in Eastern Virginia.

His three-bedroom suburban home would be the perfect nest to finish out what had been a successful life and career.

15

At age 79, he works to maintain his health and fitness, remembering the days of old when he won the title of *Mr. Virginia* in a bodybuilding contest. At night he sits in his favorite chair glued to the *Fox News* channel to continue his track record as an extreme social conservative.

But these days Herman has begun to worry a great deal. Not about his 401K or the economy. Not even about his health. He worries about his safety.

While he lives in what has always proven to be a fairly safe suburban community neighborhood he now is beginning to wonder when he may become a statistic of crime and violence in his very own home.

"There have been 46 home invasion robberies in our city just this year" he declares as we sit in his den on a hot July evening.

"If they come in here I have got something for them," he relates while detailing the number of guns he possesses throughout his home. At night and all day long, his deadbolt is secure in place, the light stays on, and the former Marine lives in fear that gang members will put an end to his life-long dream of peace and tranquility.

The unfortunate story of Herman McCloud is not an isolated issue.

America is quickly becoming victim to a homegrown insurgency that shows no signs of stopping.

In Portland, OR in June 2011, Mayor Sam Adams leads foot patrols through tough streets, hot spots for gang violence. He has had enough. The group wants to take their message right to the gang members to let them know they won't stand for the violence any more.

KATU TV News reports that since the start of 2011, there have been 44 gang-related shootings in the city. The city's Gang Enforcement Team added six new officers to help fight the rise in violence.

Adams asked Portlanders to get involved in the foot patrols and help the community stand up against gangs.

The walk, probably one of many, is geared toward teaching volunteers how to recognize gang activity. Those volunteers will then start patrolling neighborhoods and reporting to the Police Bureau's gang unit what they see.

"They (gang members) don't know which day the foot patrol's out," Mayor Adams said. "This is about engaging people that you see on the street. And it's about picking up litter. It sends a message: 'this neighborhood cares.'"

No COLORS will shatter your belief that all is well in rural and suburban America. This book is about every community in the U.S. and Canada, and in fact, in the civilized world. According to the U.S. Justice Department, 100% of American cities with a population of over 250,000 have reported gang activity.

This number is rapidly growing in smaller communities as well — 85% with a population 100,000 to 229,000 report active gang activity while 65% of cities with a population of 50,000 to 100,000 report active gang activity, according to Justice.

America is nation in denial and at war with itself. The issue is so strong that it is now impacting national, state, and local economic structures.

Finally we awaken.

We are a nation in which it is estimated that 7,300,000 children have a parent in prison, jail, on probation or on parole. Oh… My… God.

In Ciudad Quetzal in Guatemala, everyday citizens are armed with bats, machetes, and guns. They line the road, block cars and signal people to get out. Riders have no choice but to do as they are told.

We are a nation in which it is estimated that 7,300,000 children have a parent in prison, jail, on probation or on parole.

Their masks and weapons are a fearful demonstration of force, but these aren't gangsters. These are crime fighters.

One man silently keeps his gun aimed on the passengers. Another performs a pat down, another searches the car, and still another narrates the whole experience. "We are the patrol of Ciudad Quetzal. We are participating in the fight against crime and delinquency. Thank you for your cooperation with this organized community." The other masked men (and supposedly a few women, though it's difficult to tell behind their masks) stand to the side of the road, signaling other cars to stop for inspection or pass on through.

Tico Times reports that these vigilantes call themselves *La Patrulla*, meaning "the patrol." Anonymous, mysterious, and technically outside of the law, members of *La Patrulla* pull over vehicles, perform personal searches and demand entry into homes of suspected gangsters. The militia was formed in late January in response to escalating gang violence that has been targeting businesses, schools, churches, and individuals. "Ya basta" – enough is enough – is a common mantra among the patrol's members.

"We are the patrol of Ciudad Quetzal. We are participating in the fight against crime and delinquency. Thank you for your cooperation with this organized community."

The newspaper reported that Ciudad Quetzal, a slum a few miles north of Guatemala City, has a long history of gang violence. For decades, gangs have charged a "tax" on just about anything that moves in the city, a process that involves an anonymous phone call with instructions for paying a large sum of money in exchange for "protection." The cost of not paying is well known: gunshots are heard nightly, and corpses appear regularly in the homes, shops, and streets of the city.

Fed up with ever-increasing demands for gang taxes, local bus companies stopped paying. The gangs' response was swift; two days later, a bomb exploded on a bus heading from the capital to Ciudad Quetzal, killing nine. A week later, two more buses were burned. Fear is a constant element in the areas surrounding the dangerous capital of Guatemala, growing worse even than in years past.

What Can Educators Do to Prevent Student Gang Involvement?

- Know your students
- Observe students for signs of changing attitudes and personalities
- Be aware of attendance issues include truancy and tardiness
- Be aware of sudden or gradual academic performance changes
- Stay current on student trends including style, music, etc.
- Be aware of students communicating with hand signals
- Refer "at-risk" students to internal or external services
- Be aware of graffiti on books, lockers, clothes, etc.
- Talk openly about gang-related issues and concerns
- Document and report issues to administration, security, law enforcement and parents

The attacks have put Guatemala's gang problem in the international spotlight. President Alvaro Colom has responded by initiating a massive military presence in Ciudad Quetzal. Every bus traveling in or out is accompanied by two police officers (one at the front, one at the rear), and camouflage-clad soldiers now nearly outnumber street vendors.

At the National Gang Symposium in Orlando in 2011, one of the clear trends discussed was the growth of gangs near the Mexican border with the U.S.

Combine that with a Supreme Court order for California to release 33,000 prisoners.

And across America, stunned community leaders and law enforcement officials react to the migration of gangs into what many would label as "country club communities."

Police agencies nationwide are facing a cutback in resources to include gang-related education and training. The traditional means of slowing or stopping the gang movement – enforcement — is proving to be less than effective.

The nation's economic decline has made things even more difficult for big cities, like Chicago and Oakland.

Oakland is the currently one of California's worst gang and youth violence environments. Existing in a state that teeters on financial failure, this city is at the breaking point — with the state's highest homicide rate among big cities last year, 21.9 murders per 100,000 people, according to FBI figures.

In 2011, reports were issued that had the Oakland Police Department down to 650 officers from 800 a year previous. With the cutbacks, the department struggled to maintain law and order in high-crime neighborhoods like East Oakland.

Newly elected Mayor Jean Quan says more cops on the streets won't necessarily solve the crime problems. She says that Oakland will have to pay attention to how police are deployed and rely on intervention and prevention programs.

According to law enforcement experts, criminal gangs have moved from the level of graffiti to sophisticated drug cartels that rule many of our nation's neighborhoods from inner cities to suburban communities.

Local law enforcement cannot control the situation alone, so they are left to depend on state and federal task forces that work to break up powerful drug networks ruled by gangs that have woven into the business and political structure of many communities across America.

Before a community can engage fully in this effort, we believe there must be an underlying confidence in the community leaders.

Law enforcement efforts are hampered in many communities by the level of fear and intimidation that the gangs have instilled in citizens within the neighborhoods. Gang

Before a community can engage fully in this effort, we believe there must be an underlying confidence in the community leaders.

members in some cases have become the street lords in the neighborhoods where they are feared and given a style of respect through fear.

At the same time, they express a level of arrogance toward local law enforcement and their abilities to contain the problem. In one community we worked with, a gang leader phoned the local police precinct and warned the police not to step foot in his neighborhood or they would be shot.

Another example is Chicago.

Following the tragic death of an infant child being held by his father, the Chicago Police Department decided to hold a news conference to detail the incident. The conference attended by high level police officials had to be halted when gunfire from rival gangs began to ring out chasing everyone to shelter.

A high profile police event stopped cold at the hands of those who have no fear of the police or the power they possess. In many communities our police are outnumbered, out armed and not equipped to deal with the war they are asked to fight on a daily basis. This leaves communities feeling helpless.

It's been estimated that Chicago has over 100,000 gang members.

The gang insurgency issue is a national dilemma, but despite gifted and dedicated leadership at the Justice Department, funding has been greatly reduced and the burden is being delegated for the most part to local communities to solve.

Many would wonder why the gang insurgency has grown so rapidly, seemingly all over the planet.

Columnist Paul Greenberg wrote a syndicated column appearing around the United Kingdom in May 2010.

"The UK now has the highest drug usage in Europe, the highest incidence of sexually transmitted disease, the highest number of single mothers and that marriage is all but defunct, except for the toffs, upscale gays and Muslims. The whole country seems to have become downwardly mobile. Britain now has become an example to beware, not emulate.

Greenberg asked the big question.

"How can a country restore the very culture of a country, once it's been allowed to deteriorate?"

A June 2011 special report in the *Sydney Morning Herald* notes that in Glasgow, Scotland's biggest city, a stabbing occurs every six hours — and many more go unreported. The weapon of choice for many centuries has been the knife.

Survey after survey, from the World Health Organization to the United Nations, identifies Glasgow as one of the most violent cities in Western Europe. Among young males aged between 10 and 29, the rate of homicide is similar to Argentina, Costa Rica and Lithuania. Alcohol-related death rates are three times the British average while Scots have one of the lowest life expectancies in Europe.

Holland has deployed de-criminalization and has enjoyed relatively nonviolent experiences around illegal drugs for decades. Yet, despite growing discontent with the presence of marijuana coffee shops, 80% of Dutch, in a November 2008 poll, opposed the closure of the 730 shops — which pay 300 million euros each year in taxes. In many cases these establishments are fronts for organized crime. Gangs prey on them. Novices who think they can make easy money by setting up cannabis farms are preyed upon. They can't go to the law, so they arm themselves.

Yet public anger about tolerant drug laws is mounting, along the French and Belgian borders where rows of coffee shops sell to thousands of drug tourists. In 2008, Amsterdam's civic fathers shut 43 of the city's 228 coffee shops as they were "close to schools." Coffee shops offer a range of different cannabis products — which cannot be mixed with tobacco, which is now illegal to smoke in public places.

Go figure that one.

"You are standing at the precipice, the crisis is on your doorstep." That is how Dr. Mark Toten began his address to the Gang Summit in Prince George, Canada. With a Doctorate in Sociology, Dr. Toten is working with groups across the country on developing multi-year gang prevention, intervention and suppression strategies.

"You are staring at a crisis, and the question is, do you have the political will to make a change? Punishing the bad guys is needed, but we need to do less of that and look at some of the other ideas we have put on the board."

"You are staring at a crisis, and the question is, do you have the political will to make a change?

Your Child and the Gang Continuum

- Serious Gang-Related Offense
- Identified Gang Affiliation
- Early Onset of Delinquency
- Lack of Peer Recognition
- Poor Academic History
- Poor School Attendance
- Lack of Community Connection
- Lack of Family Structure

Gang Violence is a Process — Not an Event.

NCPCV
National Center for the Prevention of Community Violence

How Are Communities Responding?

Yet, even in communities where the situation has become so apparently hopeless that people are moving away, there can and will be resistance. Rival politicians will take shots at the program. Especially if you are running for office and supported street-level gang intervention, like L.A. city councilperson Janice Hahn encountered in running for the 36th Congressional district seat in 2011.

In America's fractious dialogue and debate, politicians object because it provides a target or uncovers a vulnerable position. Others are calling a clarion summons to rise and react. Amid a growing slaughter of children on the streets, devoted community leaders are trying to calm everyone down.

Amid a growing slaughter of children on the streets, devoted community leaders are trying to calm everyone down.

Budget watchdogs claim the city cannot afford to tackle this problem, immunized by a lack of funds.

Bureaucrats claim that their programming is the measure of excellence and should not be sacrificed to make way for a different gang prevention process.

Bloggers will dissect every move.

Business leaders isolated from the streets of challenged neighborhoods wonder what the ruckus is about. There is a mentality running through communities that if "I haven't seen that where I live" that it's not an issue.

Dissenters in the community may try to bully the community back into a hard-nosed suppression environment only, "reducing government waste in prevention and interventions."

Los Angeles is a typical example. They have one of the worst youth violence problems in the nation. Who has not heard of Compton or South Central LA?

It takes a strong Mayor. Luckily, the anti-gang effort enjoys the unequivocal support of LA Mayor Antonio Villaraigosa. Ever since his school reform efforts were thwarted, Villaraigosa has taken to GRYD (Gang Reduction and Youth Development) as his new flagship policy effort. He routinely touts it as "among the most innovative in the U.S.," and has the habit of making lofty claims about GRYD's impact: "The program has reclaimed our city for our citizens."

This is not for sissies. Bloggers attack his every move.

Another example of community pushback is when citizens observe cronyism. Confusion reigned in Washington, D.C. in the summer of 2010 as news broke that Mayor Adrian M. Fenty's administration was poised to award a $400,000 non-bid contract to Peaceoholics, a nonprofit organization that was co-founded by one of the Mayor's friends and biggest supporters.

Ronald Moten, a strategist for Fenty's re-election campaign, is a co-founder of Peaceoholics. Since Fenty took office in 2007, Peaceoholics has received more than $10 million in city contracts, including several million dollars from Department of Youth Rehabilitation Services.

Now planners will be spending valuable time defending what they are doing, instead of being transparent and accountable in the first place.

California made the discovery early: create a comprehensive approach, with measurements built in. But across America today there still seem to be three types of community attitudes with regards to the issue of youth violence.

"Law enforcement cannot be blamed for family dysfunction, non-performing schools, and youth's disconnection from the community, a weak economy or any of the other factors that contribute to gang proliferation."

—Jack Calhoun, Senior Consultant at the YEF Institute

Denial

The first are communities in denial that will not acknowledge and deal with the problem.

Officials are stuck in neutral.

In some communities, political leaders, school officials and those in power treat the "G" word as a form of profanity. They even refrain from using the word "gang" to describe what is occurring.

It also resurfaces the myth that gangs are just a big city problem when in fact research has shown that gang presence continues to grow in smaller communities.

In Richmond, VA the city fathers awakened one day to the fact that they were a murder capital of the nation.

Then Attorney General Bob McDonnell, currently Virginia governor, stepped up with a Department of Justice intervention that still today is used as the most successful community intervention in the nation.

Communities That Now Acknowledge the Problem

This is a difficult road to take and requires some courage by the community leadership. It creates what is known as a Morton's Fork scenario — a choice between two equally unattractive alternatives — a dilemma.

You spend considerable taxpayer money. Maybe even re-deploy services, or increase local taxation. Or you give your community away to crime and gunfire.

(The Morton's Fork concept originated in 1487 under the rule of Henry the VII as a result of tax policy to ensure everyone paid taxes. Henry believed that the rich had plenty of money to buy things and they must have enough money to pay taxes. He also believed that the poor who bought very little had saved their money, and thus had money with which to pay taxes. (Forks only had two prongs in the 15th century.)

Another way communities are dealing with the issue is by throwing disjointed services at the issue. Many believe by simply increasing recreation and youth opportunities, a community will stop the tide of gang expansion. This is a symptom of a community that has not developed a Strategic Plan. What occurs is the episodic loss of episodic services — based on the whims of the budget or political motives.

Even worse is the situation where the community's gang problem is at the direction of a single official or at the mercy of the bureaucracy.

In Madera, CA, the numbers of documented gang members boggle the mind. Despite California's two decades long battle with gangs, Madera still stands out. It's a small city of 61,000 people where over 4,000 gang members roam the streets.

In Memphis, the struggle is intense, the gang situation is ugly. Just recently, leadership rallied around a thorough Strategic Plan – and now there is a hopeful note to the future of this great city.

It's not the number of gang members that is important. After all, when you are in a crisis situation, why count? What does that number mean, anyway? Is Memphis's problem worse than Denver's?

Denver acknowledges openly that it has 8,800 gang members? Does that really matter? So many cities acknowledge the problem, count gang members and hope the numbers drop next year because they have confidence in their police chief.

But this isn't just about enforcement.

Communities That Understand That Strategy is the First Step

A growing tide of communities that finally get it: create broad community involvement in the development, validation and implementation of a strategy.

Cities undertaking a comprehensive strategy are in essence moving toward and proclaiming a new social norm, which necessitates the involvement of many elements of the community.

They are starting to combat the gang issue on all fronts. They have learned the power of solutions-driven gang approach that is showing positive results.

"Once a gang problem is acknowledged, a thorough understanding of the nature, scope and dynamics of the problem is required. The problem must be regarded as systemic in the sense that activities of youth in gangs and community response to the gang problem are interactive," said Cynthia Jackson-Speight, Project Director of the Edgecombe-Nash, NC Gang Assessment.

The now retired Mayor Joe Frank of Newport News, VA took the first bold step in 2006, asking the prestigious race relations group *People to People* to look into the root causes of the violence and make recommendations on what needs to be done. This is exactly what a city needs to do to begin to recover from this crisis — admit the problem and involve the community in solutions.

As *No COLORS* concludes, there are many paths to success. Crisis broadens the opportunities for bold action.

There are no wrong paths for communities that bubble their strategy and plans up from the community, not down from City Hall.

TEN STEPS TO PREVENTING GANGS IN SCHOOLS

1. Train teachers and support staff on gangs and gang culture

2. Train teachers and staff on effective strategies to deal with disruptive students

3. Provide proper consequences for gang-style behavior and not just appearance

4. Provide effective mentoring programs for students from at-risk homes and communities

5. Provide necessary tutoring for poor performing students

6. Provide a consistent message on gang prevention

7. Teach students their legal responsibilities under the law

8. Provide conflict resolution training for all students

9. Design effective after school programs for all ages

10. Teach-Expect-Require all students and staff to converse using proper communication and language skills. Allowing "gangsta" style talk and expression leads to a "Street" and not an educational environment

NCPCV

National Center for the Prevention of Community Violence

What Is Working

An inspirational energy comes from community leaders who have figured out what to do or at the very least, where to begin: cities like Richmond, San Jose, Minneapolis, Raleigh, Denver and Boston. We can learn a great deal from their efforts.

First, the only communities feeling any measure of success against the gang crisis are those which have deployed a community-wide effort, starting with a Strategic Plan. This effort cannot come from City Hall down. It must come from the community and be administered by the community.

Second, the strategy must attack the problem on four different fronts. Knitting together fundamental investments in prevention, intervention, enforcement and re-entry (*P.I.E.R.*) seems to be the only documented way to make significant strides. You cannot arrest your way out of the problem. It just does not work. As we can't overemphasize, it is not a law enforcement issue. It's a community issue.

On June 16, 2011, the San Jose Mayor's Gang Prevention Task Force presented their Strategic Work Plan for 2011–2013 to the city's Public Safety, Finance and Strategic Support Committee, with recommendations for resource allocation and direct interventions. Immediately the report in its entirety was posted on the Internet site. The disciplined transparency has been a key formula for success in San Jose.

Third, measure everything. Detailed measurements and independent evaluations are engineered into the plan and the metrics for success for each initiative. It is brilliant, effective, inclusive and not easy.

"They have already begun recruiting youths, parents, faith communities, businesses, grassroots groups and others to conduct a community-wide assessment of needs and resources, marshaling those who must play a role in reducing youth violence in the city. They want a full inventory of what programs, activities

and resources are available to city youths, and then they want to plot their times and locations against juvenile crimes and altercations that have occurred."

—New London, CT December 26, 2010

A fascinating white paper from the California Cities Gang Prevention Coalition takes a look at patterns over the years and noted some common factors with struggling communities:

The report noted that cities in California which are struggling with gang prevention efforts are communities where one of four problems exists:

- Mayor and police chief at odds
- Programs started with little or no connection to an overall plan
- Strategic disproportion (throwing money at enforcement, for example)
- Plan created by a single individual not by a planning body that represents the city as a whole

In cities where the Mayor does not lead, the municipal bureaucracy lacks certainty and a timid, limited plan often results.

Yet we can no longer rely on government agencies to fix this because now, after twenty years of study, we know for a fact it does not work.

Leadership within the community must reach beyond their comfort level and involve individuals who could provide valuable insight and resources to address the issue, minds unclouded by entrenched beliefs or the prejudice of long-established emotions.

A community's involvement must begin with its leadership. Local political, business and faith-based leaders must unite in an effort to bring a broad form of change.

It is important that community leaders be on the same page. The police chief should not be the only community leader making noise about gang issues. With the active, organized involvement of a joint leadership effort, a community will not only appear, but also act, in a concentrated effort.

This approach takes place in many different ways across America. But the good news is that it is beginning to take place — there is already an understood common bond to think and act beyond government.

There are communities that organize leadership task forces or summits. This is one way to bring people together in a concerted way.

As a strong community voice, civic organizations help spark action with consistently loud and articulate communications on the horrors of gang violence. A strong voluntary service organization has been a common denominator over the years in most communities that have been successful. This has been proven over and over again in California.

As a community begins this process, there is an underlying fear of finger pointing. This is unnecessary and inappropriate. The reality is that it is difficult to point out one risk factor that created the growth of gangs in a community. The years of denial are what they are. Looking back and wringing our hands has no benefit.

Local government leaders should not try to defend their actions but should embrace new opportunities for direct citizen involvement.

Looking back and wringing our hands has no benefit.

And we must remember that voluntary civic groups need to be recognized. It is easy for citizens to get frustrated when local government leaders do not identify them as a vital part of the solution.

Yet this should not be about who deserves funding or credit. Civic and government officials must enter into a new paradigm of team building to achieve what is in the best interest of the entire community.

It is then that the entire community becomes the overall winner.

In July 2011, Salisbury, MD got the good news that the $324,623 grant from the *Governor's Office of Crime Control and Prevention (GOCCP)* is secured; the *Safe Streets Coalition* will enter a third year.

DelmarvaNow reported that the countywide crime-fighting initiative, born in Annapolis, was implemented in 2009 in Salisbury and has reportedly lowered Part 1 violent crimes by 35%.

Salisbury is a different place today than where we were two and a half years ago," *GOCCP* Executive Director Kristen Mahoney noted at a press conference.

"The program is working because you are all relentless, you're being honest with each other, you're sharing information and you're holding each other accountable. Your citizens should be very proud because you're working very hard," *Delmarva* reported.

A Tale of Two Cities That Have Emerged as Cultivated National Models

San Jose

Some of the best news in California at the turn of 2011 involved significant drops in violent crimes during 2010. Cautious celebration among members of the gang prevention coalitions began as the statistics came in.

UC Berkeley criminologist Franklin Zimring, noted in news reports that a depressed economy usually portends a spike in violence.

"Everybody is amazed this year because the arrow is still pointing down," Zimring said.

The homicide rate in San Jose in 2010 was "as low as American big cities ever go," he noted. "More important, it's way down during a year when nobody had any reason to expect that.

San Jose had a good year. Jacob Stowell, a Massachusetts-based professor of criminology, pointed out that the number of police officers has gone down in San Jose along with killings. There were 1,365 sworn officers in 2000. Now, after several years of deficit-era budget cuts, with more to come, there are 1,252 officers.

Local officials gave clear credit to police and the city's comprehensive approach to gang prevention.

"While there are many factors that lead to a low homicide rate, credit must be given to the outstanding work of the San Jose Police Department and their diligence in solving homicides," said incoming District Attorney Jeff Rosen in the *Mercury News* report.

Mayor Chuck Reed agreed.

"That's good news to end the year with," said Mayor Chuck Reed, crediting his own gang prevention task force. He added, "both Salinas and L.A. have seen significant drops, and both cities have been implementing gang prevention programs like we have in San Jose, which has been a state and national model."

Over the last decade, the news has been up and down for San Jose. The celebration was tempered by a spate of gang turf murders in early 2011. Mayor Chuck Reed said he was "mystified" by the homicide trend because other violent crimes and property crimes have been trending downward.

But the trend lines over the decade are pure gold.

But the trend lines over the decade are pure gold.

They have committed to a sustained community-wide effort to tackle their tough gang problem and they have stuck with it. The desperate state of the economy in California jeopardizes the comprehensiveness of this city's initiatives.

There is clear progress in a state that has focused on community collaboration and involvement, strategic planning and steady funding of anti-gang initiatives.

In 2010, one community had already noticed the diligence and steadiness with which San Jose had been tackling the gang problem.

An outspoken activist group focused on race relations and quality of life sought an inside look at why San Jose's model is producing both a sense of community pride in gang prevention and measured successes year after year.

When youth violence began to escalate, the leadership of Newport News, VA's *People to People* sought insights by sending in freelance writer Tom Emswiller to view the inner workings of their highly acclaimed gang intervention program.

Tom, who lives in San Jose after a career in Denver, was eager to help with this assignment, as he is proud of his adopted community's efforts.

He was commissioned by *People to People* to go behind the media reports and talk to the people with "boots on the ground." He presented his findings to *People to People* in a white paper analysis.

San Jose is often cited as the most effective program in America, having been fine-tuning their measurements and processes for almost two decades. Over time, San Jose has reduced youth violence by almost half, and cut the school dropout rate.

It's a city with a population of 912,332, the tenth largest in America.

The city's initial plan, developed in 1991, has thrived through three Mayors, four city managers and three police chiefs.

The Mayor effectively delegates day-to-day staffing decisions for Parks and Recreation programs and the Police — but makes team members create tight liaisons with these departments. The key leverage, final authority of the city budget — is used to set aside funds each year for grants.

And most importantly, the Mayor takes charge with personal leadership of the effort through ongoing public appearances and announcements.

Newport News listened carefully to our colleague's report, which we now share with you in its entirety:

Committed, Collaborative and Community-based: An Overview of Gang and Youth Violence Prevention In San Jose, CA

By Tom Emswiller

Preface

Information on gang prevention in the United States is both voluminous and easily accessible. Any online search will provide an extensive compilation of initiatives from the private sector and from a full gamut of federal, state and municipal government sources. In addition, this information is geographically and often demographically diverse with strategies, programs and documentation highlighted from Miami to Seattle and from Boston to San Diego.

Similarly, there is no dearth of information regarding the work that has been carried out in San Jose, CA, with regard to the beginnings, evolution and current state of anti-gang interventions and accompanying youth development efforts. Readily available resources include the latest strategic work plan developed by the (San Jose) *Mayor's Gang Prevention Task Force (MGPTF)* as well as comprehensive gang-related material created or disseminated by the *California Cities Gang Prevention Network (CCGPN)*, a collection of 13 cities, that examines the issue through the filters of criminal justice, social theory, behavioral science and economics.

As a result, this presentation will not attempt to reiterate or re-format the wealth of information that is available to the online researcher or other interested parties. Instead, the purpose of this paper is to provide some particular insights and critical thoughts related to the San Jose model as described by individuals who have been part of the program since its inception or close to that time.

The San Jose Plan

Vision Safe and healthy youth connected to their families, schools, communities, and their futures.

Mission We exist to ensure safe and healthy opportunities for San Jose's youth, free of gangs and crime, to realize their hopes and dreams, and become successful and productive in their homes, schools, and neighborhoods.

GUIDING PRINCIPLES We value our youth. We cannot arrest our way out of this problem. We will address this community challenge with a community response. We will hold our youth accountable for their actions and assist them to get back on the right path. We will not give up on any youth and are committed to facilitating personal transformation.

Strategic Goals

Service Delivery Education and Public Awareness Capacity Building * Crisis Response * Local, State, and National Collaboration

Outcomes

Reduced Gang Violence * Informed and Engaged Community * Well Trained and Funded Direct Service Providers * Safe Schools, Community Centers, and Neighborhoods * Seamless Delivery System * Action, Collaboration, Transformation * A plan to break the cycle of youth violence and foster hope

San Jose Mayor Chuck Reed's Gang Prevention Task Force Strategic Work Plan 2008–2011

Note: The *BEST (Bringing Everyone's Strengths Together)* Program staff will negotiate with service providers to provide activities under the following eligible services categories for 2011–2012:

1. Personal Transformation through Cognitive Development and Youth Support Groups

2. Social Recreation, Cultural, and Community Service Intervention Activities

3. Group Mentoring Life Skills — Curriculum Based Short Term

4. Gang Mediation/Intervention Response

5. Outpatient Substance Abuse Services

6. Services for Adjudicated Youth

7. Parent and Family Support and Youth and Children Domestic Violence Services

8. Truancy and Educational Support for Schools

9. Community Gang Awareness

10. Unique Service Delivery for High-Risk Youth

Rather than a re-telling of the significant body of information itself, this paper represents some of the interstitial tissue that holds the story together, gained through formal interviews and informal conversations with a representative group of the program's stakeholders.

A Brief History

As with many gang prevention programs throughout the country, San Jose's began with a public outcry. In the 1980's, communities, activists and individual citizens wanted to reduce the expanding gang violence, drug usage and other criminal activities that threatened their neighborhoods. In growing numbers they began making their concerns known to local government. Initially, police responded with law enforcement strategies and specific suppression tactics. What they learned, an experience that has been frequently repeated across America, is that no matter how effective or zealous the suppression efforts, a city can't arrest its way out of a gang problem.

Then, for the first time in the city's history, a number of municipal departments joined with the San Jose Police in their work to improve public safety.

In a relatively short time, this effort enjoyed the participation of schools, community groups, faith-based organizations and neighborhood associations. In addition, the city reached out to state and federal resources related to gang prevention. In 1991, after several years of increasing momentum that included extensive community outreach and input, San Jose Mayor Susan Hammer formalized this growing collaboration through creation of the *Mayor's Gang Prevention Task Force (MGPTF)*.

This partnership, which has become the center point of San Jose's anti-gang initiatives, has now been incorporated into its third Mayoral administration. The current work plan for the *MGPTF* is in place through 2011 and the strongly held expectation is that it will be sustained beyond that time.

What the San Jose Model Tells Us in 10 Lessons

Lesson 1: Call it what it is

Gang activity can affect a community beyond the obvious public safety issues. Concerns about gang problems can affect real estate sales and values, they can damage the retail economy of impacted areas and they can divert needed funding from other infrastructure. There is also a persistent feeling on the parts of some people, in both the public and private sectors, that acknowledging serious gang activities validates gang members and can even lead to a self-fulfilling prophecy. So the forces of denial are understandable.

But while they may be understandable, they are not tolerable. Like virtually every other problematic issue in the life of an individual or a community, admission of the problem is the first step in an effective remedy. Public officials and community organizations in Newport News have already made this acknowledgement, but equally important is making certain that the information has been disseminated on as extensive a scope as possible. Simply put, let people know what's going on through whatever media are available in the clearest and most straightforward manner possible.

Lesson 2: Only a community can deal with a community problem

Once the existence of a gang problem has been acknowledged and announced, the conversation often turns to how law enforcement can solve it. And even municipalities that do their homework, have their community forums and gather input from a diversity of sources, sometimes continue to over-rely on law enforcement. Interestingly enough, this mandate and the traditional "hook and book" mindset behind it are often as likely or even more likely, to be driven by members of the community than by the police department and elected officials.

The thought in San Jose is that if it takes a village to raise one child then imagine what it takes to offer alternatives and hope to many children. What that meant initially and what it continues to mean is a very inclusive and comprehensive community response that includes city agencies, businesses, schools, community organizations, regional partners, faith-based groups – anyone who has a stake in a safer more livable community, and that includes everyone.

The awareness that every strategy has to find its roots in the community and that, suppression policies, while part of the overall picture can't be your primary approach, are the cornerstones of gang prevention 101. But they always warrant mentioning and remembering.

Lesson 3: Get consensus for your ultimate objectives

It is critically important for the stakeholders in gang control initiatives to agree on what they want to do about gangs. And that depends on how the problem is defined. For example, is the objective to reduce gang violence, bring about a decrease in gang-related crimes, especially gun carrying crimes, or to try to eliminate the gangs themselves?

Several years ago in Los Angeles, the head of the city's homicide bureau compared gang members to insects and called for their total eradication. Other more measured perspectives on what gang control efforts should try to accomplish include working to change behaviors, particularly criminal behaviors, thereby defining success as a reduction in crime. Some city leaders and even some police officers may acknowledge, usually off the record, that what they want to accomplish is reduced levels of crime and violence, not to eliminate or even necessarily curtail membership in gangs.

There's no right answer to the questions about objectives, but it is an issue that should be considered by everyone involved in gang prevention efforts.

Lesson 4: Separate the facts from the not so factual

Members of the Newport News community with an interest in gang control have already noticed the exceptionally large and growing body of literature on the subject. It's more than enough to keep researchers busy for a long time. The problem is what to believe, or more appropriately, what to use as a foundation for decisions and actions.

In an example here in the state of California, civil gang injunctions have been used in a number of municipalities, including San Jose in the mid 1990's, predominantly in the southern part of the state. These legal tools are generally seen as a very serious intervention and require large and sustained police presence to enjoin alleged gang members from engaging in what are otherwise lawful behaviors. The intense use of resources is worth the cost *if* these measures work and that's where the questions lie.

In response to gang injunctions carried out some years back in the city of Irvine, CA, local law enforcement agencies and the media reported impressive reductions in crime. As a result, Irvine's particular example is often cited as a success in practitioner literature and is most certainly a compelling story. The problem is that the story may not be entirely accurate or statistically supportable.

After examining actual crime patterns before and after the injunction, researchers found that there is little actual evidence that the measure had a positive effect on reducing gang activities. So what and whom do you believe? For the most part that's a case-by-case question. The point is, do your homework and get confirmation and verification or at least some type of additional support for anything you communicate to your collaborative partners and to the general public. That confirmation is even more critical when it comes to the policies you develop and execute related to actual gang prevention efforts.

Lesson 5: And keep an eye out for the myths

Along with questions about what is verifiable in the world of gang prevention, there are also some out and out myths. One good example is that once in a gang, always in a gang. A lot of research shows otherwise. In fact, a large multi-state survey found that most youths who join gangs remain involved for about a year.

...a large multi-state survey found that most youths who join gangs remain involved for about a year.

And why did they quit? The "myth" is that they fear arrest or criminal penalties within a society that is increasingly under surveillance and a judicial system that may well have sentence enhancements in place for gang affiliated crime. More likely, according to self-reporting, they were concerned about the high levels of violence within the gang and many former members say that they simply grew out of gang activity.

Some of these misconceptions stem from the popular media, which among its other distortions often portrays leaving a gang as a potential act of suicide. Most surveyed gang members, however, report that they ended their gang affiliation without harm. Again, as with dueling claims and statistics, it is important that everything you read and hear should be subject to scrutiny and placed in the questionable category until proven—or at least strongly indicated—otherwise.

Lesson 6: Understand the real issues

Any official response made by a municipality as well as any action or communication generated from a grass roots coalition should share one common factor: they should be based on a solid understanding of gang issues (and not just in a general sense but relevant to the locale) and a coherent idea as to what an intervention should accomplish.

Consequently, there are some basic questions that should be asked in any effort at gang prevention. These questions include: What are the objectives of the model, the program, or the specific intervention? Whom will it most precisely target and what demographic and psychographic characteristics are at play (for example, is the initiative(s) directed toward gang leadership, hard core members, fringe members or nonmembers who may be at-risk)? What effect will the initiative have on the target or targets in order to achieve the objectives?

These questions are inherent in every overall or individual effort you begin and having a satisfactory answer is essential. Once you do have an answer, make sure it exists within a context that includes a very accurate assessment of the actual gang contribution to crime problems in Newport News.

Lesson 7: Never underestimate the pull of gang culture

Why do kids join gangs? Is it because that's where the parties and the drugs are? Does it offer a sense of security to someone who feels threatened or a sense of belonging to someone who feels adrift? How about the perception (and often reality) of risk to young people who want to show their independence? Prestige, status, respect? Pride of current locale or place of origin? The potential for monetary gain? A family or intergenerational pattern? Yes to all the above.

> *"The battle may be fought in the streets and the neighborhoods, but the war itself is being waged over the souls of our young people."*

The fact is gang problems can be deeply rooted in a way of life and going up against the gang mentality can run as deep as questioning somebody's personal identity and self-worth. It is a complex and ongoing psychological contest that cannot be won by programs based on "just say no" approaches. As a member of the San Jose clergy active in gang prevention put it, "The battle may be fought in the streets and the neighborhoods, but the war itself is being waged over the souls of our young people."

Simply understanding the difficulty of a situation doesn't give you the tools you need to overcome it. But it does help you realize that you better be prepared for a long and difficult challenge. It also helps you realize that you better offer some good, and realistic, alternatives.

In some cases, these alternatives may not be what you think they are or what has been traditionally viewed as productive. Keep in mind that young people who have been marginalized for most of their lives and are innately mistrusting aren't typically served well by mainstream service-oriented organizations. So before you conclude what represents a viable alternative to gang activity, make sure you talk with some people who have had the experience.

Lesson 8: Get the right balance

What the San Jose model for gang prevention has shown from the beginning, and what we can't overemphasize, no matter how hard we try – is that enforcement activities can't exist alone. Although as mentioned, it's always prudent to be wary of research and studies, the Department of Justice is usually a reliable source, and its Bureau of Justice Assistance noted in its evaluation of gang programs that traditional law enforcement efforts are, in the long run, not effective at addressing gang activities. To quote its website, "most stand-alone gang intervention and suppression programs in the community that have generated positive results can be characterized as having only modest and/or short term impacts."

What experience shows clearly is that education, job promotion, specialized services for gang afflicted communities, support for gang-involved and at-risk youth and some attention to the obvious and the subtle barriers that make it difficult for former gang members to be re-integrated into society have to be part of the equation. How you get the right balance depends on the particular nature of the gang issues facing a specific community, as well as the resources at hand to address the problems. But the need for the balance itself is unassailable.

Lesson 9: Keep your eye on the prize

Developing and implementing anti-gang measures involves casting a wide net when it comes to accessing the research, relying on your own experiences and taking advantage of what existing initiatives have already learned. Once the direction is in place, however, the field should narrow considerably.

At that point, specify the role of law enforcement, of private and public agencies and of all other resources by delineating which tactics support the overall initiative and which should be avoided because they could be counterproductive. By clearly communicating the initiative there is a lot less chance that your efforts will be derailed by political or institutional considerations.

Lesson 10: Stay flexible

When we look at the strategic work plans developed over the years in San Jose for the Mayor's Gang Prevention Task Force there are a number of strong threads that remain from the first plan to the current iteration. But there are also some important differences. These differences are generally related to shifts in the community, human and organizational resources, the acquisition of new information and the simple evaluation of what's working and what isn't.

It's very likely that some sense of movement can already be seen from the first stages of gang prevention efforts to the present time. Among all that we've learned over the past twenty years, this is one of the most basic: things change. Pay attention and make sure you make the appropriate adjustments. That's what a continuous improvement organization is all about.

What about replication?

Gangs differ in their ethnic and racial makeup and the cultural competencies needed to interact with them, their identifying signs and symbols, their origins and affiliations, their activities and their creation myths. That doesn't mean that best practices and evidence-based approaches can't be translated or in some cases even moved intact to other locations. If they hope to be effective, however, gang prevention initiatives have to, at the very least, take these differences into consideration.

But among the variance, there are a few broad areas that most likely would have universal application. In closing, these areas and attributes include:

Commitment: Since Chuck Reed, Mayor of San Jose beginning in January of 2007, made gang prevention a priority - thereby continuing the work of his predecessors and honoring a major campaign platform. The action necessary for effective gang prevention is grass roots at its core, but the commitment has to continue at the top with willing and able leadership.

Sustainability: Keeping a major initiative like gang prevention alive over time takes more than desire and will. It takes money. And during times of mounting city and county budget problems, funding becomes an even greater challenge. During the past 13 years, the *MGPTF* has maintained a funding mechanism that enables the task force to strategically deliver significant amounts of money in grants to critical community, school and public safety programs that help curb gang violence. These efforts are guided by the *MGPTF* strategic work plan.

Another approach that enables San Jose and the Mayor's Task Force to pursue gang prevention efforts is a coordinated plan to periodically convene stakeholders with assets and experience in leveraging resources. The fact that the budget for the work of the *MGPTF* and its community network has been reduced only minimally at a time of declining resources is testimony to the positive results that have already accrued as well as evidence of the city's steadfast commitment to healthy and safe communities.

Collaboration: The question of "why" to collaborate has been addressed, but the question of "who" may remain. Who do you want to come to the table to share skills, ideas, resources and hopes for gang prevention in Newport News? Our experience has been that we welcome any group or individual who believes in the continuum of services approach and the proposition that every child and young adult should have the opportunity to succeed.

At its most basic level, gang prevention programs models are about people and our feeling was that it should begin here.

Relationships: One of the least quantifiable but no less important foundations for the effectiveness of the *MGPTF* is that we took the time to get to know each other. With so many agencies and organizations and so many agendas, we needed personal connections and interactions far more than bureaucratic responses. At its most basic level, gang prevention programs models are about people and our feeling was that it should begin here.

Acknowledgments

The author gratefully acknowledges the input and assistance of various officials of the San Jose city government, the San Jose Police Department, the Mayor's Gang Prevention Task Force and the San Jose Department of Parks, Recreation and Neighborhood Services with special thanks to Angel Rios, Esther Mota, District 7 Councilwoman Nancy Pyle and Pastor Tony Ortiz.

Richmond, VA

The most effective crime prevention program in America, according to the International Association of Chiefs of Police in 2009, is the Richmond, VA *Gang Reduction, Intervention and Prevention (G.R.I.P.)* program.

When he was Attorney General of the Commonwealth of Virginia, Virginia Governor Bob McDonnell noted, "When it comes to gang reduction we know what works. Now we just have to find a way to fund it."

> *"When it comes to gang reduction we know what works. Now we just have to find a way to fund it."*

The Richmond program was originally funded through a grant from the *Office of Juvenile Justice and Delinquency Prevention (OJJDP)* in the amount of $2.5 million. This initiative involved the leadership of the co-writer of **No COLORS** Bobby Kipper, who managed the *G.R.I.P.* Program in Richmond for the Attorney General.

G.R.I.P. was one of the three winners for the prestigious *2009 Webber Seavey Award for Quality in Law Enforcement* and received the award during the Annual International Association of Chiefs of Police Conference.

Jointly sponsored by IACP and Motorola, the *Webber Seavey Award* is presented annually to agencies and departments worldwide in recognition for promoting a standard of excellence that exemplifies law enforcement's contribution and dedication to the quality of life in local communities. G.R.I.P. is listed as a national best practice. The difference in the Richmond community after four years of G.R.I.P. was nothing short of miraculous. Along with Richmond, three other localities were awarded the original grant by OJJDP: Milwaukee, Los Angeles, and North Miami Beach.

The State and local political leadership worked together to seek what the best path for Richmond and not their individual party. The Richmond model stands out as an example of how local, state and national politicians can exist together for common cause and agreed upon purpose.

Politically speaking, the issue of posturing around the gang reduction effort is not a good political strategy.

Gang reduction is clearly a bipartisan issue. The opportunity for a community to embrace a solid proven strategy has a place in political circles as long as we do not continue talking about the problem, but focus on proven solutions.

Bobby Kipper believes something special happened in Richmond.

"Something very unique evolved with the partnership of the police department and the Richmond Outreach Center, a central faith-based effort in south Richmond."

"We worked closely with the Sheriff's office, the probation and parole department, and the Commonwealth's Attorney to develop a solid re-entry program for returning inmates into the community," Kipper noted.

A total of forty-four partners worked on the Richmond project. They came from state and local government, nonprofits, faith-based, and citizen groups. All worked together to insure that the project succeeded. The biggest gain for those involved clearly became the building of relationships. In Richmond, walls that have separated agencies for years fell into rubble.

"Within the program, no one agency claimed to be the lead and everyone involved worked hard to insure inclusiveness," Kipper said.

The program has been so successful in Southside Richmond that it has expanded to the Northside as well, with the city's *One Stop* Center opened in early 2011 in the Gilpin Court neighborhood.

Organizers hope that *G.R.I.P.'s* continued success will allow it to be used as a model in other parts of the Commonwealth, and across the country, as they work together to combat the growing problem of gangs. Indeed, portions of this strategy have been adopted in dozens of cities across the country, including neighboring Newport News.

The *G.R.I.P.* program includes over forty programs focusing on the strategic areas of primary and secondary prevention, intervention, suppression, and re-entry. More specifically these strategies target the following populations:

- Primary Prevention: Targets the entire population in high-crime, high-risk communities. The key component is a *One Stop* resource center that facilitates effective distribution of health and other support resources for youth and families.

- Secondary Prevention: Identifies young children, ages 7-14, at high-risk of becoming involved in gangs and juvenile delinquency. It involves schools, community-based organizations, and other community partners in providing age-appropriate services.

- Intervention: Targets active gang members and their close associates ages 10-24. It requires aggressive outreach, ongoing recruitment, and careful planning and coordination of services. The primary goal is to provide youth with positive alternatives to the gang life.

- Re-entry: Targets serious and gang-involved offenders who face multiple challenges to reentering their community. *G.R.I.P.* provides appropriate, individualized services and juvenile justice supervision to ensure a reduction in recidivism.

- Suppression: Gang leaders are targeted for aggressive suppression efforts. Enhanced sentences, federal charges, and vertical prosecution are used to effectively remove the most dangerous gang members from the community.

Programs are designed to address the full range of personal, family, and community factors that contribute to high levels of juvenile delinquency and gang activity. Young people have the capacity to make better choices if they have better choices available to them.

The commitment to public safety is strengthened because the community is administering prevention and intervention programs prior to the use of necessary suppression efforts.

The Office of the Attorney General for the Commonwealth of Virginia details how they set up the initiative.

"*G.R.I.P.* provides youth on the wrong track with the resources and skills to make positive choices and ultimately build better lives. All ages in the community are provided services through these programs, but many of the programs begin with very young at-risk youth.

Available *G.R.I.P.* programs range from health care, after school care, Class Action Camp, ESL (English as Second Language) and SSL (Spanish as Second Language) Classes, job development, community revitalization, and a host of other programs, which offer the community, and specifically youth, a positive alternative to gangs."

Building relationships toward gang reduction is important. But even more important is maintaining relationships.

No one wins within a community if we all work together on a grant program but dissolve our partnerships when the funding runs out.

In Richmond, the relationships formed around the *G.R.I.P.* model became solid and long lasting.

On recent trips back to the project area, we were met by members of the police department and the Richmond Outreach Center who provided us with a tour and a presentation of the model approach to reducing gangs.

It was evident by what we heard that relationships matter, but more importantly, they can be sustained.

Three Strategies for Success

It's been about two decades that careful measurements have been put into place in communities across America and in Canada to investigate what is effective in keeping kids out of gangs and setting a moral compass for at-risk children.

We suggest that there are three primary findings are the result of benchmarking research across the nation and in Canada.

A Community-wide Strategic Plan

These plans are created by a multi-disciplinary group of citizens, not laid out by city government or drawn up by City Hall. The role of city government is changed to supportive participant, and a new social paradigm results.

You will find detailed guidance in the following tactical chapters to assist in the creation of this plan, which is a living, breathing, moving document that changes as you find out what is effective in your community.

Community Strategic Plans to address crime and violence began in the United States in 1987 when the U.S. Justice Department and the Office on Juvenile Justice and Delinquency Prevention launched a juvenile gang suppression and intervention research program under the direction of Dr. Irving Spergel of the University of Chicago.

Gang Violence

The Process that Leads to the Event

- Gang members are connected in a type of "family" emotional bond
- When gang members perceive a threat from a person, whether individual or gang-related, they tend to bond closer
- Gang-to-gang threats increase the move towards violence
- The process will include verbal threats and insults
- One gang typically will commit an act of violence
- A period of silence may exist
- Violence once again erupts in the form of retaliation

NCPCV

National Center for the Prevention of Community Violence

Since their initial research, strategic planning models have been successfully implemented in a number of small, medium and large communities throughout the U.S. Examples include: San Jose, Los Angeles, Memphis, Salinas, Boston, Minneapolis, Pittsburgh, Milwaukee, Richmond, and North Miami Beach, to name a few.

The research nationally has clearly indicated the need for a community to develop and maintain a Strategic Plan that acknowledges the issue as well as provides a direction to address it. Currently the United States Justice Department under the direction of Attorney General Eric Holder, continue to endorse the philosophy. The power and advantage of strategic planning is that it emphasizes:

- Problem Identification
- Community Mobilization
- Collaboration of Efforts
- Assessment of the Results

P.I.E.R. Model

Successful youth violence initiatives are organized into four broad categories of simultaneous programming: Prevention, Intervention, Enforcement and Re-entry (*P.I.E.R.*).

The Operational Council is the critical support organization for a city's gang and youth violence reduction effort. This working group represents a comprehensive, community-based structure outside of the command and control of city government. The individuals selected to serve on the Operational Council should have proven, direct service delivery experience within the community. These individuals go beyond the decision-making process to the ground level implementation process of citizen outreach and service delivery. The Operational Council should be divided into four operational strategic subcommittees:

- Prevention – This subcommittee focuses on recommending proven strategies for implementation for the community's youth (birth – young adulthood). Such strategies should involve existing nonprofit groups, youth sports leagues, the local public and private schools and the faith-based community.

- Intervention – This subcommittee focuses on recommending proven strategies for implementation for the community's young people who are identified as being at-risk of becoming or have already been involved with the criminal justice system. Street outreach through community and faith-based organizations and parents supplements partnerships among public agencies to make well-integrated services available to the youth. Intervention efforts include job training and placement, recreation at safe locations, and mobilization of neighborhood residents and police in identifying community resources that serve youth.

- Enforcement – This subcommittee focuses on working with the public safety community to recommend proven strategies for implementation to reduce crime and gangs throughout the community. Police, probation personnel, prosecutors, and court services share information with the community about gang activity, diffuse crises that arise from gang conflict, and refer at-risk youth to community-based services. New roles for law enforcement officers in the prevention and intervention realms are encouraged.

* Re-entry – This subcommittee focuses on recommending proven re-entry strategies for implementation with the young adults returning to the community from incarceration in probation and parole services to implement strategies that focus on job training, placement, and employment retention; housing assistance; and other community-based services, as needed. They also create methods to encourage nonviolent gang members to "re-enter" mainstream society.

Measurement Is Built In

Communities that are making progress against this domestic terrorism are funding measurable programs and discarding programs that fail to clearly measure their results and impact.

No COLORS is filled with suggestions regarding funding, measurement and evaluation – vital links in creating a successful initiative in your community. Make this the most important aspect of your plan. Make it independent, transparent and credible.

Let Us Begin

Part of what we hope to accomplish is to help get the word out to all of our children – in schools, in neighborhoods, in churches, in recreational programs – that the time has come to stop the violence; to get out of the gang; to come home.

> *...the time has come to stop the violence; to get out of the gang; to come home.*

We suspect that at least some of these young people already know, in their hearts, that the path they're on leads nowhere. Something bad evolved here and it must stop.

And just as other cities and nations are clearly struggling with this crisis brings little comfort, it also presents no license to throw up our hands. On the contrary, it should steel our resolve and direct us to study what has been working across the country and the world, and then reach out to the young people we have lost or are losing and make every effort to bring them back.

It's time to stop backing up.

We may be angry at these young people for turning into domestic terrorists. But we can get many of them back and we can make gangs very uncomfortable if they seek to destroy the fabric of our community.

To those young people just stepping into gang culture - we refuse to abandon you. We understand your need for acceptance but we challenge your decision to go through a life of brutality, life threatening drug use and gunplay to succeed.

Our message to the nonviolent young people in our community who are already in gangs should remain steadfast. "Know that we will be there for you when you are ready to quit gang life, that we value each young person's life. We will not label you forever because you have been in a gang. We will welcome you back when you're ready."

To those who have already become brutally violent – we will send you to jail.

To those who have not, we will be reaching into your life; we seek to bring you back.

We must give kids access to people in their lives, mentors, who will care about them every day — someone who does not want these kids to carry guns, hang around with gang bangers; sell drugs; go to jail; become criminals; lead brief lives.

Someone who can reach in and help bring out the goodness in directionless young people, demonstrate how to listen to and follow your own voice.

Let our efforts be about the kids.

Let our efforts be motivated not by being against gangs per se – but against youth violence. Let us be about a brighter future for the many young people in our communities who do not have a level playing field. Show them a better way.

Let us draw a line in the sand here, now. We can't win this with arrests. We have to win the hearts of our young people and show them a better way.

Here we present 100 bold interventions and processes. Think of it as a menu. Select what is most appropriate for your specific community. Make your plan. Be creative. Enjoy the process and the challenge. Win your young people back. Cultivate their better angels. Reach in to shape their character and mind and instincts for inspiration, not despair. We have left them behind. Now we are returning for them.

Win your young people back. Cultivate their better angels. Reach in to shape their character and mind and instincts for inspiration, not despair.

No city, town or county shares the same circumstances. Different measures are needed. The important thing is to bring together the entire leadership of your community. Then make the plan carefully and balance the attack, adding measurable programs in prevention, intervention, enforcement and re-entry.

You will know which of these initiatives resonates with your community. You will know because of your awareness, your experience and your research. And you will know because of the small, quiet voice inside you whispering, "We could do this. It would work here."

It may take a while.

To nonviolent gang members, the American young people who have lost their way — we are in awe of the burdens you have had to carry.

You can come home now.

PART TWO

100 TACTICS FOR
SAVING YOUR COMMUNITY
FROM GANGS

Quick Reference Guide

Here is a useful guide to help your community leadership view how the 100 tactics presented in *No COLORS* fit together by topic, in a solid, benchmark planning process.

Strategic Planning

See Chapters:

Prevention

See Chapters:

Intervention

See Chapters:

Enforcement

See Chapters:

Re-entry

See Chapters:

Measurement

See Chapters:

✸ 1 ✸
Proclaim a New Social Norm: Citizens Set the Strategy

Executive Summary

Organized communities large and small must move toward a new social norm. Through the efforts of their citizens, they now need to undertake a comprehensive strategy focused on youth violence reduction.

This necessitates the involvement of many elements of the community.

Many communities are starting to combat the gang issue on all fronts. They have learned the power of a solutions-driven gang approach that seems to be showing positive results.

In May 2007, California Governor Schwarzenegger announced new initiatives to combat gang violence, calling it the *California Gang Reduction, Intervention and Prevention Program (CalGRIP)*.

In a press release from the Governor's office, the program was introduced:

"For the past several months the Governor has met with Mayors, law enforcement, faith-based and community organizations, local officials and legislators to discuss how communities across the state are fighting gangs and what resources they need to strengthen their success."

At every meeting the Governor heard about the same problems: lack of coordination between state and local agencies and programs, lack of funding, and lack of a comprehensive approach to anti-gang efforts.

"Everywhere I went, local law enforcement would say the problem is just being pushed from one city to the next. They say gang leaders come out of state prisons and go right back to terrorizing their communities – law enforcement finds out they have gang leaders back in their communities when gang-related violence spikes," the Governor said.

"Prosecutors say they need more tools to protect witnesses. Community leaders say they can get kids out of gangs but they need help with job training and education. The state spends hundreds and hundreds of millions of dollars on education, job training and substance abuse treatment every year – with no focused coordination on gang activities. We need a comprehensive approach to gang violence that provides a statewide framework with long-term solutions," Governor Schwarzenegger said.

This measure, for the first time, took some bold steps with re-entry, giving law enforcement the tools to closely track gang leaders both inside state prisons and when they are released on parole.

At the 4th Annual All-City Teams Meeting of the *California Cities Gang Prevention Network*, the spirit of openness and sharing is evident. This May 2010 meeting featured U.S. Attorney General Eric Holder who said that solutions were at hand. The years of research have paid off.

"To succeed in protecting the safety and potential of our children, we need a variety of perspectives; we need to test multiple strategies; and, above all, we need a comprehensive, collaborative approach." Holder said.

The Formula for Success

Create a Community-wide Strategic Plan

Communities feeling a measure of success against the gang crisis are usually those that have deployed a community-wide effort, starting with a Strategic Plan. This effort cannot come from City Hall down. It must come from the community and be administered by the community.

CREATE THE TASK FORCE LEADERSHIP

Gather community leaders from every part of the community. These are the police chiefs, schools superintendents, civic club leaders, key business leaders and prominent ministers.

This is the policy-setting body which appoints the Operational Council – which consists of key players at ground level.

CREATE THE OPERATIONAL COUNCIL

The Operational Council is the critical support organization for a city's gang and youth violence reduction effort. This working group represents a comprehensive, community-based structure outside of the command and control of city government. The individuals selected to serve on the Operational Council should have proven, direct service delivery experience within the community. These individuals go beyond the decision-making process to the ground level implementation process of citizen outreach and service delivery. The Operational Council should be divided into four operational strategic subcommittees:

P.I.E.R. MODEL

The strategy must attack the problem on four different fronts. Knitting together fundamental investments in prevention, intervention, enforcement and re-entry (*P.I.E.R.*) is the only documented way to make significant strides. You cannot arrest your way out of the problem. It just does not work. As we can't overemphasize, it is not a law enforcement issue. It's a community issue.

> *You cannot arrest your way out of the problem.*

Developing and implementing anti-gang measures involves casting a wide net when it comes to accessing the research, relying on your own experiences and taking advantage of what existing initiatives have already shown. Once the direction is in place, however, the field should narrow considerably.

Think of what follows as a menu of potential tactics; some may fit your community, some may not be appropriate for your setting and circumstances. Enjoy the journey. Choose well.

Prevention

This subcommittee focuses on recommending proven strategies for implementation for the community's youth (birth to young adulthood). Such strategies should involve existing nonprofits, youth sports leagues, the local public and private schools and the faith-based community.

Intervention

This subcommittee focuses on recommending proven strategies for implementation for the community's young people who are identified as being at-risk of becoming or have already been involved with the criminal justice system. Street outreach through community and faith-based organizations and parents supplements partnerships among public agencies to make integrated services available to the youth. Intervention efforts include job training and placement, recreation at safe locations, and mobilization of neighborhood residents and police in identifying community resources that serve youth.

Enforcement

This subcommittee focuses on working with the public safety community to recommend proven strategies for implementation to reduce crime and gangs throughout the community. Police, probation personnel, prosecutors, and court services share information with the community about gang activity, diffuse crises that arise from gang conflict, and refer at-risk youth to community-based services. New roles for law enforcement officers in the prevention and intervention realms are encouraged.

Re-entry

This subcommittee focuses on recommending proven re-entry strategies for implementation with the young adults returning to the community from incarceration in probation and parole services to implement strategies that focus on job training, placement, employment retention, housing assistance, and other community-based services, as needed. They also create methods to encourage nonviolent gang members to "re-enter" mainstream society.

Measure Everything

Communities that are making progress against this domestic terrorism are funding measurable programs and discarding programs that fail to clearly measure their results and impact.

Operate Transparently

Publish everything. Stay in constant contact with the news media. Share information with all stakeholders constantly. Accept criticism as well as praise.

✳ 2 ✳

Face Down Community Denial

At the direction of President Obama, the U.S. Departments of Justice and Education officially launched the National Forum on Youth Violence Prevention in Boston in October 2010.

The administration created the forum as a context for participating localities to share challenges and promising strategies with each other and to explore how federal agencies can better support local efforts.

At working sessions, teams from the cities of Boston, Chicago, Detroit, Memphis, Salinas, and San Jose met with federal agencies and each other to share information and experience about what works in preventing youth and gang violence.

"Our effort to combat youth violence isn't about federally-imposed fixes, it's about changing the way we do business on this critical public safety issue," said Attorney General Eric Holder.

"We must come together to share knowledge and experience about what works, creating networks of local law enforcement agencies, educators, public health providers, community and faith-based organizations, parents and kids to stand together in the fight against youth and gang violence," Holder stated.

This administration will continue to do what it takes to reclaim our communities and our youth from crime and violence. The lives of our nation's children are at stake."

"We know that if children aren't safe, then they can't learn," said U.S. Secretary of Education Arne Duncan, who met with the forum.

"We all have a stake in public safety and a responsibility to keep our children out of harm's way. But the bigger issue of community denial is that it drives a credibility stake in the ground between citizens and local government officials."

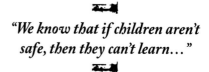

"We know that if children aren't safe, then they can't learn..."

"While every day citizens see signs of community gang involvement to include graffiti and increased fear and intimidation, local leaders downplay the actual events that are taking place in the neighborhood where they live," Duncan said.

Imagine how teens across America feel when the find themselves in school with known gang members only to be told that their community is gang free.

In communities that have not faced up to the gang issues, the responsibility falls completely on the shoulders of federal, state, and local law enforcement.

Police chiefs and sheriffs across the country are feeling a greater burden to save their communities from the spread of crime and disorder caused by gangs. Local law enforcement officials are scrambling to put together gang units and special task forces to deal specifically with the issue of gang crime and violence.

Communities are now hiring special prosecutors to enforce existing criminal statutes in hopes that it may deter the presence and growth of criminal gangs. At the state level, political leaders are scrambling to enact new laws and increase sanctions of current laws in an effort to fight the problem.

Law enforcement officials schedule training conferences and presentations to learn and provide information on what gangs look like and how they operate. Parents and school officials are trained to look for gangs in their communities.

While law enforcement officials continue to seek solutions on how to address this new insurgency, gangs continue to grow.

From local, state and federal jails and prisons, gangs are becoming stronger every day. The population of gang members in incarceration in America has grown to epidemic proportions; not to mention when these individuals are released many return back into society to go to the very neighborhood they came from and repeat old patterns.

It is vital that citizens who are willing to address the issue get together and face down those that would ignore it or just call it a police problem. Ask for and insist on the violence data. Ask the police officers on the street. Ask the kids what they are experiencing. The first step in effective community-wide planning is to change the dialogue.

The first step in effective community-wide planning is to change the dialogue.

3

Develop Overall Community Ownership of the Plan

There are certain roles that diverse partners will play in an effective gang reduction strategy. The successful programs across the country are the ones that have had community participation as its key aspect.

Gang reduction is not the role of government, although government at the federal and state level can serve as a catalyst for funding through much needed grant related programs. This is clearly a community issue and it must be met with a community and not a government solution.

When the United States Justice Department under President George W. Bush decided to get involved with model gang reduction strategies it did not dictate what the exact community-based solution would be.

Demonstration grants of $2.5 million were appropriated to Los Angeles, Milwaukee, North Miami Beach, and Richmond. The scope of the effort allowed for each city chosen to come up with a community-based strategy to reduce gang-related violent crime in their respective area.

The key to this effort was that the noted Urban Institute in Washington, D.C very closely evaluated it.

Every dollar spent was examined to measure the overall impact on the community. Several of the targeted communities used the funding to increase the role of government while others tried to embrace and grow community involvement. It became very clear that the funding used for growing community involvement led to a dynamic change, which included a reduction in crime and a higher quality of life.

> *When the voices of the community are heard loud and clear — the quality of life seems to improve.*

When it comes to gang reduction, local government agencies and leadership should be viewed as equal partners and not a controller of the overall strategy. When the voices of the community are heard loud and clear — the quality of life seems to improve.

This issue should not become another way to grow local government. It is not about creating or securing local government positions, but about providing employment for individuals trying to leave gangs or coming out of state or local incarceration. Most communities have enough government — they just do not have a solution to an issue that is at its base a deep-rooted social problem within the community.

In working in various communities across America, we are gratified to see them moving away from bureaucratic answers and into adoption of community-based strategies.

This is not to say that government at all levels does not have a role in gang reduction. What it points out is that the role does not assume that government will lead the effort.

There is evidence of this in the phrase, "As funding goes, so does government." And with gang reduction, that is the case. When grants are issued and funding is available, government leaders are quick to respond, but that response appears limited when the funds dry up.

Gang reduction programs are typically sustained through strong community support to include citizens, nonprofits, and faith-based organizations. Government sustainability is limited. The efforts of a passionate faith-based organization within a community will outlast government action every time.

> *The efforts of a passionate faith-based organization within a community will outlast government action every time.*

Another great example of this issue is the community-oriented policing push of the 1980s and 1990s. Communities across America were quick to apply for funding to put more police officers on the street. When funding left so did the positions in a number of cities and towns. There was not a solid plan to sustain the effort. While putting more officers on the street was a good idea, it was not a passionate, community-driven solution.

Gang reduction is too important to rest on the whims of government. It must be driven and sustained by the community.

Greensboro, NC had such an awakening. They partnered with University of North Carolina - Greensboro and prepared a thorough study of gangs in their region.

There were approximately 1,300 confirmed or suspected gang members in Guilford County, NC, the university's location, according to the study.

A 327-page study was conducted by UNC-G's Center for Youth, Family and Community Partnerships. According to the study, there were 38 unique gangs with 462 members in Greensboro. More than 450 crimes in Guilford County in 2009 were gang-related, officials said.

Fox8 Television News reported the words of Police Captain J. Wolfe, "We all own this problem. This is a community problem. This is a Greensboro problem."

Some of the gang members are as young as seven years old, the study reported.

❖ 4 ❖

"View the Seeds of the Problem"

Enabling concerned citizens and leaders to view the seeds of the problem in a specific community is the first step to healing this dysfunctional culture.

This is going to take some research, persistent research, because all this is not in one place – yet:

- Gang Unit Intelligence
- Third Graders at Reading Level (DOE)
- Underweight Births (HHS)
- High School Graduation Rates
- High School "Graduation on Time" rates
- Violent Crime (Dept. of Justice)
- Juvenile Crime (Dept. of Justice)
- School Dropout Rates (Dept. of Education)
- Households in Poverty (Moody's Economy)
- Prison Discharges to the Community (DOJ)
- Number of Subsidized Housing Units per Capita (HUD)
- Unemployment (Bureau of Labor Statistics)
- Self-reported student surveys

Each of these factors play a role in creating an atmosphere for a thriving gang culture and the drugs, guns and violence that always accompanies this dysfunction.

We know that activities of youth in gangs and the community response to the gang problem are interactive.

As part of its Comprehensive Gang Model, the *Office of Juvenile Justice and Delinquency Prevention (OJJDP)* has published *A Guide to Assessing Your Community's Youth Gang Problem*, a user-friendly resource to assist communities that are conducting a gang-problem assessment.

Ideally, the assessment should provide an understanding of the "evolution of gangs in time and space"

This guide simplifies the data-collection process, helping communities determine types and levels of gang activity, gang crime patterns, community perceptions of local gangs and gang activity, and gaps in community services for gang prevention.

Ideally, the assessment should provide an understanding of the "evolution of gangs in time and space" within the city, community, or neighborhood (Hughes, 2006). Your community's assessment should answer these questions:

- Who is involved in gang-related activity and what is the history of these gangs?

- What crimes are these individuals committing?

- When are these crimes being committed?

The next step is to identify program gaps and develop and coordinate an array of prevention and intervention program services and sanctions, in concert with a targeted strategy of community and government agency responses to serious and violent gang activity.

Prevention and intervention services should be directed to the neighborhoods, schools, and families from which gangs emanate.

The *OJJDP* stresses the importance of community factors, which can come into play at any point during childhood and adolescence.

- Where is gang-related activity primarily occurring?

- Why is the criminal activity happening (e.g., individual conflicts, gang feuds, gang members acting on their own)?

- In addition to helping communities answer these questions, *OJJDP*'s Comprehensive Gang Model promotes a problem-solving approach to gang-related crime, asking communities to identify:
  - Neighborhoods with many risk factors for gang involvement
  - Schools and other community settings in which gangs are active
  - Hot spots of gang crime
  - High-rate gang offenders
  - Violent gangs

To assist with these identifications, the *OJJDP* Strategic Planning Tool provides the following:

- A list of risk factors for delinquency and gang membership organized by age

- Data indicators (i.e., measures of risk factors)

- Data sources (from which relevant data can be retrieved)

- Community Resource Inventory, where community planning groups can record information on existing programs, identifying gaps

- Information on promising and effective juvenile delinquency and gang programs

- Hyperlinks connecting risk factors with effective programs that address them

- Strategies that address specific risk factors for various age groups

✹ 5 ✹

Pick a Civic Group Champion

The gang issue is forcing communities into partnering that is traditionally not common among local government officials.

Community leaders are now learning that in order for a gang reduction strategy to be successful it must focus on involvement of various key components of the problem and possible solutions.

A strong civic group can be the social consciousness of a community. They have a realistic human stake in the welfare of the community. No one wants to live in a community that is deemed unsafe and civic groups have an energy that is totally independent in thought.

Strong civic involvement may not always be welcomed.

Where there may exist passivity on gang issues by local government leaders, the involvement of local civil groups and their leadership may be viewed as a threat.

Local government is not usually designed to offer inclusive solutions. To avoid this issue it is important to open a dialogue about the role each will play in the gang reduction strategy.

In many communities, a widely recognized nonprofit organization is often a huge advantage because it represents a large body of "like believers" already organized to do something good for the betterment of all.

There is already an understood common bond to think and act beyond government. And usually, such groups are composed of thought leaders and influencers within the community.

A disadvantage to the "fire starter" civic group beginning is that such efforts are often mentally delegated by other community leaders and groups to take care of the matter, both financially and strategically - and that is not the desired outcome.

One of the most credible and powerful civic groups is the faith community. When church leaders begin to act in concert, the earth can be moved.

One of the most credible and powerful civic groups is the faith community. When church leaders begin to act in concert, the earth can be moved.

The real key is the gathering of policy makers and decision makers in the same room to establish a clear direction for the community plan. Gang reduction strategies without broad key leadership involvement are destined to fail.

When we directed our examination across the country, one of the most community-involved cities in America consistently comes up as San Jose, CA. There hasn't been a mayor in two decades whose platform hasn't included strong vocal support for their gang intervention program. Citizens there are very proud of their outreach to young people. And they know it is working as the organization established reaches deep into the community.

San Jose shows a strong commitment to a very transparent way of pursuing its strategy.

In the white paper *Implementing a Citywide Violence Reduction Strategy*, the *California Cities Gang Prevention Network (CCGPN)* articulated how the two decades old program got its start.

The community voice that helped spark action has been consistently loud and articulate over the years.

Representatives of *People Acting in Community Together (PACT)* participate actively in Task Force and related meetings, and bring their particular emphasis on leadership accountability to many settings. *PACT* members and others express the "moral voice of the community" that is a necessary component of any comprehensive gang strategy.

Blending the elected leadership with the voices and passions of the community is San Jose's formula for sustaining its gang strategy. While the Mayor and police chief convene meetings, provide leadership, and rightfully take a degree of credit for the effort, community members feel a strong sense of ownership.

The *CCGPN* white paper summed it up this way:

"When asked recently whether the new Mayor would continue the Task Force, one longtime community activist responded: 'Of course it will continue. It's not his, it's ours.'"

The faith community is the "civic" group that led the transformation of Richmond. It is very difficult to tell the difference between the city programs and the faith-based programs throughout the community.

The *Richmond Outreach Center (ROC)* united the efforts of 140 different ministries. Most notable is the manifestation of a vacant mall into a magnet for at-risk youth throughout the city.

The Big House is one of the most impressive initiatives we have ever seen for at-risk kids.

It was a great celebration at the Grand Opening of *The ROC* at *The Big House* located on 5501 Midlothian Turnpike in Richmond on April 10, 2010.

Thousands came to hear Senior Pastor Geronimo Aguilar dedicate the new Center. Governor Bob McDonnell spoke (when he could be heard over the continuous ovations) at the opening in the 4,500 seat theatre/sanctuary. Both Pastor G and the governor helped create the award-winning gang reduction program in the city.

Buses fan out to challenged neighborhoods all over the city and provide free transportation to and from *The Big House* after school, during the weekends and during the summer. This state-of-the-art building houses the *ROC* Café, Fitness Center, Dance Studio, Food Pantry, Computer Lab, shops including: The *ROC* Bookstore, Jesus Couture, Laundromat, and the Hair Salon and Spa.

In a number of cities and towns it has been nonprofit and faith-based civic organizations that have carried the torch that has led to addressing the gang issue.

In Newport News, an interesting civic group deserves a great deal of credit for encouraging local government to benchmark the nation and deal openly with the gang issue.

Founded in 1992, the race relations group *People to People* and its leadership started a dialogue within the community about the presence and growth of criminal street gangs three years before the discussion developed traction among city leaders.

This organization refused to allow the issue to go away. They began to hold community meetings on the issue and went after funding to address the issue.

Newport News' *People to People* secured a federal grant through Rep. Bobby Scott (D-VA) to initiate a community Strategic Plan to address the issue.

The power of this effort led the local political leadership to agree that the community was at-risk of social and economic decline due to the gang situation. The secured funding provided a spark to developing and bringing to life a plan to address gangs in the city.

This is one of a number of success stories where a civic organization has led the charge to address community gang issues. These organizations are generally made up of not just ordinary citizens, but they also attract local business leaders who can help not only in the planning of a community's initiative, but can also provide insight into the important issue of sustainability.

Civic involvement focuses on how the gang issue is impacting everyday citizens. It's apolitical.

Usually, those who lead these organizations are driven to action-based solutions.

✹ 6 ✹

Empower Your Mayor to Lead — Or Elect a New One Who Will

America is beginning to understand that the presence of gang activity signals a community in distress. The growth of gangs within communities in the U.S. and Canada has moved community dialogue to a new level as we all face extreme changes in violent crime and a gang population that is frightening.

The role of the Mayor stands out in communities that are successful at gang resolution. Successful gang reduction strategies in many communities have become a direct extension of that vision and leadership.

Conversely, communities that have disinterested Mayoral leadership appear to struggle with the ability to develop and operate a comprehensive Strategic Plan. In cities where the Mayor does not lead, the municipal bureaucracy lacks certainty and a timid, limited plan often results.

It has taken a couple of decades, but community leaders now accept some responsibility for leading the charge in violence prevention.

Dramatic attention from Washington, D.C. and the Department of Justice has been focused on the gang epidemic as they have stepped in to assist many severely distressed communities.

Community leaders must have an accurate assessment of the nature of the gang situation. For far too long, law enforcement has downplayed the gang issue unless crime and violence statistics demanded an explanation.

Law enforcement leaders traditionally have been reluctant to hang the "Gang's Rule" banner out in fear of embarrassing the local political leadership, namely the Mayor of the community.

Bob Flores, former Director of Juvenile Justice and Delinquency Prevention has stated that gang issues are signs of community dysfunction. Gangs can typically be labeled as a community risk factor to economic decline. This issue alone should ignite a Mayor to act in a bold and responsible manner.

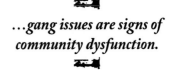

...gang issues are signs of community dysfunction.

The Mayor's role in gang reduction should be a great deal more than ceremonial. It is not enough to talk about the issue in high profile settings. The Mayor must provide vision and stay in tune to the overall development and operation of the gang reduction strategy.

In addition, the Mayor must insist on the cooperation of city staff, challenge the bureaucracy to embrace the challenge and be willing to seek out resources to assist in addressing the issue.

An effective Mayor must also rally other local political leaders. Even if the community has a strong two party political environment, the Mayor often is in a position to use the "Bully Pulpit" to keep the high ground of combating gangs in everyone's resume.

The *California Cities Gang Prevention Network (CCGPN)* published a strategy paper recently that expressed clearly that the Mayor, in close cooperation with the Chief of Police, must lead the community in three areas:

* Moral — crimes must be prevented

* Conceptual — Mayor must lead the planning

* Bureaucratic — must be willing to re-deploy city staff in support of the program

In Newport News, the voters elected local dentist and community leader McKinley Price, DDS on a platform of collaboration and youth violence prevention, intervention and reduction.

Price championed the phenomenal success of the Richmond *G.R.I.P.* Program, which reduced the violence in that city significantly.

"We don't have to re-invent how to reduce gangs in our city, we only have to look at our neighboring city of Richmond," Dr. Price said as he campaigned. Dr. Price united the city in developing the Strategic Plan.

Following his sweeping election in 2010, Dr. Price held a community forum with Rep. Bobby Scott, (D-VA) on the legislative progress of the *Youth Promise Act* and his plan of attack for the troubled city.

Dr. Price's outline provides a wonderful template for a community just beginning to wake up to the crisis. Here are the first fledgling steps taken by this troubled community to get their arms around a community-driven Strategic Plan.

Mayor McKinley Price's
Ten Steps to Reclaiming our Youth and Neighborhoods

1. *Appoint the Mayor's Task Force on Gang Reduction, Intervention and Prevention.*

2. *Assess the current gang situation from multiple perspectives.*

3. *Identify current gaps in services in the critical areas of prevention, suppression, intervention, enforcement and re-entry from incarceration or gang membership, with new focus on young adult services (18-25).*

4. *Adopt a BEST Practices model (Bringing Everyone's Strengths Together) empowering the most effective programs with grants.*

5. *Increase citizens' involvement substantially through targeted neighborhood outreach.*

6. *Nurture civic involvement through community presentations to civic organizations, churches and high profile special events in targeted neighborhoods.*

7.   *Identify Best Practices on a national and state level and integrate proven, measurable programs into measurable Best Practices already in place locally.*

8.   *Encourage active involvement by major employers and business leaders, especially in jobs training and incarceration re-entry support.*

9.   *Select and motivate the most committed faith-based leaders to bridge their efforts together.*

10.   *Increase success by continuous measurement and evaluation. Assign accountability for this to the Task Force.*

A prime example of positive leadership is San Bernardino CA, where Mayor Patrick Morris funded more police officers and anti-gang crime prevention programs. As a result, crime dropped 38% in the city's most crime saturated 20-block area.

In Richmond, VA, Mayor Doug Wilder made gang reduction a priority during his term and ordered a shift in city services to fit into a total community strategy. The 5th most dangerous city in America until Wilder became Mayor, Richmond's ranking dropped all the way to 119th under his leadership.

Richmond was named the number one crime prevention program in America, dropping murders from 148 in 2004 to 32 in 2008 after the Office of the Attorney General implemented the community-wide Strategic Plan.

With the *G.R.I.P.* (*Gang Reduction, Intervention and Prevention*) program in place from 2004-2008, Richmond saw double digit decreases in overall crime for four straight years. That impact continues today as the faith community has accelerated their intervention in dramatic ways in Virginia's capital city.

❋ 7 ❋

Reach Deep into the Community for Your Plan

When Salinas, CA was developing their Strategic Plan for their *G.R.I.P.* program, 25 different meetings were held in a 90-day period to gather ideas on gang issues throughout the city.

Since 1981, gang violence had claimed the lives of 15,000 Californians and citizens within individual communities before they were ready to get involved and work towards a solution.

The *California Cities Gang Prevention Network* (*CCGPN*) learned, after 32 months of study, that developing a *comprehensive plan* is essential. They have also learned community, police and social services must know gang members' names to stop them, engage with them and help them.

The gang issue in California attracted a great deal of attention and led to the forming of this thirteen-city coalition. The purpose of the network is to provide a conduit for information on gang intelligence as well as promising practices that would lead to community-based gang reduction solutions.

The *CCGPN's* six goals:

1. Get in front of the gang issue before policies based on fear alone dominate decision-making and divert funding from essential community services

2. Reduce gang violence and help build communities that do not provide violence

3. Forge and sustain a comprehensive municipal community partnership

4. Create strategies that combine prevention, intervention, and enforcement

5. Create a peer-learning network of urban leaders who work on local anti-gang strategies

6. Recommend legislative-administrative changes at state and federal levels

Solid community involvement remains in place within each of the thirteen cities that included Fresno, Oakland, Oxnard, Richmond, Sacramento, Salinas, San Bernardino, San Diego, San Francisco, San Jose, Santa Rosa, Stockton, and Los Angeles. This involvement in each community began with a total emphasis on citizen outreach.

In the Richmond *G.R.I.P.* program, staff spent countless hours reaching out to the community through meetings, forums, and special events. When the project first started, meetings occurred where the community appeared to show anger and hostility toward what they called "just another program."

Citizens were tired of the status quo, which is a typical government-lead program where a group of suits show up and tell the community how it is going to fix the problem.

In Richmond, it was obvious that this was not going to be received well. So staff ventured out to ask the community members how the team could join with them to seek solutions to their gang and crime problems.

In one meeting, an elderly African-American woman protested,

"Who are you to come to us and tell us how to fix our community?"

The staff was humbled by the question and *G.R.I.P.* provided an excellent response to this concern.

"We have come here tonight to have you tell us what the problems are and how to fix them."

This theme continued through the project and may have had the greatest impact leading to Richmond's success.

Citizens are the ones that are mostly impacted by the issue and they must be involved in the solution.

National guru Jack Calhoun has described the erosion well. "In crime besieged neighborhoods, kids fear going to school, parks become un-usable and shopping and taking the bus to work are dangerous ventures for residents. In short, communities plagued by gangs become aggregations of frightened isolated individuals."

❋ 8 ❋

Separate, Empower the Operational Council

A planned strategy will never work without the necessary foot soldiers to carry it out. It is not enough to establish that there is a gang issue within the community; citizens should expect that bold and decisive steps will be taken to address the issue.

Once the leadership has established that there is a problem, they must turn to those who are actually in a position to do something about it.

The careful creation of a strategy to reduce gangs is only a milestone in the journey.

Each agency and organization that provides service delivery and outreach can play a valuable role. But a key to the success evolves around thorough understanding of roles.

Clear separation between policy makers and operational personnel helps. The policy making team or "Executive Task Force" should involve leadership level representatives from direct service government agencies to include city agencies, law enforcement, courts, nonprofits, faith-based, and other citizens groups.

This is the group that would feature individuals that can assist in making policy and financial decisions on behalf of the overall effort. Examples of this group include the Mayor, the police chief, chief probation officer, director of social services, a prominent clergy member, selected citizen leaders from businesses, and the overall community. This leadership team will look different in each community that develops a program.

The second group that "actually does the work" should be formed within the community and is usually referred to as the technical operations team.

Local nonprofits, government service workers and community youth advocates must unite in their efforts. This group is typically assembled as the Operational Council. Members must agree upon and advocate for solutions-based, measurable plans to address the problem. This team should be described as the "boots on the ground." The Operational Council should meet at least monthly and operate in a dynamic environment, open to information sharing with a built-in level of confidentiality.

... new avenues of support are beginning to open up at the medical field discovers that this slaughter of young people is a public health issue.

Key prevention and intervention strategies are discussed, planned, and put into action. Accountability and performance become key factors. They should know when a specific strategy is working and be quick to recommend and or build in changes. Funding is an issue for the leadership team. Once a need or a gap in service is identified, the leadership team finds the necessary resources to address the issue. The good news is that new avenues of support are beginning to open up as the medical field discovers that this slaughter of young people is a public health issue. In fall 2010, the new Milwaukee Family + Youth Center got a huge boost when the Medical College of Wisconsin's Youth Violence Prevention Initiative, a program that views youth violence as a public health issue, awarded the Holton group a million-dollar grant to plan and operate the center over five years.

During a very stressful economic period for all agencies, it becomes easy to relax the plan, to put off funding the necessary gaps in service delivery. But a community should resist this impulse. The very existence of the effort depends upon trusting that resources will be there.

The technical operations team needs to be focused on the business of reducing gangs and preventing violence within the target area. The team should not operate with the fear or pressure of failure due to resources.

Positive efforts de-railed because of funding shortfalls can impact the entire community. In Los Angeles, the funding for gang reduction is constantly targeted, challenged and questioned.

The success of an overall gang reduction strategy is not in boardrooms or Council chambers. While endorsement and consent to the strategy are paramount, once funding is in place, the emphasis shifts fully to the Operational Council.

From outreach to citizen involvement, the role of a successful program will greatly depend on a community's understanding of the role of leadership with a clear separation of individuals who should be supported and left to do their jobs.

A typical operational council should include, but not be limited to:

- Government agencies
- Law enforcement
- Schools
- Social services
- Parks and recreation departments
- Nonprofit organizations
- Youth serving agencies
- Business representatives
- Faith-based leaders
- Citizens and parents
- College partners

This combination of perspectives, influence and wisdom comprises a leadership team that examines policy, scope and direction. As an Operational Council they should focus on applying the strategy through direct services — and this composition will insure that a community is involved and represented at all levels.

At the end of the day, no one organization has all the solutions.

9

Focus on the
Worst Problems First

In most communities across the United States there are areas that fall under the definition of "at-risk."

This could have a different meaning and definition depending on the agency that is conducting the assessment. When it comes to the issue of gang reduction, the measurement of selecting a community to address the issue unfortunately often falls into the lap of law enforcement.

The central risk factor that is constantly measured boils down to crimes that take place within a geographical area of the community. The central reasoning behind relying on crime statistics is because it is driven by fear and public perception.

But the neighborhood in the community that may be in the greatest need often is overlooked. One of the primary reasons that this occurs is that many community leaders have a misunderstanding of the risk factors that contribute to gang involvement. Dropout rates, unemployment, poverty, and available services all play an important role in looking at a neighborhood poised for increased gang activity.

The issue of selecting the right neighborhood is often hampered by delays — until gangs predictably come into existence and put the public in a state of fear and then we start to look at how to address the problem.

Communities will find it difficult to spend resources on risk factors that may not make the 11 o'clock news. But the reality is that we would save a great deal of resources by addressing the risk factors earlier instead of waiting until they become major issues.

The power of strategic planning will assist in selecting the right neighborhood for immediate action if the right assessment of the proposed community is completed.

During the *G.R.I.P.* program launched by the Justice Department, each selected city was mandated to select a targeted neighborhood for immediate action and planning purposes.

Within Los Angeles, which is nationally known for its gang-related issues, a targeted community had to be selected.

After careful consideration, the city's leadership decided to address the program in the *Boyle Heights* area of the city. The flexibility of the *G.R.I.P.* program allowed for the selection to be made at the local level.

A similar situation occurred in the Richmond project when it was decided that the South Richmond *Broad Rock* community would be the target for the Gang Reduction Program.

Clearly, by narrowing the focus of the reduction efforts to one part of the community, it allows for a specific model plan to be implemented toward a given set of risk factors and activity. It is very difficult to adopt an entire city for a planned strategy.

Following Boston's highly effective *Operation CeaseFire* in 1995, the next generation of intervention was based on careful research. The Harvard Kennedy School of Government found that approximately 1,600 to 2,200 Boston young people are at-risk for committing violent offenses.

> *...researchers found that 1% of Boston youth aged 16 to 24, from 5% of the city's geography, are committing more than 50% of the city's youth violence.*

In other words, researchers found that 1% of Boston youth aged 16 to 24, from 5% of the city's geography, are committing more than 50% of the city's youth violence. *StreetSafe* was designed based on this research. Launched in 2008, this is supported by a partnership of funders who built measurements into the strategy for the $26 million six-year project.

Operation: Safe Community is a collaborative effort in Memphis that seeks to reduce violence by young residents, under 24 years of age, by 25% over the next five years. The first phase of its *Memphis Youth Violence Prevention Plan* will focus on the city's northwest quadrant, where 50,000 children and youth live in poverty. The city will work with neighborhood networks to provide a continuum of evidence-based services from prenatal to career, and will promote data sharing among law enforcement, schools and service providers.

In San Jose, targeted neighborhoods are identified by operational teams and approved interventions are recommended, depending on the issues those neighborhoods face. This plan then goes forth to Council for funding.

✹ **10** ✹

Create the Vision and Clear Goals

The process starts with the deliberate shaping and adoption of a vision. It's a very lofty perch from which we craft a vision. Following some open discussion, create a very small group of engaged citizens and have them offer a vision that everyone can understand and accept.

In Salinas, it's "*A City at Peace.*"

In Santa Rosa, the vision is "*Reclaiming our youth for their families, schools, communities and futures.*" In Minneapolis, it's the "*Blueprint for Action.*" In Charlotte, it's "*The Gang of One.*"

Once the vision is developed, clear goals need to be set.

In Santa Rosa, the goal has been to cut gang violence in half in the five years 2006–2011. Their plan details the specifics on how they hope to achieve that goal.

Specific strategies should be selected, such as Santa Rosa's five targeted strategies:

- Awareness
- Prevention
- Intervention
- Enforcement
- Systems/Metrics

In Fresno, they have four goals:

- Tough enforcement
- Removing gang members from the gang lifestyle
- Preventing "wanna-bes" from escalating into gang membership
- Increasing the number of gang members in the legitimate workforce and/or back to school

Measurement is next. Fresno adopted these broad measurements to tell them if their program was on track:

- Rate of violent incidents
- Surveys of self-reported gang-involved youth (in school surveys)
- Recidivism rate for gang-involved youth
- Academic performance index improves
- Truancy rates decline

What is immediately apparent is that the more focused the vision, the clearer the goals become. Once the community has clear goals, measurement of the interventions is much easier.

In most mature markets, the measurements are conducted by the community's college or university faculty – independent from city bureaucracy and politics. The community usually compensates the school for guidance and involvement.

❋ 11 ❋
Tear Down the Walls — Relationships Matter

Since the beginning of the spread of the gang movement in America, one of the classic activities that have been a common theme among street gangs is the adoption of "neighborhood turf" issues.

In most communities, gangs typically take ownership of one or more streets and neighborhoods to build and show a source of strength and power.

In many communities in America, another form of turf issue arises when local leaders begin to develop a plan to reduce gangs.

When we start developing a strategy to address the problem, there seems to be a great deal of interest in agencies that seek involvement.

This is a clear shift from working with individuals who for a long period of time refused to acknowledge that a gang problem existed.

Little will be accomplished until community partners engage a team approach and not work in isolation. This becomes extremely important to the outcome of the project.

While helping a community develop a strategy to combat gangs, we made contact with the commander of the police department's gang unit. He requested a meeting to talk specifically about the rising tide of gang activity. It was refreshing to hear this tough, street hardened suppression expert plead for "more prevention and intervention services to address the issue."

We inquired about his department's working relationship with other community serving agencies, to which he replied "we can't get anybody to the table around the issue."

... "we can't get anybody to the table around the issue."

It is not law enforcement that usually displays barriers. Many local government departments do not play well together. And many nonprofits are huddling around their lifeblood funding.

The best gang reduction models in the country are the ones where team members unite their efforts behind a central mission. In San Jose, part of the formal measurement is a survey of all stakeholders asking if they have developed new and abiding relationships through their involvement with the Task Force. That is reported to the community and City Council. Measure everything.

Law enforcement, schools, social services, and key nonprofits all have to work together to insure that the developing strategy is a comprehensive approach.

The Richmond *G.R.I.P.* program, from the beginning, fed off of cooperation between the partners, many who had never worked together before. The model was developed with the theme of relationship building as a key component.

A powerful partnership was founded with the police department and the Richmond Outreach Center, a central faith-based effort in South Richmond. In addition, the team included the Sheriff's office, the probation and parole department, and the Commonwealth's Attorney to develop a solid re-entry program for returning inmates into the community.

A total of forty-four partners worked on the Richmond project. They came from state and local government, nonprofits, faith-based, and citizen groups. All worked together to create the project's success.

The biggest gain for those involved was the building of relationships. In Richmond, walls were torn down that had separated agencies for years. Within the program, no one agency claimed to be the lead and everyone involved worked hard to insure inclusiveness.

❊ 12 ❊

Fund Measured Programs That Work

Those who work in the field of social action observe one unfortunate fact on a regular basis: there is consistent funding to programs that have not been evaluated or have not proven to be successful.

In most cases, these programs are noble in their intent.

The issue is that they may not be relevant to what is needed to address the current issues.

The indicators would support that a directional change is needed in service delivery within communities when it comes to gang reduction.

One key indicator of widespread systems failure is that gang involvement across the United States is dramatically increasing. If our traditional strategies were having an impact, would the numbers show such a noteworthy increase?

Another indicator of systems failure is the fact many of the young people immersed in gang culture are young adults ages 18-25. Yet few communities fund programs that provide support services to this age group.

It's an obvious need to program for young people to set their moral compass. But it's a vacuum out there for programs going after the majority of existing gang members over 18 years of age.

... it's a vacuum out there for programs going after the majority of existing gang members over 18 years of age.

Funding for gang reduction must be used to support actual services that will help with this issue. Granted, a vast majority of these older gang members have been immersed in the lifestyle for years. Some began gang involvement at age 10. Many have attained high status and rank because of their brutality. And in most cases, suppression and enforcement strategies are the smart bet for tackling this aspect of the gang problem.

But an even more important issue is that funded programs should be able to show measureable results.

The key issue is not only that we address seasoned gang members, but also that we measure everything we do.

That's been the problem – accountability and measurement. With the proper evaluation procedures in place, the results should speak for themselves.

When we say fund programs that work – we are referring to measured results.

For example, Boys & Girls Clubs, which connect young people to caring adults and constructive activities after school, found that housing projects without clubs had 50% more vandalism and scored 37% worse on drug activity than those served by the programs.

Or, another example of measurement is Big Brothers Big Sisters. Young people who were randomly assigned to a Big Brother or Big Sister mentor were about half as likely to begin illegal drug use and nearly one-third less likely to hit someone compared to those who were assigned to a waiting list.

Diverting or cutting funding to nonprofit programs has never been a major issue. The larger issue is how we get a fair evaluation of local government services and what steps will be taken to change the course of that funding.

Can all of the youth serving agencies in your community measure up with data like the Boys & Girls Club?

This becomes very difficult owing to the fact that it can become extremely political.

When you divert public funding, it rarely goes without some form of political backlash at the local level.

At times, we would rather continue supporting a program without measureable results than calling into question the issue of diverting funds. Once a local government has a fixed budget it throws its complete focus on that inertia. Suggest altering that and watch the bureaucracy look at you like you were a diamondback rattler.

In most communities this might be interpreted as an event that would precipitate loss of jobs. Well, not necessarily at all. What it does mean is that many jobs could well be re-purposed, re-engineered; job descriptions could be drastically changed.

We cannot let our new way of doing business be a "witch hunt" or a blame game. Well-meaning and talented people have labored for years to create their niche in the community. If our evidence does not support that role, we must pry that individual up from the trench and send him or her on a new mission with firm measures. That will protect rather than threaten job security.

The one central theme that should remain in our planning and funding requirements is that we must move beyond the status quo of believing that we are truly making an impact on reducing gangs by providing the same service year after year.

Change is the norm in this field. It's insane not to change up what you're doing.

Change is the norm in this field. It's insane not to change up what you're doing.

"The definition of insanity is doing the same thing over and over and expecting different results," we often hear.

This definition of insanity still works for us - when community leaders keep applying the same strategies over and over and over and over without any change in the outcomes.

If our efforts are not effective we must be willing to ask the serious questions of what is effective and what do we need to support to succeed.

After two decades of diligent measurement, it is of interest to note that San Jose has distilled their funding interventions into ten eligible services that can be funded by city dollars.

For FY 2010–2011, a total of $4.6 million was allocated for direct intervention services. Of this, the city of San Jose contracted with 26 community-based organizations (for a total of $2.3 million), providing a range of gang intervention services throughout San Jose. Services are provided based on priority service areas and need in each Police Division (Central, Foothill, Southern, Western and City-wide). Some of these services include gang mediation and intervention, truancy intervention, services to adjudicated youth, outpatient substance abuse services, parent trainings and parent/community gang-awareness trainings. The following is a breakdown of the funds distributed to each Police Division:

- Central $265,066
- Western $428,959
- Foothill $1,151,310
- Citywide $158,650
- Southern $311,065

Additional services including late night programming, *Safe School Campus Initiative*, staffing and activities, tattoo removal, and other diversion activities were provided through *BEST (Bringing Everyone's Strengths Together)* funded San Jose intervention programs for a cost of $1.4 million. The remaining $900,000 was used for administrative costs, an independent program evaluator and the emergency reserve fund. A program evaluation report will be completed by January 2012, and results brought forward to City Council.

Again, deploying the local university or experienced independent national consultant to conduct measurements is a common strategy that pays big dividends in credibility and effectiveness.

❊ 13 ❊

Expect Resistance after Years
of Heads Buried in the Sand

In Los Angeles, Mayor Antonio Villarigosa constantly finds himself in a political battle. Not just for his office, but for funding for a gang reduction and youth development program. With a city facing regular annual budget shortfalls, the Los Angeles City Council must do some serious trimming in their budget.

The gang reduction effort within the last several years has become the central target with a price tag of $26 million. Political objections take many forms, depending on how divisive the politics in a given community have devolved.

Lying in wait are people looking for evidence that the community's elected leaders are wrongly funding hapless efforts.

Budget watchdogs chirp at every expenditure, penning their letters to the editor and testimony before Council.

The violence prevention task force must vocally lead the effort from a community Strategic Plan and defend the decisions as both worthy and community-driven. This removes the target from the Mayor's back.

The key to this effort is a highly visible, transparent approach. Make it someone's job to assure this is the atmosphere in which the community takes on this task.

But in most communities, the resistance is passive-aggressive.

Lawmakers dismiss the symptoms of crisis in the challenged neighborhoods.

Golfers line up their tee shots lamenting the black-on-black crime in town. It's not happening in their neighborhood, thank goodness.

Golfers line up their tee shots lamenting the black-on-black crime in town. It's not happening in their neighborhood, thank goodness.

The only people who really seem to know what is happening on the streets are the cops, judges and physicians and nurses in the ER.

People who live in subsidized housing and tough streets have lived with drugs, guns and violence for decades. They have no one they trust to go to, so the meek and dignified voices from the projects are muted by the other priorities of the city. But in communities across the country, for varying reasons, the awakening came slowly and the slumber ended with the tragic death of many young people.

In the city of Rochester, MN, a community known for world-class medicine and technology, the first crack cocaine arrest leading to an awareness of gangs setting up shop was in 1990. In 2010, thirty years later, the United Way lays the foundation for a gang prevention plan. It's by no means unusual. In fact, this is a typical response curve in most American cities.

❦ 14 ❦
Harness Faith-Based Interventions

Faith-based groups have a unique power to effect change in violence-prone populations.

The Diocese of Monterey and a community organization organized a 5,000-strong peace march against gang violence *in 2010. Communities Organized for Relational Power in Action, (COPA),* a collaborative network of churches, synagogues, schools and nonprofits in Monterey and Santa Cruz counties, helped the diocese create the "*Procession for Peace*" march.

The Bishop's *Covenant for Peace* is aimed at creating healthy activities for youth, improving familial relationships, forging partnerships with law enforcement and applying the strength of prayer. The diocese has said that it's making gang-violence prevention a priority.

They have also collected over 12,000 signatures of support. We think this is brilliant because it gives volunteers a mission. It enables everyone to help gather signatures and tell others about the prevention initiative. It spreads the word and can be used when applying for grants as a demonstration of community readiness.

In Salinas, all 29 homicides in 2009 were blamed on gangs. In 2010, the city had 15 gang-related homicides. This year at least two of the three homicides were gang-related.

The key is to bring together church leaders – which is a dramatically successful formula for success. Create a Clergy Council as a coalition of faith-based communities.

In Oxnard, CA, the Clergy Council offers *Peacemakers*, who do street intervention; *HopeBoyz*, who do school interventions, offer alternatives and long term mentoring and *Next Step Re-entry*, which offers services to inmates and soon to be released parolees. *Granny's Love* is a group of grandmas who do intervention at middle schools — showing unconditional love, Grannies-style, during the students' lunch break.

This, from a gang interventionist blog in San Jose:

"*Today, Tony is an extremely influential man throughout the entire country. 29 years ago, the Lord led Tony to found a ministry that is today known as the California Youth Outreach. He and his team go into the streets and talk to youth who are caught up in gangs. They are working on gang prevention. They are not armed with weapons. They are armed with the Word of God. I...well, I have nothing more to say about that. I think that it speaks for itself. I encourage you to pray for Tony Ortiz, his staff, and the hearts of the men and women on the streets. Pray that the Lord and His principles will go ahead of them and calm the storms."*

We love the Boston model and its focus on *Season of Peace* activities that all partners can participate with. It would be a great template for your community's ministry.

The model established in Boston for deep and abiding involvement by the local faith community is being replicated across the nation. The *Boston TenPoint Coalition (BTPC)* is an ecumenical group of Christian clergy and lay leaders working to mobilize the community around issues affecting Black and Latino youth.

> ... *"shattered lives and dreams are reflected in their violent and oftentimes callous and/or self-destructive behaviors."*

TenPoint is a nationally recognized model for mobilizing faith communities to serve as full partners with public safety, local government, schools, and human services providers to work with at-risk youth and prevent violence. The *BTPC* focuses on "troubled youth," youth that other agencies most frequently are unable to serve, specifically high-risk youth. The faith community refers to these young people as those whose "shattered lives and dreams are reflected in their violent and oftentimes callous and/or self-destructive behaviors."

The local clergy operates in collaboration with other community-based, governmental, and private sector institutions that are also committed to the revitalization of the families and communities in which our youth are raised. The work of the *TenPoint Coalition* is to transform the culture of violence in the Greater Boston community, one neighborhood at a time, one young person at a time. The mission is to end the era of violence in Boston, and demonstrate the vital need for faith-based institutions to participate in city-wide crime reduction strategy.

The *TenPoint* Plan, as described on their website:

1. Promote and campaign for a cultural shift to help reduce youth violence, both physically and verbally within the Black community by initiating conversations, introspection and reflection on the thoughts and actions that hold us back as a people; individually and collectively.

2. Develop, as churches, a curriculum regarding Black and Latino history with an emphasis on the struggles of women of color to help young people understand that the God of history has been and remains active in all our lives.

3. Acknowledge and respond to the impact of trauma as a physical and emotional reality on the lives of our young people and their families as a direct result of violence.

4. Build meaningful relationships with high-risk youth by recognizing their reality on their terms and in their spaces.

5. Focus specially on connecting and rebuilding the lives of youth who have been incarcerated and stigmatized by mainstream society.

6. Provide youth advocacy and one-on-one mentoring for high-risk youth.

7. Provide gang mediation and intervention for high-risk youth with the goal of establishing cease-fires and building the foundation for active peace.

8. Establish accountable, community-based economic development projects that are organic visions of revenue generation and demystify the accumulation and power of money through financial literacy.

9. Build partnerships with the social/secular institutions of our city, with suburban and downtown communities of faith to help provide spiritual, human and material support.

10. Provide ongoing training for individual churches along with a systematic program in leadership development to create, maintain, and sustain community mobilization."

The organization's website serves as a portal for new partnerships.

"At the heart of the Boston *TenPoint Coalition* is the building of partnerships. We have long realized that police and law enforcement cannot arrest the city out of violence, that District Attorneys cannot prosecute the city out of violence, and that sheriffs cannot incarcerate the city out of violence. Partnerships are needed because the best approaches to violence involve a multi-pronged intervention, prevention and suppression strategy, and multi-stakeholders with community and faith groups as leaders in the effort."

Conversely, some of the most unsuccessful community efforts have a notable absence of the faith community in their planning.

As we have seen and observed, San Jose is often cited as the best gang prevention program in the U.S. San Jose's program began with the faith community in the early 1990s when passionate faith-based leaders asked the Mayor to do something about the 300% rise in the juvenile crime rate.

Note this continuing theme as we continue this tour of programs around the nation and in Canada – almost every one of the dramatically successful efforts has deep involvement by the faith community.

Perhaps the most vital contribution by the faith community comes in street intervention.

Street outreach programs have not been measured as closely as many of the prevention programs around the nation.

Yet in terms of mayhem, these programs are likely the most effective. You never heard about the gang gunfight that did not occur because a peacemaker was on the street and convinced the gang leaders that having this war would be bad for business.

You never hear about the murder that did not happen when a former gang leader was released from prison and came home to re-claim his territory, because a gang interventionalist stepped in and negotiated a nonviolent outcome.

The key element of street outreach programs is outreach workers, sometimes courageously, working with at-risk youth in their communities.

They work with kids that have rejected mainstream mentoring, Boys & Girls Club membership or church programs. These workers need strong networks with social agencies and police, yet distance themselves enough to establish trust on the street. They often have a history of being in gangs themselves.

There was an independent study of Chicago *CeaseFire* cited by the National Council on Crime and Delinquency as significant.

This study found clear "reductions in shootings, gang involvement in homicides, retaliatory murders, and a cooling of 'hot spots' in target areas compared to similar areas in the city that are not served by *CeaseFire*."

The National Council's white paper is an excellent resource for the planning of street interventions. The study is available online at *California Cities Gang Prevention Network* website.

One of the key findings in this study is the fact that nonprofits and faith-based organizations have an easier time of organizing such an effort and have strong street credibility.

The National Council on Crime and Delinquency's report evaluated ground-level street outreach.

- Outreach workers ("gang interventionists") must be able to connect with the youth targeted; in other words, they need to be ex-gang members. These street smart young people know when a situation is too dangerous to enter. Yet passion and commitment are equally important, even if the worker has no street experience.

- Outreach workers should not work for city government. There are too many restrictions and requirements. A prison record would remove them for eligibility in many cases, for example. A strict drug testing policy would eliminate many candidates. The most successful outreach programs are faith-based, as they give the targeted kids a very legitimate reason to leave the gang.

- There will be high turnover and significant dangers. Forming and establishing an outreach program is delicate work. Only in 2010 did a city actually graduate the first class of interventionist training (Los Angeles).

- Outreach workers need to be highly connected to services as they cannot solve all a kid's problems by themselves. For safety, they often work in pairs. Some are given uniforms to deter gang violence in their presence as well as keep law enforcement from sweeping them up in an action.

Some hard core gang members may not be willing to alter their lifestyle, but they may be willing to reduce the violent behavior, or at least stop using gun violence.

This report notes that one of the best places to begin outreach is in juvenile and adult lockups, receiving lists of those about to be released from the Probation Department, initiating a re-entry strategy for the client.

Sometimes the goal is different. Some hard core gang members may not be willing to alter their lifestyle, but they may be willing to reduce the violent behavior, or at least stop using gun violence. In these instances, drug selling or gang involvements are not emphasized. Violence Interrupters mediate conflicts between gangs and work situations such as with returning prisoners expecting their territory to be returned to them.

The faith community also excels at prevention initiatives.

Tony Lowden has attracted over 800 students to after school programs at several *Campus Clubs* in Macon, GA. Tony grew up in the Philadelphia ghettos lacking hope, and for a while, purpose. He created these 21st century learning centers with the latest software, computers and engaging curricula in science, technology, engineering and math. He has these kids building rockets and robots. Tony notes that many children from poverty and broken homes aren't usually rooted in faith and morals - so *Campus Clubs* addressed that with these church-based programs.

A firm believer that government and public education should not advocate the practice of faith, Lowden says these entities should not run from religion either. All can co-exist, with a common goal of uplifting at-risk youth.

The most powerful view of street interventions we have seen appeared in late 2010 on *A&E*: "*The Peacemaker: L.A. Gang Wars,*" five half-hour episodes following gang mediator Malik Spellman as he tries to keep gang tensions in South Central Los Angeles from erupting into violence.

In season one, Spellman works with opposing gangs run by brothers, tries to prevent a war in his own neighborhood after a gang member's pregnant girlfriend is killed, and tries to calm tensions after a game of dice erupts into gunplay in the Imperial Courts housing project. Viewing this powerful documentary will convince you that violence can be averted with properly done interventions, demonstrating respect for the people involved. But it is absolutely essential to hire those who can operate in this world.

Teny Gross, executive director of the *Institute for the Study and Practice of Nonviolence* in Providence, RI, notes in the white paper that "programs housed in a city agency do not allow flexibility in worker schedules necessary to do this kind of work, which occurs at all hours of the night. It also keeps the program from becoming a 'dumping ground' for city employees."

"Furthermore," he notes, "it allows the program to be more aggressive and flexible in responding to the ever-changing nature of violence in the city."

He suggests that street interventions not be organized and operated in a large, bureaucratic nonprofit organization.

From a street perspective, when a faith-based worker approaches a gang member on the street, that faith motivation is apparent to the community — and it is evident that the former gang member has actually changed ways, and why. Many challenged neighborhoods already have strong churches, so the "boots are already on the ground."

Street outreach also challenges the need for full and complete transparency — it is sensitive and misunderstood by the omnipresent budget watchdogs of city government.

Reassurance is the operative word — and funding a church's effort provides a level of trust that is important to the program's ongoing credibility.

A faith-based organization can do miracles as we have seen in Richmond, VA, where you really cannot tell the difference between faith-based programs and city run programs. It is seamless.

The cause and effect of former gang members serving in a solutions-driven role within reduction programs is an issue that many government leaders reject.

The Los Angeles issue is if public dollars should ever be used to pay individuals whose past, certainly by traditional means, appears shady and questionable. These are legitimate questions, considering the financial crisis in that state.

In directing Virginia's *G.R.I.P.* gang reduction program, it was clear that that this issue is important. It can be a dividing issue both politically and operationally on a subject that requires consensus.

We funded a way for former gang members to have tattoo removal to prepare them for re-entry into the workforce — a move that brought forth a tremendous amount of criticism from a number of people in leadership positions.

Politically, prevention, intervention, and re-entry programs face a great deal of pressure as they seek funding and political backing.

These efforts go against the political sound bites of "let's get tough on crime," and "three strikes and you're out." Few if any candidates ever ran a political campaign on "let's give gang members or felons a second chance."

One very powerful retort to the naysayers is, "How's your incarceration cycle working for you so far?"

The reality of the matter is that gang reduction efforts that are successful go against the grain of political and public policy.

In order to reduce gangs you must first believe that there is value and worth in each nonviolent member of a gang. That factor does not win elections.

> *We urge communities to be against violence, not the young people drawn into gang membership.*

We urge communities to be against violence, not the young people drawn into gang membership.

The politics of gang reduction can greatly reduce a community's ability to deal with the problem. The continued growth of gang issues in the United States allows us to realize that the critical issue facing a community is to agree on a proven strategy that will provide solutions.

In Los Angeles, the Mayor has created a new academy in charge of training interventionalists and overseeing gang violence intervention. LA currently has over 400 criminal groups and spends over $26 million a year in fighting them.

Up until this year, the city has not been able to gain traction and creditability with street intervention. The 15-week academy graduated its first class in June 2010 and law enforcement officials across the nation are watching and monitoring the results.

Mayor Antonio Villaraigoso marked the occasion well by stating that "these brave men and women have chosen to correct their life's path, to work side by side with our police department, to bridge the gaps of cooperation for the sake of saving lives."

The Oakland Police Department works closely with their outreach team, and they are mutually supportive in every way. Close partnership with other interventional agencies are also key to Oakland's strategy – tying up closely with the alternative high schools and helping to mediate gang conflicts and provide community support following shootings and violent acts. Groups such as *Youth Alive,* a Catholic Charities effort, support families of homicide victims and prevent retaliation in Oakland hospitals.

The program tracks street outreach workers' daily location and activities and workers file incident reports.

✹ 15 ✹
Set Clear Goals from 10,000 Feet

We encourage communities to set clear goals, but to site those goals from altitude. Many folks want tactical programs to be goals. The goal setting we recommend includes many tactics beneath an umbrella goal.

The clearest broad-reaching goals we have seen across the U.S. and Canada reside in Minneapolis. In fact, if we could give an Oscar to the best violence prevention goal setting in the country, we would open the envelope and announce, "and the Oscar goes to… Minneapolis."

Published prominently online is the City's Preventing Youth Violence in Minneapolis *Blueprint for Action:*

"The city of Minneapolis recognizes that youth violence is a public health epidemic that requires a holistic, multi-faceted response. Drawing on a mix of increased law enforcement and public health strategies to address the root causes of violence and significantly reduce and prevent youth violence in Minneapolis, the city, in partnership with a host of community stakeholders, created the *Blueprint for Action.* Goals identified in the *Blueprint:*

- Connect every youth with a trusted adult

- Intervene at the first sign that youth are at-risk for violence

- Restore youth who have gone down the wrong path
- Unlearn the culture of violence in our community"

The actions plans developed in the Strategic Plan all vividly fall under one of these four action goals.

An effort equally as commendable comes from the national leaders in California.

One of the most seasoned veterans of gang intervention is Jack Calhoun.

Calhoun notes that since 1981, gang violence has claimed the lives of more than 15,000 Californians. Most of this violence occurs in cities. Death is just one measure of victimization.

National League of Cities Institute for Youth, Education and Families partnered with Oakland-based National Council on Crime and Delinquency to launch the *California Cities Gang Prevention Network (CCGPN)*.

The 13 participating cities have six goals and they meet regularly to share best practices. Again, extreme clarity from 10,000 feet:

1. "Get in front of the gang issue before policies based on fear alone dominate decision-making and divert funding from essential community services.

2. Reduce gang violence and help build communities that don't produce violence.

3. Forge and sustain a comprehensive municipal-community partnership.

4. Create strategies that combine prevention, intervention and enforcement.

5. Create a peer-learning network of urban leaders who work on local anti-gang strategies.

6. Recommend legislative-administrative changes at state and federal levels."

In Salinas and Monterey County, the *Community Alliance for Safety and Peace (CASP)* aims to reduce violence caused disproportionally by the county's 71 gangs and 5,000 gang members. *CASP* has developed a comprehensive strategy built on four principles:

- A single operational structure for coordinating violence prevention work by multiple agencies
- Data-driven action and data sharing
- Putting youth needs at the center
- Promoting meaningful community engagement

❧ 16 ❧

Measurement Is Everything — Indicators to Steer By

The National Center for the Prevention of Community Violence was created to respond to the steady demand across the country for assistance in helping communities select the right course for violence prevention.

Other nonprofits also offer good and noble counsel.

Whatever counsel or consultant works with the community, we recommend the use of very broad benchmarking as we believe that one solution does not fit all communities.

It is also a wise counselor who while offering guidance on making critical decisions, assures that those decisions are made during critical conversations among community leaders.

Benchmarking across the nation, we always urge insistence on tight, disciplined, independent measurement.

Communities large and small, usually have three things in common:

- Their present strategy (if any) is not working
- The gang and violence measures are going the wrong way
- A true community-wide Strategic Plan has not been collaboratively developed

When we go into a community, we ask to see the data that can be gathered to give us some idea of how far the erosion of the culture has advanced. It's the first step in analyzing the most acute needs in the process.

Transparency and frequency of reporting are paramount with gang reduction efforts. In Los Angeles, people complained about transparency despite a $900,000 contract with the Urban Institute to evaluate the gang reduction efforts.

"No comment" and the stonewalling of inquiries caused a deficit of trust, which initiated investigative reports and a great deal of public scrutiny of the program.

America's financial crisis has forced most local and state government officials to cut back to basic core services.

In Los Angeles, the crisis has caused grave cutbacks in the city's services. Yet the gang strategy and funding is holding on despite these pressures. *Homeboy Industries* is suffering the worst, but is reviving.

*Public money is followed
closely by public perception.*

Public money is followed closely by public perception.

This is a key reason why open transparency is crucial especially during a time of severe budget restraints. The issue with funding gang reduction is that there is still a great deal of public discourse over exactly what works.

In Richmond, VA, the *G.R.I.P.* program, deploying the Urban Institute, published the measures and the progress reports. Many in government were cautious and wanted to hold back. But it is important for the community to know and understand that measurement is ongoing and independent evaluators will assure their investment is being monitored.

People begin to become distrustful if they do not know the process of spending public funding. The reality of it is that there should be no reason to hide anything. With Sunshine laws and the Freedom of Information Act, there is little point to secrecy.

It is our duty to inform the taxpayers. The days of unexplained government spending at the local level have already come to a close. With an issue as important as gang reduction, the more transparency — the better.

A bigger question may be how do you measure successes in gang prevention/reduction?

Is it measured by a reduction in crime?

Or is it a drop in individuals that are repeat offenders?

What about an increase in incarcerated individuals gaining employment once they return to the community?

It is difficult to place a hand on what one figure would indicate success of a program. In reality, if a community's gang reduction strategy is working, then many indicators should improve.

Early in the process, a community may actually experience a slight increase in crime. One of the by-products of an effective violence reduction program is an increase in neighborhood trust, and consequently, an increase in crime reporting.

So, it's vital to measure active citizen involvement.

In Richmond, this dynamic actually showed an increase in police clearance rates, which was a great measurable victory against the "No Snitch" policy that has held the community hostage. In law enforcement lingo, "clearance" refers to solved crimes.

We must ask ourselves, do citizens feel empowered to report crime and then work with police to solve it?

By looking at baseline numbers it may be hard to sell this logic. But the reality is that our overall goal is to bring a feeling of safety and security to our streets. This feeling is central to the quality of life in any community.

Gang reduction must be transparent. We should not get lost in political fighting over funding simply because people are not informed. Measurement and transparency may take extra time from our efforts, but it is central to public trust.

Tracking the effectiveness of gang reduction efforts can be tricky and misleading if not done properly.

> *Measurement and transparency may take extra time from our efforts, but it is central to public trust.*

One example would be the tracking of ex-gang members and offenders that become gainfully employed.

In most communities, this would be difficult to track because there has never been a concentrated effort to offer employment to this group. So our tracking must begin with a documentation of our community needs and a clear division of our current risk factors and the assets that we are putting in place to address the issues.

This factor again highlights the need of the development of a multi-faceted Strategic Plan that is specific for the community.

Traditionally many communities have been counting the number of gangs, gang members, and the arrest rate of those identified to be involved.

This measurement alone simply lets us qualify the work of law enforcement and judicial officials as we stockpile and send to Gladiator School all the individuals who have committed gang-related offenses.

The issue with law enforcement numbers is that they do not give us a sense of success in turning the lives of young people and gang members.

Tracking results in gang reduction should not be an expensive or complicated process. It all begins with the community assessment. This starting point will allow for us to track the number of involved citizens in our process.

We may be working in a community where citizen outreach and involvement is weak or non-existent. This is an identified risk that should be documented along with a tracking of any increase in involvement.

This and all other aspects of our efforts should be tracked to measure where we are in comparison to where we need to go. Within all of our efforts, we should be constantly reminded that our overall goal is not just related to numbers but overall quality of life.

While this factor may seem hard to prove, it really can be made into a fairly simple equation. By tracking citizen involvement we start to see a community where the key stakeholders are becoming part of the solution.

Recently, we were assisting in the development of a Strategic Plan in a city that had gang infested neighborhoods, full of blight.

In a planning meeting, we were able to determine that the area was extremely low on citizen involvement. The police department in the area had been busy answering gunfire and crime related calls to the point that efforts to develop a citizens' outreach program had been replaced by a mentality of "putting out fires."

With one question, "What about starting a crime watch group?" we began to measure citizen outreach and involvement.

Where a traditionalist may not see this as a major step, those who work with this issue routinely would view this as a victory. We have gone from having zero citizen involvement to establishing a baseline for citizen input.

An additional measurement would be attached to our service delivery.

It is easy to cut funds to what we cannot quantify. With the proper tracking we will not only measure the overall impact of the project, we will quickly identify project strengths and weaknesses.

Tracking gives us valuable information for funding, service delivery, and success measurement and this is essential to any gang reduction effort.

Measures can be simple or complex.

In Norwalk, CT, the local Youth Services Department received a federal grant for $200,000 to enhance their gang intervention programs and help the Youth Services Department establish a program that hopes to curb angry and aggressive behavior.

"*Norwalk Online Hour*" reporter Steve Kobak reported in September 2010 that the goal is to curb gang-related violence and stop gang recruitment by reaching at-risk youths before they sink into the gangster lifestyle.

The measures going in to the program were impressive. They had documentation that the majority the gang intervention program's clients are "dabbling" in gang activity and 37% are "willing to admit" that they are involved in a gang.

At the Justice Department's 2011 annual gang summit, Salinas' efforts were reviewed and suggestions made. *Herald* Salinas Bureau reporter Julia Reynolds reports that Salinas is in dire need of two components that experts say are required to surmount its gang problems: "better information on its youth and gang crimes, and resources to deal with prisoners returning to the community."

Just reporting outcome of gang-related crime statistics does not make us a believer that suppression is the only dog in the fight.

Sometimes, a community focuses a bit too much on one-dimensional reporting. We must ask what prevention measures look like, what interventions have been measured. Just reporting outcome of gang-related crime statistics does not make us a believer that suppression is the only dog in the fight.

Here is a press release from the Public Affairs Department, city of Raleigh, NC from June 14, 2010:

56 known gangs in Raleigh, 3070 gang members

"Raleigh's Police Chief Harry Dolan issued a report that lists gang-related crime in the Raleigh area down by 49% in 2009, to 1,417 gang-related crimes.

Gang-related drug cases were down 43%. Firearms cases involving gang members dropped 53%. Assaults by people involved in gangs decreased by 67%. In 2009, the Police Department began tracking gang-related crimes. The department reports that there are 56 known gangs with a membership of 3,070. Statistics show that 76% are between 16 and 25 years of age. Half of the gang members are 18-22."

We honor the work of Raleigh's law enforcement community. Yet we yearn for deeper measures than counting gang members and measuring violent crime and we worry that by reporting only enforcement and suppression initiatives, the community will limit focus on equally paramount prevention and intervention tactics.

We should always be asking who is making the measurements, how long they have sub-divided gang-related crime from non-gang-related crime, and what is being done about preventing more from joining the three thousand gang members in town. What are they doing about prisoner re-entry? Where's the faith community? What's the third grade reading level looking like? What percentage of high school graduates are finishing on time?

All that being said, Raleigh and North Carolina are doing great – sporting the lowest crime rate in 25 years in 2010 – and feeling good about an aggressive movement toward prevention.

In 2010, crime measures went down across America. Cities were triumphant in claiming their police departments were proud of the evidence of their violence reduction measures. But crime went down across the board. Many cities have been raising the victory flag.

Results Minneapolis is a management tool the city uses to systematically track performance toward achieving the city's five-year goals and 2020 vision.

A review panel of city leaders meets with a different department head each week to track progress and discuss strategies on key performance measures. By regularly tracking performance data at these "progress conferences," city leaders identify areas where the community is excelling, as well as opportunities for improvement.

Again, we look to San Jose as the benchmark for measurements. Here is an excerpt from the City Council Agenda of June 21, 2011 whereby the performance of the funded programs of the Task Force was reviewed:

Highlights of the San Jose *BEST* *(Bringing Everyone's Strengths Together)* Final Evaluation Report for 2009-2010

For FY 2009-2010, a total of 5,781 ongoing unduplicated participants were served by 22 agencies. Of these youth, 49% were gang-impacted with the remaining 51% at-risk or high-risk youth.

Results included:

- 88% of *BEST* participants were satisfied with services received

- 89% of the parents of the *BEST* participants were satisfied with the services their youth received

- 78% of the *BEST* participants reported that the services received were effective in producing a change for the better

- 74% of the *BEST* participants reported that the services received were effective in producing positive changes in their attitude and behaviors that were important to a civil society

- 91% of parents indicated that they improved their skills and knowledge about youth and gangs, accessing youth intervention resources and how to advocate for their child due to their participation in the workshop

Other notable findings include:

- 806 youth who were arrested previously were not re-arrested during the service cycle

- 658 youth who were previously not in school, re-connected to a school during the service cycle

- 50% decrease in the number of gang-related incidents over the past four years, with a 30% decline in the last year

- Through re-enrollment and reduced dropouts, San Jose schools have reduced lost revenue by 50% since school year 2006

✸ 17 ✸

Assure an Independent Audit

Once the tracking and evaluation system is in place and project data is received, what agency will be responsible for channeling the results?

This question is one that is an important as tracking the data itself.

Can government and nonprofits conduct an objective view of their own program?

As part of the United States Justice Department's benchmark gang reduction and intervention program, Richmond required an independent audit by the Urban Institute in Washington, D.C.

This audit was essential to tracking the funding that had been provided as well as the service results that were achieved in the four chosen communities.

The Urban Institute was charged with making site visits as well as accumulating the data on each community project. This independent audit was not a surprise; it was planned as a part of the program from the beginning.

During the funding period, a report was generated listing the strengths and areas in need of improvement for each project. Most projects are evaluated at the conclusion of the funding cycle, but the mid-term audit allowed for program changes to gain the greatest return of public investment. Additionally, upon completion, a second audit was conducted to measure program effectiveness.

Independent audits are a crucial form of evidence to define the project impact from planning to service delivery. They do not have to be expensive and should be conducted by a group or an individual that has experience in managing or evaluating gang reduction efforts.

There are a number of choices when it comes to independent audits. Some communities partner with local colleges and universities to conduct the audit, or consultants.

The proper audit should first consist of an assessment of the problem. This is important so that auditors will have a starting point in an effort to manage results.

In addition, an independent audit will track the resources that have been expended for the project and present a clear picture of cost benefit. This will assist as decisions are made about funding. This audit should include a review of government resources and their effectiveness.

A community is often quick to measure the outcomes of a nonprofit yet fails to measure the effectiveness of local government services. This tendency reflects the insular culture of city and county governmental organizations, and should be resisted - an audit is not simply a way to rubberstamp the efficiency in service delivery.

Make the audit one that is independent without allowing project stakeholders to control funding and outcomes.

overall measure is still elusive and troubling to leadership:

Make the audit one that is independent without allowing project stakeholders to control funding and outcomes.

In July 2010, Wendy Greuel, the City Controller of Los Angeles sent out a letter to the community with some concerns about the independent auditing. Even though the Urban Institute was conducting the audit for the city, the

> *"This morning I released a follow-up audit of the City's Comprehensive Citywide Anti-Gang Strategy. I strongly believe that this audit is among the most important I will conduct, because the safety of our children and communities is the city of Los Angeles is our city's most important responsibility.*
>
> *Unfortunately, our city has become known as the gang capital of the United States, despite the best efforts of the Los Angeles Police Department (LAPD) and community partners. According to the LAPD the city currently has over 400 gangs and nearly 41,000 gang members.*
>
> *In 2008, the Controller's office completed a report that revealed the city was wasting millions of dollars a year on disparate programs that were supposed to be addressing the gang crisis. The programs were highly disorganized and lacked accountability — clearly something needed to be done.*
>
> *The Blueprint for a Comprehensive Citywide Anti-Gang Strategy was created to show a path forward for how the city could reclaim our streets and our children through a strategy of prevention, intervention, and suppression. At the time, I was still serving on the City Council, and I introduced a proposal to consolidate all anti-gang programs into a coordinated office, which was created in 2008.*
>
> *The Blueprint made about 100 recommendations, one of them being that the Controller's Audit Division conducts periodic follow-up audits. The audit I released today is the second follow-up, and the results give me mixed feelings: I am happy to see the progress the Mayor's Office of Gang Reduction and Youth Development (GRYD) has made, but am disappointed that there is no way to measure the success of this progress, which I believe is vital if we are to continue putting our efforts to fighting against gang violence,"* the Controller wrote.

Wendy Greuel closed her open letter with this summary:

> *"Progress has indeed been made. My audit found that 52% of the original 109 recommendations have been implemented or are no longer relevant, and 47% are either partially implemented or still in progress. In fact, only one recommendation has not been implemented. Efforts such as the Summer Night Lights Program are clearly successful and heartening to hear about — but that is not enough."*

☀ 18 ☀
Conduct Baseline Survey
of Student Perceptions

We believe that a baseline of student body perceptions, especially among middle and high school students, can be a useful measure as time passes.

The first year of such a survey will produce numbers that are what we call a baseline. We have no basis for saying whether this response is good or bad, improving or sliding. But we do a baseline survey of student perceptions so we can come back later and see if we have moved the needle with our community-wide Strategic Plan.

In a perfect world, we would suggest surveys of teachers, parents and the general citizenry. But the expense of that notion, as well as the degree of difficulty in getting city and school leadership to allow such an effort, we do not feel is essential until a community's mutual trust level is at a high point.

In February 2011, it was refreshing to learn of the Durham School System's open discussion of the gang problem as it affects their student body. Many school systems would back away from such a public revelation.

Just over one in three Durham middle schools students and one in two high school students say gangs are a problem at their schools, according to the *Durham News*.

The 2009 Youth Risk Behavior Survey found 37% of middle schools students agree gangs are a problem at school, compared with 29% of their statewide peers. The survey showed that 54% of Durham high school respondents think gangs are a problem, compared with 36% of their peers.

The survey, released by the *Partnership for a Healthy Durham*, gives educators, health officials, and others information on students' risky behaviors, along with mental health and nutrition information.

Surveys are important for several reasons. It's a public event. The survey act in itself sends a message to the community that movement is afoot; that the community cares about their perceptions. And it provides a legitimate measure of the fears of the young people in the community.

Separate surveys are suggested for middle and high school students, teachers, parents and concerned citizens.

> *The survey act in itself sends a message to the community that movement is afoot; that the community cares about their perceptions.*

Internet survey providers, such as *Survey Monkey*, enable you to post the web address on the Internet and simply ask your citizens to go there and fill it out. The surveys should be brief and provide opportunity to comment.

How the results can be used is illustrated very well in Charlotte, NC, which partnered with the University of North Carolina-Charlotte to measure these perceptions.

In October 2010, Dr. Paul Friday, a criminal justice professor at UNC Charlotte, presented the results of his gang assessment surveys to the *Juvenile Crime Prevention Council (JCPC)* in Concord, NC.

The *Independent Tribune* reported the results.

Data was collected from community demographics, law enforcement and juvenile justice databases, surveys of school youth and staff, school disciplinary reports, community surveys of community leaders, citizens and parents of middle and high school students, and a survey of community agencies that provide services to youth.

The press report by Jessica Groover noted that "there appears to be a gang problem in Cabarrus County, and it is small but increasing."

Professor Friday's surveys uncovered a key finding regarding drug usage among teens that surprised a lot of people and altered their planning.

In addition to his conclusions about the gang problem existing and being small, Friday said gang members represent a small proportion of all delinquent offenses, and gang members are getting younger, especially among minorities.

"Forty-seven percent of them have smoked (marijuana) by the age of 13, so if you don't have something in the middle schools for drug and alcohol prevention, you're going to pay for it later," Friday said.

Prevention was something JCPC Chairperson Carolyn Carpenter said needed to be addressed.

"Looking at the age group of substance abuse is something I was not aware of, and it was alarming to me how young they are starting out," Carpenter said. "Substance abuse is not in one of the areas we have addressed."

In 2011, *People to People* conducted a survey of the children who are members of the Boys & Girls Clubs in the Newport News, VA area. Almost 600 at-risk kids responded to the survey, which asked direct questions about gangs, drug use and perception of personal safety in schools. The baseline results will be useful a year or two down the road when the effort can be repeated and the most at-risk children can once again be surveyed, comparing the results to 2011.

❀ 19 ❀

Make Sure the News Media Understands

The local news media in your community needs to fully comprehend the strategy and process your community has developed.

It is vitally important that planning leaders approach editorial writers, columnists, crime beat reporters and local television reporters to brief them fully on the initiative.

You are not necessarily seeking news coverage with this briefing, though. We encourage that as much as possible. Rather, the goal is to open up the transparency of the effort and answer any questions they may have. If this is done, a misinformed media will not be your problem.

We recommend high transparency, a chronological flow of meetings, listing of committee and task force members, presentations, documents, speeches– all published on a website.

When something new is added, push it out to a comprehensive list of reporters and editorial writers so that they have the opportunity to stay abreast of the effort – and by viewing the chronological flow of events, have a deeper appreciation for the community-wide involvement.

Automatically send updates to everyone on the task force. Also, enable citizens to opt-in for these updates.

An unacceptable outcome is to have community journalists think that gang prevention is a quick fix.

> *An unacceptable outcome is to have community journalists think that gang prevention is a quick fix.*

In Calgary, Canada, the gang prevention team did a superb job of briefing the local *Calgary Herald* newspaper about the program and its intent. The editorial below illustrates the vital role the media play in keeping public understanding at a high level and long-range in scope.

"A new anti-gang strategy announced this week by the province seemed, on the surface, to be wrapped in motherhood-like mission statements. It committed to funding 14 projects and agencies with track records of working with vulnerable youth — essentially a province-wide prevention program for kids who are at-risk of criminal behavior and ripe for gang recruitment.

Keeping kids out of trouble by increasing their participation in sports, leadership programs, music and academics is nothing new.

The gang-reduction strategy has more than two dozen such action plans, as well as initiatives to 'deglamorize' the gang lifestyle and exit strategies for gang members who want out.

One cannot argue with such measures. Every dollar invested in prevention results in far greater savings down the road to the health and criminal justice systems, not to mention saving lives and saving families from being destroyed by drugs and murder. But the payoffs are so long-term that such initiatives rarely capture the attention of the public.

That was not the case this week. The day after the anti-gang strategy was announced, Calgary police involved in a two-year organized crime investigation raided 11 homes and seized 4.5 kilograms of cocaine and luxury cars including two Lamborghinis and two Porsches.

It drove home the reality that gang life is often seen as the road to the good life for many disadvantaged youth.

If the gang strategy pays off, it will be worth every penny of its $2 million cost."

20

Train Community Leaders as well as the Providers

For years, the bulk of training surrounding the gang problem has been limited to law enforcement personnel.

This training helped law enforcement identify gangs more precisely, and how they operate. Law enforcement deploys such important training in educational seminars and conferences throughout the country.

While recognition training is important, it is not the total picture.

What gangs look like in one community is not the way they may appear in another community. The gang movement is not set in stone. Gang appearance and gang activity changes daily.

While it is gratifying to be introduced as experts in gangs, those of us immersed in the subject know better. The real gang experts are the individuals that are actually gang members, or people who have left that lifestyle.

From law enforcement to social services, every agency that is going to be part of a community gang reduction strategy should be involved in understanding that strategic planning is necessary to accomplish the goal of reducing gangs. This process is important because it defines the purpose of operating as a team.

Once the stakeholders are assembled, do not assume everyone is on board or in full appreciation of the need for a community-wide Strategic Plan.

With proper research and a community needs assessment, agencies should engage in training to establish the current risk factors. This should be highlighted by presentations regarding local data to establish where gangs exist and how that relates to community demographics.

The issue in San Diego will look completely different than what Miami will experience. This is the factor that should drive the training content.

With everyone up to speed on the latest intelligence about gangs and exactly what the community is facing from a situational analysis, team members can then focus on the second part of the training on how to go about making a comprehensive plan.

The training format should include a period where each agency represented can give a quick introduction and a perspective of their role in dealing with the gang issue. It is important that each agency is clearly recognized as a stakeholder in the process — and that will begin during the training process.

The briefing should also include a view of prevention, intervention, and enforcement resources and initiatives so that the team will begin to be comfortable with what is being planned.

The key to this important educational event is that it has a multi-faceted approach to existing problems and a proven strategic approach to the solutions. The presentation needs to be inclusive, professional and involve a great deal of interaction between the agencies involved.

Gang reduction planning is essential, but these initial steps will be the experience that binds the effort together.

At a minimum, all enforcement, detention and sworn staff should receive training in:

- Legal requirements of gang prosecutions and testifying as a gang expert
- Issues for gang investigations procedures and prosecutions, questioning, report writing and testifying
- The need to coordinate and share information willingly with regional substations, the District Attorney and neighboring jurisdictions

In Denver, where an estimated 8,800 gang members roam the streets, a federal grant is helping attack the problem. This community has been birthing this effort for several years. The city leadership has been briefed and trained and the community-wide task force has been educating Denver about the problem and the Strategic Plan for a long time.

The $2.2 million federal grant to Denver allows the city to hire two new "violence interrupters" to join the four that currently go to gang strongholds when violence flares. They are mentors, often former gang members, tasked with urging peace when drive-by shootings start.

The *Denver Post* report interviewed community leaders, all seemed on board and supportive.

"Gang violence is a very public form of violence," said Regina Huerter, executive director

"Gang violence is a very public form of violence"...

of the Denver Commission on Crime Prevention and Control. "Without it being managed and contained, it can spread."

An extra probation officer also will be hired to join the two who currently shadow adult gang members and tailor services to them.

Police are pledging to conduct home checks and community outreach three times a month to increase supervision of gang members. The extra work means more home visits to determine whether those with felony convictions are hiding guns at their homes.

A new social worker also will train and steer people living in the areas toward jobs.

"All this collaboration has caught the attention of two California criminologists, Cheryl Maxson and Malcolm Klein, who have developed a screening system to predict those youth at-risk of becoming gang members," The *Denver Post* reported.

The screening program has rolled out in Los Angeles. Now Denver has secured permission to become the second test-pilot site for the screening tool.

✳ 21 ✳

Communicate Aggressively, Continuously

Working on gang reduction in isolation is never a good thing. This issue requires open communication and dialogue with all leaders in the community.

> *We are battling for the lives of a generation of children who have the gangster life marketed to them...*

We are battling for the lives of a generation of children who have the gangster life marketed to them on television, on the radio, on the Internet and in their music. We are battling a choice between poverty and gangs, loneliness and belonging. We may speak in organizational terms and express ourselves in a very organized, accountable way in this business of saving our children.

But the pure essence of our communications with each other and with the community and the media must rest on a compassionate understanding of the brutal choices so many of the kinds are making and how important it is to help these kids change.

There needs to be open communication about the nature of the gang problem. People who join gangs are actual members of the community.

Citizens need to be informed about the scope of the problem and educated on how to identify and report gang activity. There is a clear answer to the question, "What can I do?"

In developing the Strategic Plan, communicate aggressively by scheduling dozens of meetings throughout the community.

When Salinas, CA was developing their Strategic Plan, 25 different meetings were held in a 90-day period to gather ideas on gang issues throughout the city. They entitled the meetings "*A Community Dialogue for Change.*"

Communication is the key to citizen involvement. Many people want to get involved as long as they feel they are in the information loop.

Law enforcement officials hold the key in providing the necessary information needed to help involve citizens. But the real issue is the involvement generated by these forums.

Parent-teacher meetings, teacher training, faith-based groups, civic groups are all vital communications channels on the nature of the gang issue in a community.

Communicating with the service providers actually working on the problem needs to be planned and deliberate. The worst outcome is a group of agencies continually grumbling that no one ever tells them anything and that they do not feel connected.

Silent service providers, those who do not communicate for the greater good, need to be left on the bench during the next round of funding. The Strategic Plan cannot work if everyone sews up the cocoon. Once the marching orders are released from the leadership, this needs to be monitored regularly. Dissent is likely. This is a "change event." It's only human. But reward it with zero funding.

Not discussing the gang issue is a decision. It's a wrong decision, very wrong.

In a period of diminishing resources, there is a natural tendency to view information as power. This needs to go out the window.

A mandate comes along with embarking on a Strategic Plan. Local leadership needs to not only be behind the plan, but needs to talk about it passionately and publicly.

One of the best strategies we have seen solid leaders deploy is to ask for the advice of many. Beginning a conversation with a community leader with a query about his or her opinion regarding a segment of the program is a terrific way to enable everyone to feel as if they were architects of the plan, or helped to shape it. Then, active listening embodies that viewpoint into your planning.

This openness also enables some honest vulnerability. It has taken us decades to get into this mess. It may take a while before we find traction and solid results. And we are going to need your understanding, talent and support.

So, exactly who and what provider should be responsible for assuring the flow of reporting and information?

Information needs to be a priority of the working group. Responsibilities and expectations should be clear. In some communities, the local government expects to fill that role. Resist that impulse. It is best managed by a non-governmental agency that is not part of a naturally defensive bureaucracy.

Early in the development of the strategy, it is absolutely predictable that false information will get around to many of the service providers. An atmosphere of jealousy will arise as agencies see funding opportunities. Rumors will rule the day.

Again, the chain of communication and the transparency of the process are the only remedy for this negativity.

Another communication crisis will occur if the strategy only involves local government officials and agencies. Governmental agencies tend to keep information internal and only express it out when directly asked. Community groups will be the first to protest about this non-inclusiveness.

The community-wide development of a gang strategy is a whole new way of doing business with each other. It's a major change in the social paradigm. Its must involve a wider cross-section of the community than has ever collaborated regularly for an extended period before. Ongoing communication needs to reach everyone effectively.

Communications initiatives obviously include minutes of task force meetings as well as operational council meetings.

Gang members are smart people and they read a lot of content on the Internet. So, certain operational information just cannot be shared widely. Yet the highlights need to be available for information purposes.

Obviously, a robust website is a wonderful resource, with interactive features enabling surveys of students and parents and citizens and connecting people who want to help with opportunities to do so. This provides the level of transparency so necessary for success.

It is important to establish a style of respect for all young people. While we are against gang membership, never use language that insults or threatens these young people. Be about stopping violence. Be against gang membership as it leads to crime and violence. But never lower the standard of respect to name calling or threatening. It serves no purpose.

Other channels are also vital – newsletters, public service campaigns, school publications, community message boards, church programs – it helps if the program recruits someone to assume the daily responsibility to enhance the communication of the effort.

Here's the reward for all this — citizens will feel more comfortable knowing that a gang reduction strategy exists and that the community is engaged and working on the problem.

The public will not be satisfied to know that a program exists – they want to know what direction the program is going, how they will be involved or impacted and how the effort is being measured.

The unspoken expectation from almost every citizen in the community is "make me a believer." Citizens will become skeptics until convinced otherwise. A steady flow of information builds that sense of comfort with the effort.

The unspoken expectation from almost every citizen in the community is "make me a believer." Citizens will become skeptics until convinced otherwise.

Local governments have operated on a "need to know" basis for decades, keeping service providers and agencies at arm's length. In fact, the reason we are here, the reason we have to figure this out, is that we have kept each other in the dark too long hoping it will go away or not be noticed by the community.

In Novato, CA in early 2011, the leadership issued a three-page letter to every citizen advising them that the town has a rising gang problem, and what they are doing about it.

The letter, posted on the city's website and signed by Police Chief Joe Kreins and City Manager Michael Frank, addresses the issue head-on and lets people know that Novato police are working closely with other police agencies to deter gang activity and violent turf battles.

The local newspaper commended the communication.

"It is unusual to issue such a detailed letter on a crime-related issue. Frank and Kreins deserve credit for taking such action."

🐾 22 🐾

Partner with Your Local University

One of the most powerful ways a school of higher education can lead a community's efforts is in the identification of young people to target for intervention.

As Newport News's community-wide strategic planning began to take shape, the entire process is mentored and modeled by deeply involved faculty members and senior student interns from Christopher Newport University, who helped the Mayor's Task Force bring hundreds of leading citizens to the table to develop the plan.

The *Harvard Youth Violence Prevention Center (HYVPC)* is an innovative, multi-disciplinary Center dedicated to "working collaboratively to build community capacity for youth violence prevention in Boston."

Located at the Harvard School of Public Health, the Center's activities have evolved from the premise that effective prevention evolves from synergy between researchers, community members, and policy makers.

HYVPC collaborates with 11 Grassroots Community Partners, as well as with the Mayor's Office, Public Health Commission, Centers for Youth and Families, public schools, and the police department. *HYVPC's* primary goals are to work across multiple levels of the community to:

Define the problem of youth exposure to, victimization by, and perpetration of violence

- 🐾 Identify risk and protective factors for youth experiences with violence
- 🐾 Develop and test youth violence prevention strategies
- 🐾 Assure widespread adoption of strategies shown to be effective

Many other universities are immersed in the violence prevention initiatives in their community.

For example, experts at the University of Southern California work with Los Angeles in standardizing methods and measures. To do so, all of the gang reduction investments in 12 contracted prevention agencies are required to use the *Youth Services Eligibility Tool (YSET)*, a lengthy questionnaire designed by a team of experts at the University of Southern California.

In theory, the *YSET* gauges which kids are most likely to be headed for gang membership based on nine risk factors.

So, instead of judging a young person by his or her tattoos or behavior at school, the test isolates a set of psychosocial components that may lead to future gang membership. The *YSET* looks at home life, past trauma, drug use and general mental health among other factors.

Gang prevention agencies administer the 60 question test to the kids who agency personnel deem good candidates, and then send the resulting data to USC for scoring and analysis. Kids who show four or more risk factors are considered to be adequately "at-risk" and are therefore eligible for prevention services.

The *YSET* is designed to be highly selective.

Matthew Fleischer, who wrote a powerful analysis of Los Angeles' gang intervention funding, reported this analysis from the university viewpoint.

"In the past, the paradigm was the Boys & Girls Club-type model, which was open to anyone and everyone," explained Karen Hennigan to Fleischer. She heads USC's involvement with the gang reduction program.

"There are plenty of youth with family issues, but it's not one or two issues that pose the greatest risk. It's the piling on of risk factors," she said.

"The *YSET* creates a sample of youth with higher needs."

"There are plenty of youth with family issues, but it's not one or two issues that pose the greatest risk. It's the piling on of risk factors,"

When cities were invited to have their programs reviewed in Washington, D.C. at the 2010 forum, a Department of Justice analysis pointed out weaknesses in one city's ability to collect and analyze its gang crime data, The most critical need pointed out by government officials, and by Salinas' partners from other cities, was what Washington called its "glaring deficiency in data collection and sharing."

One major difference between Salinas and cities showing success in lowering gang crime is that most of them have forged close relationships with universities. Academic institutions have offered cities in-depth analysis of individual gangs, their rivalries and recent activities. That means not only being able to evaluate programs that are, or aren't, working, it means being better able to predict the groups likely to start shooting in the near future.

This kind of information could prove crucial in preventing the kind of retaliatory violence that in Salinas reached critical levels, despite an impressive overall drop in gang homicides. The Washington summits demonstrate what is working. For instance, how police are able to provide real-time crime data to a University of Memphis team.

Boston, where the violence intervention program was developed, has worked closely with Harvard University, where citywide studies are under way to track how demographic and neighborhood factors affect youth violence.

In Chicago, a study conducted by Northwestern University correlated drops in violence with the city's version of *CeaseFire* on a neighborhood-by-neighborhood basis. Academia has helped school leaders, police and outreach workers know when to step in to help troubled kids.

Among Salinas' strong points shared at the Washington, DC sessions are its multi-agency efforts, including *CeaseFire*, as well as its ability to sustain ongoing prevention and intervention programs, such as *Silver Star* and the *Rancho Cielo Youth Campus*.

In Columbus, Ohio, the connection between the gang program and the academic community is seamless.

Time for Change (T4C) was formed after the results of a community survey showed citizens perceive gang activity to be both great and increasing over recent years.

Goals include implementing programming that will interrupt gang recruitment and retention efforts, providing youth with alternative ways to establish an identity, pride and sense of community connection, ensuring parents have the tools and community support to keep children from being recruited and setting a clear community standard disapproving of gang activity.

Based on an *Office of Juvenile Justice and Delinquency Prevention* model, *T4C* functions as a partnership. The partners include the University of Nebraska at Omaha School of Criminology and Criminal Justice, local and state law enforcement, area schools and community members.

❈ 23 ❈

Reconnect Community and Schools

One major strategy that will pay dividends for every community in America is to become inspired by what other communities have done to help the school system keep kids out of gangs.

If what the schools have been doing so far had been working, we would not be in this situation in America and Canada.

They just need help. A school program has many masters. It is a treadmill of never ending SOL guided learning. Many programs that keep the kids off the streets and are now considered fundamental key gang prevention efforts have been eliminated by budget cuts, especially in the last few years.

Where is the middle school sports program on the agenda? Where is after school music and drama in the middle and high school life? How well is the facility being used after the bell rings in the afternoon and on weekends.

Our schools can be neighborhood bastions of hope for these kids. Where are the scouting programs, mentoring programs, school enrichment trips, parenting classes? How are we using our school buildings as neighborhood centers to draw people into a safe, secure environment, to connect with the many support services people in poverty need?

What would happen if a committed group of community leaders took ownership of prevention activities in the schools, freeing the faculty and staff up to focus on academics and student encouragement?

We don't know if this would work everywhere, but it apparently did in Baton Rouge — amazingly, over 30 years ago.

In 1980, several community and educational leaders with great insight and incredible commitment created a model prevention program to address the issues of alcohol and drug abuse in the Baton Rouge community. The *I CARE* program has been nationally recognized for being the epitome of a successful grassroots program.

Initially supported by the taxpayers of East Baton Rouge Parish, it was placed in the East Baton Rouge Parish School System to better reach the students, teachers, and parents, as well as the community. *I CARE* is jointly owned by East Baton Rouge Parish School System and the Baton Rouge community.

Bette C. Levine, Chairman of the *I CARE* Advisory Council can brag a little. She writes in her annual report:

"It is worthy to note here that many of the components of successful prevention programs, according to the current research–based findings, would include such things as a community

...hundreds of trained volunteers go door to door to offer non-enrolled students encouragement to return to school.

advisory council, community assessment and support, science–based prevention curricula in schools, and evaluation of the program. While we have these components and are constantly striving to improve the *I CARE* program, the original Advisory Council had the foresight and vision to include many of these components in the original plan of the *I CARE* program."

Charleston, SC Mayor Joseph P. Riley learned about the *First Day of School* Initiative from Nashville Mayor Bill Purcell who encouraged the city to sponsor this event to celebrate education and generate community support and excitement for the beginning of a new school year.

The 1st annual *First Day Festival* was held in 2003 at Joe Riley Stadium.

The families who attend receive information on educational programs and student support services in addition to participating in recreational and enrichment activities. The *First Day* Festival serves parents and children in need of help and assistance with support services and additional resources to motivate success in school.

First Day is the result of partnerships and extraordinary community support. Key partners provide financial, in-kind and volunteer support for the *First Day* Festival. This allows the city to provide this event at no cost to parents and families.

The community has embraced this initiative and established a model of public engagement in support of education.

The greatest benefit of the *First Day of School* Initiative for teachers is that when parents feel welcome starting on day one, they are more likely to be allies instead of adversaries throughout the rest of the year.

Parents, students, teachers and principals begin the year together on a positive note.

Mayor Riley created the vision and provided the leadership in stressing the importance of mobilizing the community to build better parent/teacher relationships.

Each year, he spearheads a campaign to engage more businesses to allow parents time off to take their child to school and be involved in their child's education throughout the school year.

The *First Day Festival* is an initiative that positively impacts parents' relationships with their child's school and teachers.

As the United States Conference of Mayors *Best Practices Guide on At-Risk Youth and High School Drop Out Prevention* notes, *First Day* is a "successful public engagement activity that can occur on an ongoing basis to reconnect the community and our schools."

Only 42.2% of the Houston Independent School District class of 2004 graduated. A high dropout rate results in personal deficits for individual students and a host of economic and social problems for the wider community.

Relationships play a big role in a series of programs under the umbrella of *Expectation Graduation,* whereby students are inspired by the efforts of the Mayor, school officials and hundreds of community volunteers.

A *"Reach Out to Dropouts Walk"* takes place after the first week of class each school year. The Mayor, the Superintendent of the Houston Independent School District, representatives of other area school districts, and hundreds of trained volunteers go door to door to offer non-enrolled students encouragement to return to school.

Resources are provided to alleviate root causes of dropping out such as lack of immunizations, transportation or school supplies, gang problems or the need of students to earn money.

Advance training is held for community volunteers on what to expect and how to handle specific situations.

For example, one teen dropout told volunteers she thought she was prohibited from attending while pregnant. The volunteers quickly got her back into school.

This program has now expanded to 22 cities across Texas and 18 Houston-area school districts, and involves over 20,600 volunteers.

To promote a culture of staying in school and prevent students from dropping out, Mayor White engages in a letter and *Commitment Card* Campaign aimed at ninth–graders.

In the late fall, the Mayor mails a personal letter to each student. His letter outlines the importance of staying in school and the financial implications of a student's decision to continue with education. The Mayor challenges students to make a commitment to completing high school by signing a *Commitment Card* included with his letter. In 2010–11, 19,000 kids returned their pledges to the Mayor.

Many students have written personal letters to Mayor White in response to his efforts, and the Mayor always sends each student a reply speaking to the unique content of each student's letter.

The *Mayors Best Practices Guide* also notes other ways the city gives support to the students.

The Houston Independent School District created positions for dropout prevention specialists to work with students who returned after dropping out.

The Mayor's Office schedules special events throughout the year to recognize the commitment made by students, educators and community partners to *Expectation Graduation.*

One year, students who signed Commitment Cards were invited to participate in NBA All-Star Week events, and this year, students attended a Harlem Globetrotters game and a Beyoncé concert.

The Mayor and other civic leaders participate in special school assemblies dedicated to teaching Houston's youth the importance of staying in school.

A pilot mentor program pairs students with mentors who they see at several group events throughout the year. The students are supplied with *BlackBerrys* to allow frequent and prompt communication among the student, mentor and teacher, and e-newsletters are sent to the students on the devices.

☀ 24 ☀

Publish a Gang Awareness Resource to the Community

Once you become immersed in this work, you begin to take some things for granted.

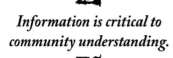

Information is critical to community understanding.

You take for granted that everyone in your community recognizes the gang problem. You take for granted that all your parents understand the danger of gangs to both their children and to the future of the community. You take for granted that most people care. Information is critical to community understanding.

A great answer to this is to publish an educational resource that would actually communicate those informational areas you may take for granted. We have looked all over the United States and Canada for what we thought was a benchmark community handbook for gang awareness and prevention that is written to a mainstream audience in terms everyone can understand.

We found some outstanding websites and some good articles, brochures and handouts. The one publication that impressed us with a comprehensive, sensible approach to educating their citizens about the gang problem is found in Canada. It is published in hard copy and online. It comes with hotlines, anonymous tip lines and a variety of social media applications.

We salute and congratulate the Manitoba government for their 96-page booklet developed by the Province with project partners, which includes the Winnipeg Police Service and the Royal Canadian Mounted Police.

Manitoba Justice also recognizes all the community-based organizations in Manitoba working to make their communities safer and more caring places to live.

It's called *Project Gang-Proof.*

Manitoba Justice notes that collaboration has been important. The information contained in *Project Gang-Proof* is based on solid research and the advice of law enforcement agencies, community members, teachers, youth child and family services, social workers, agencies and counselors.

The guidebook describes the government's actions as strong and decisive in partnership with community groups to address gangs.

"Gangs form in all types of neighborhoods, and across all cultures and ethnic groups. The provincial government has developed a comprehensive coordinated response that focuses on dealing with gang issues and creating positive alternatives for Manitoba youth. These initiatives are enhanced by crime prevention programs, educational opportunities and community and economic development initiatives which help address social and economic challenges."

Peruse just the contents list of this 96-page booklet *Gang Proof* and be inspired by this benchmark publication.

- Let's act now
- When a gang isn't a "gang"
- How Manitoba Justice determines gang
- Why determining gang membership is necessary
- Legal definition of a criminal organization
- How gangs are organized
- Gang life
- Initiation
- Different levels of gang activity
- What gangs do
- Females and gangs
- The link between gangs and drugs
- Drug activity
- The link between drugs and sex
- Why kids join gangs
- Children and youth at-risk
- Children with Fetal Alcohol Spectrum Disorder (FASD)
- Common reasons kids join gangs
- Impact on communities
- Signs of gangs in your community
- Gang graffiti
- Tagging
- Gang identifiers
- *Project Gang-Proof*
- Strategies for parents, caregivers and families
- Protecting a child from gangs
- Warning signs a child may be involved in a gang
- Strategies for schools
- The link between bullying and gangs
- Prevention strategies for communities
- Community-based, crime prevention strategies
- Intervention techniques (strategies for parents)
- Talk to your child about gangs

- What to tell a child about the realities of gangs
- Warning signs a professional is needed
- What if I suspect a child is in a gang
- How do I help a child get out of a gang
- Back to school
- Back to work
- You can get out of a gang
- Drugs – a brief guide for families and communities
- Teaching children about drugs
- Signs a child is selling drugs
- Drug descriptions
- Common street drugs and paraphernalia

25

Expand After School Activities,
Police Athletic League

Expanding after school programs and increasing youth sports, especially in middle schools, is clearly a measurable and effective tactic for prevention.

... after school programs can help shut down "prime time" for juvenile crime (2:00 pm – 6:00pm).

Whether because of the scope of the crisis, or just because it's one of the more progressive places in America, California spends three times more than the remaining 49 states combined on after school programs targeting gang reduction. As much as $550 million annually has been funded to these programs. Their research clearly shows that after school programs can help shut down "prime time" for juvenile crime (2:00 pm – 6:00pm).

Police Athletic Leagues (PAL) are a great way to bring sports into challenged neighborhoods.

There are over 300 *PAL* affiliates in more than 700 cities across the nation. The first *PAL* formed in 1910 by New York police officer Captain John Sweeney.

Being involved in sports promotes friendly competition and camaraderie among teammates. In areas where kids do not have the most desirable family and economic situations, it is important for them to have a place where they belong and a reason to be proud.

Charlotte proudly opened a neighborhood center in 2011 featuring the *Police Athletic League* headquarters.

The Southern Nevada *PAL* operates programs in various community centers and sports facilities in Las Vegas. The *PAL* also sponsors sports teams to provide an alternative to the violence that is created on unstructured time. Boxing, tennis, martial arts, workforce connections, indoor soccer, golf, homework assistance, tutoring and community service projects are only a few of the programs offered by this progressive organization, which is led by retired as well as active law enforcement officers, and key community leaders.

PAL recognizes that trusted relationships between law enforcement and at-risk youth reduces criminal activity and fosters self-fulfillment and civic responsibility.

All *PAL* of Southern Nevada program sites provide safe havens in which to meet, play and learn for hundreds of youth ages 6-17, usually in community centers.

All programs involve local law enforcement as coaches, instructors, mentors, and role models. Police employee involvement helps promote a positive view of law enforcement and leads to life changing attitudes and relationships.

In Oklahoma, Oklahoma City's gang prevention unit are winning kids away from crime with their strong personalities, supportive after school program and a push for education.

Oklahoma City police officers ditch their uniforms and pick up kids in unmarked cars for an after school gang intervention program in the northeast part of the city. The program, officially known as *Family Awareness and Community Teamwork (FACT)*, was launched in 2007 and has more than 200 youth, with 50 members who spend time in an after school program run by four officers.

"We get referrals from the people who see it firsthand," said Lt. Paco Balderrama, who supervises the *FACT* division and truancy programs for the Oklahoma City Police Department.

"Principals, teachers, pastors, friends, family — they refer kids under the age of 18 who are obviously at-risk of getting influenced and getting into a gang," he said.

"We show up in plain clothes and unmarked cars. We talk to the family. We talk to the kids, and tell them there's a better way, there's a better life. We try to connect the family with whatever resources they need to improve their situation."

✸ 26 ✸

Seed Each High School with Student Leaders Trained in Mediation, Inclusiveness, Race Relations, Non-Violence

The best program we have seen in the nation for sowing the seeds of non-violence, inclusiveness and understanding in a high school population occurs in Virginia.

Since 2001, the Virginia Center for Inclusive Communities has held the *Project Inclusion* program (formerly *Unitown*) for high schools across the Commonwealth.

Designed for students and educators from a single school or district, *Project Inclusion* brings together up to 60 students and 15 educators for an intensive four-day residential experience.

While at *Project Inclusion*, participants explore issues of diversity and prejudice, gain insight into their own lives and values, and develop action plans to share their learning with their school.

Administrators have credited *Project Inclusion* with improving school climates, reducing incidents of bullying and violence, and building stronger connections between students and educators.

The experience involves student leaders of all kinds – athletes, student government leaders, social leaders, and even kids-from-the-projects leaders.

They choose exciting and interesting places for their retreats – a 4H camp on a beautiful lake, or a Chesapeake Bay beach YMCA resort. Teachers, coaches, school staff and even involved parents take four days out of their life to volunteer for the experience with the kids.

Facilitated by Virginia Center for Inclusive Communities Executive Director Jonathan Zur, the benchmark to create this program then as now, was San Jose, CA.

Youth "leadership" retreats like these are taking place all over the country. It takes a lot of inner courage to open up the way these young people (and faculty) do about their values, their struggles with race, gender, and inclusiveness.

In Manchester, NH in early 2011, sixty students immersed themselves in these tough self-examinations for three days.

Seacoast Online reported that "Manchester teens who held a retreat this weekend in Portsmouth and New Castle, focused on violence prevention… some of whom were born abroad and others who are first generation citizens from Sudan, Puerto Rico, Kosovo and other countries — are a part of the peer education group *Manchester Violence Prevention Teens*, a partnership with the *Manchester Weed & Seed Strategy* and *Friends Forever* based in Portsmouth."

☀ 27 ☀
Let the Kids Design
"Stop Bullying" Programs

Everyone is watching. A live audience and millions of national television and on-line viewers gawk as the presenter tells us that that Taylor Swift has won the award for Best Female Video.

Immediately, a defiant Kanye West invades the stage to grab the award from a shocked Swift to protest the winner. According to *MTV News*, the crowd is silent and confused as to how they should respond.

While this scene from American pop culture is fading, should the style of this interaction be forgotten? Well maybe not, as Kanye West is still a popular hip-hop artist among teens and young adults.

Maybe this incident is just a snapshot of the attitude that prevails in popular teen culture today. From pop to hip-hop, or what can also be defined as "gangsta."

Does this style of attitude have an impact on the actions that many define as bullying today? While we can't blame artists like Kanye and his followers for why kids bully, we can certainly propose that for many young teens the impact of teen culture in American speaks loudly to the attitude of defiance and domination.

We label it "the art of thug-ism," which translates to the art of being a "thug" and creating social discourse. In today's society, to be crude, rude, and socially unacceptable is now grounds for some type of celebratory trophy.

The sense of human entitlement and domination has clearly replaced our previous ideal of civility.

This was best defined in the *PBS* documentary *Merchants of Cool*, featuring media correspondent Douglas Rushkoff.

He closely defined the rise of the "new American bully" when he declared kids' culture and media culture are now one and the same, and it becomes impossible to tell which came first, the anger or the marketing of the anger.

This commercialism has emerged to give us a backdrop for the style of bullying behavior we are now seeing. The "new American bully" operates well outside previous social norms.

It goes to the power of a culture that has its base in major financial investors who want to cash in on the latest trend at any cost. Just listen to the music influencing our kids. Then watch the awards show.

Clearly we can all agree that the cost could be basic human civility. With the backing of the large empire of wealth that supports youth culture, the new style of bullying behavior is never in isolation. It operates with an unspoken power of the mass that is represented in style and entertainment.

Moreover, the bully believes they have the power of culture. That power, in many cases is interpreted to be a so-called "license" to insult or injure without consideration of the consequences.

At stake here is the fact that bullying is just a word that has lost any connection to real self-definition. In today's culture many do not see put downs, profanity, threats, and even physical abuse as bullying.

In reality for teens, they see it as part of an existence, and in some cases a means to survival in the growing "in your face" world.

So how do teens escape this new form of abuse? For some, they did not have the strength and took their own lives. For others, it is molded through depression and acting out. Finally, for some, they escape by transforming into a bully themselves.

The October 11, 2010 issue of *TIME Magazine* described how scientists are searching for characteristics associated with youth aggression and bullying.

TIME notes that a 2008 study of nearly 2,000 children, published in the *Archives of General Psychiatry*, found that the "trajectory of victimization" begins as early as age two. The aggression of young children who are unable to peacefully negotiate solutions to social problems can lead to those kids' being bullied."

This helps explain why a number of anti-bullying initiatives have taken a victim-focused approach, teaching bullied kids how to handle social situations and manage their emotions more effectively.

Bullying in schools is a significant problem locally, nationally and internationally.

Stories of tragic suicides moved through news cycles regularly in 2010. Celebrities weighed in. School administrators, motivated by a watchful press, concerned parents and the life-and-death stakes now clearly on the table, set up bullying hotlines and deeply involved the kids in designing anti-bullying campaigns.

A 2009 U.S. Department of Education study found that "one-third of all students ages 12-18 felt that they were being bullied or harassed at school." Such situations can lead to tragic outcomes including poor academic performance, youth dropping out of school, and even self-harming behaviors including suicide.

Europe is gathering the best minds in academic research to tackle bullying. In Finland, an innovative anti-bullying program developed by Professor Salmivalli at the University of Turku focuses on influencing the bystanders and empowering young people to support the victim rather than encouraging the bullies.

The *University of Cambridge Research News Bulletin* notes "the *KiVa* program, which won the European Crime Prevention Award in 2009, uses new technologies such as computer games and virtual learning environments to provide students with

- information ("I know")
- skills ("I can")
- motivation ("I do")

These will "enable them to behave constructively when witnessing bullying."

The *Cambridge Research News* reports "a carefully conducted large-scale evaluation showed that the programme resulted in a reduction of victimisation by about 30% and of 17% for bullying perpetration."

KiVa was launched in Finnish schools in 2009, and is now being implemented by more than 80% of the country's schools.

Achievable Dream Academy, an internationally acclaimed school for at-risk children in Newport News, VA, set a high standard this year for the elimination of bullying.

Their benchmark program created regional acclaim with the school's rally and pledge to stop bullying. The middle and high school students created "pledge cards" signed by nearly every student. The pledges are posted in hallways and walls throughout the school.

The "*Anti-Bullying Pledge*" signed by 480 students affirm that they will "refuse to watch, laugh or join in when someone is being bullied" and that they will help or tell an adult when they see bullying happen.

A team of eleventh-grade students at Achievable Dream created the campaign. And that's the key. Let the kids design their own anti-bullying campaign.

The Virginia Center for Inclusive Communities and The Conciliation Project joined forces to address this critical and timely challenge.

"*Pushed: Explorations into Bullying*" is an engaging theatrical performance that leads to facilitated discussion on the sources and consequences of bullying. Through storytelling and drama, "*Pushed*" examines the consequences of bullying for an individual, organization, school, and community. The program helps participants consider what a bully is, who bullying hurts, and how to stop a bully.

More activities were initiated as a result of participation in Virginia Center for Inclusive Communities programs:

A group of middle school students and teachers have developed a website called "*Words Hurt*." Students can anonymously post information about bullying situations that they have observed or experienced, and the message is automatically sent to school administrators and counselors.

Eighth grade students at one middle school developed an assembly focused on the negative consequences of name-calling. Students acted in skits to model interrupting prejudice, and then read personal statements sharing how hearing put-downs makes them feel. The assembly was followed by student-led workshops for fifth and sixth graders.

High school students developed a week of activities called *Black out Bullying*. Throughout the week, students heard morning announcements focused on inclusion, signed a pledge banner to stop bullying, and participated in a *Mix-It-Up Lunch*. Additionally, students and educators wore black to signify a commitment to end bullying.

Another high school group planned a pep rally focused on ending bullying that featured skits, statistics, personal testimonials, and the identification of resources and support for those who are victims of bullying.

Students at two high schools and two colleges partnered to implement the *Clothesline Project* to raise awareness about domestic violence. T-shirts featuring messages and statistics related to domestic violence were painted by students, and the shirts were displayed throughout the community.

At one college, students created a new student organization called *Inclusive Alliance*. The group meets regularly to lead conversations and plan campus programs to educate and facilitate dialogue.

One thing is predictable — you have gang members in your schools, recruiting for members, and wearing gang signs.

One thing is predictable - you have gang members in your schools, recruiting for members, and wearing gang signs.

Gang colors can be changed, and gangs will often do so as soon as a particular garment or color is banned. Lately, there has been a switchover in many gangs to jewelry - in Virginia, a large cross or crucifix is now gang sign.

In Manitoba, Canada, which is often the home of some of the best anti-violence programs in the Western hemisphere, they even pay attention to school hallway patterns.

Some schools have worked with students to determine which times of the school day are the busiest and might pose a bigger threat to student safety; or which locations in the school may be more vulnerable to bullying.

For example, a map of the school hallway is presented to the students, who secretly identify the most dangerous area of the hallways by putting a red sticker on the map. The school can then determine how to better monitor this section of the school.

Writer Julie Gray was posted on *The Huffington Post* website with these important thoughts on bullying:

"These monsters are our children and neighbors, not some 'other' that we'd rather not claim for ourselves. We don't have the luxury. It's tempting to think that we are above such things and that the parents of these bullies are in some way ignorant, lazy or selfish. But these bullies, these children, belong to all of us."

The most challenging aspect of creating a bully-free school environment is the use of social media to attack someone who is gay or different.

Okay, no app is going to "stop" cyber bullying, but perhaps the most lauded recently is the "Find Help" application on *Facebook*.

Often blamed as an easy venue for cyber bullies to target victims, *Facebook* has partnered with the monitoring site *SafetyWeb* to create an app that allows users not only to immediately report inappropriate behavior to *Facebook* officials, but also to connect to various support organizations. These include suicide hotlines and child abuse prevention centers, such as *Partners Against Hate*, which offers anti-hate crime education and strategies.

At the elementary level, students experiencing an anti-bullying curriculum called *Steps to Respect* are getting lessons on respecting themselves and others and doing what they can do to identify and eliminate bullying in the school hallways and beyond.

The research-based *Steps to Respect* program teaches elementary students to recognize, refuse, and report bullying, be assertive, and build friendships. In fact, a recent study found that the program led to a 31% decline in bullying and a 70% cut in destructive bystander behavior.

Where are most incidents occurring? When students completed a 21-question confidential survey about bullying, the results ranked buses as the most frequent bullying location.

✸ 28 ✸

Small School Efforts Pay Dividends

It sounds like a modest number of kids, but a small, intensive program targeted well can change lives, as is done by the school district in San Diego.

The program, *Ten to Succeed*, begins with ten students just entering high school that have been underperforming in both school attendance and academics. The focus is simply making sure the students attend school and fully understand the

... respect, responsibility, integrity and tolerance.

steps to be successful. They adopted four tenants — respect, responsibility, integrity and tolerance.

Memphis is tackling this problem. They have come together as a community to create a community-wide plan as the crime crisis has escalated.

Memphis schools have created *Gang Reduction Assistance for Savings Society's Youth (Grassy)* which targets gang members and recruits, giving students an alternative to gang life.

Memphis has one of the most challenging gang problems in America. The creating of *Grassy* in 2008 was a start in the right direction. Four hundred students have gone through the program since it began.

While the gangs are luring students with a sense of belonging, *Grassy* is providing structured activities to keep them busy and engaged. Students in *Grassy* have their regular classes, but also get tutoring, social skill development, and mentoring with a listening ear and words of advice to counter the words from the gangs.

Students who are in gangs or who are being approached by them are targeted for the program or referred by others.

All this can be frustrating, even with smaller efforts.

One citizen in Salinas, CA expressed her frustration in a public letter in October 2010:

"The Second Chance gang diversion program has been in existence since 1989. My daughter was 10 when Brian Contreras came to speak at a Loma Vista PTA meeting to educate about gangs. He said it takes 20 years to 'break the cycle.' My daughter is almost 30 now, and we are no closer to "breaking the cycle." I have many times expressed to our City Council the need to partner with the schools; it fell on deaf ears. The schools are filled with thousands of children. This is the place to break the cycle. There should have always been a partnership between the schools and the city, wherein a couple of times a year, there would be week-long focus on "saying no to gangs," with rallies and literature going home with children. Gang-prevention programs should target all grade levels until "saying no to gangs" is a part of everyday life."

29

Deflect Violence with Non-confrontational Conversations

About 25 men in the Yonkers *Peace Keepers* spend an hour a week reaching out to young men to reduce conflicts among them and to serve as positive role models. The chapter got active just as 2011 summer began, when shootings on the city's west side traditionally have increased, according to Lower Hudson Valley website *lohud.com.*

The Yonkers Violence & Gang Prevention Coalition and *Peace Keepers* national founder Dennis Muhammad presented some members of Yonkers' *Peace Keepers* at a public meeting at Nepperhan Community Center.

David Ancruem, 60, a Yonkers *Peace Keeper*, said his members will go "wherever the trouble is," citing a 2011 shooting in a Mount Vernon park as an example of how they operate.

The website quoted Ancruem as saying "the *Peace Keepers* will target an area, go there, make their presence known and hopefully someone will come up to them and say something." Based in Columbus, OH, the group also has a presence in Mount Vernon.

The Yonkers *Peace Keepers* are intended to complement a program called *SNUG*, in which five Yonkers men are paid to meet with young men on the streets.

At the coalition's community introductory meeting, Capt. Frank Invervallo of the Fourth Precinct said *SNUG* workers have made an impact since starting in November 2010.

"We noticed right away," Intervallo said. "They're doing difficult work under dangerous conditions."

In Chicago, the spring of 2010 brought new non-confrontational actions by the police department in area high schools.

Chicago Tribune reporter Annie Sweeney, in her October 15, 2010 article, noted that Chicago police officers are moving "beyond gang-conflicted streets and into public high schools to meet with students for non-confrontational conversations about what drives the violence and how to prevent it."

The pilot program throws up a challenge to the image of gang officers chasing and collaring offenders. In this case, officers listen, lend help and speak frankly about what kind of trouble the student might be in, Sweeney reported.

"I don't want them to arrest," Cmdr. Leo Schmitz, head of the gang enforcement unit, said of the officers. "That's not why we are there."

"We're getting guys who can be potential victims or potential offenders and trying to talk them out of the violence."

Officers assigned to the Gang School Safety Team held more than 300 interventions in the first few months.

Officers assigned to the Gang School Safety Team held more than 300 interventions in the first few months.

The *Tribune* reports that the ten-man team sometimes meets with large groups of students if there is a conflict brewing inside a school, but most meetings happen privately — between the gang officers and the students they think need help. A parent or school representative is present, Schmitz said.

Cmdr. Schmitz said the officers assigned to the team go into schools based on daily reports of violence or shootings. They meet with friends and associates of those involved in shootings — especially victims, finding out what was behind the shooting, with an eye on prevention of further violence.

Sgt. Kenneth Boudreau, who leads the team, said he usually starts a meeting by finding out how much violence the students have witnessed and asking them to think about a friend who has been killed. He asks what they are afraid of — and most say getting shot on the way to school.

Boudreau said that they shed all of that hardness, and they become a youth again, Sweeney reported.

"The conversation then winds back to whatever conflict is happening."

Boudreaux asks the youth what he or she thinks they could do. He asks, how did it start?

After an intervention at a school that had two shootings in the first week of classes, violence around the school stopped for a month, officials said.

Ms. Sweeny reports that some students have asked for help in getting tattoos removed.

"Fathers have stood up at meetings to support the officers. And a student council just extended an invitation for the officers to talk to an entire school."

"We can't arrest ourselves out of the problem," Boudreau said.

When police calls are a daily occurrence to stop fights in the hallways, it's time for serious intervention. At George Wythe High School in Richmond, VA, the *G.R.I.P.* program hired an intervention provider to staff the school with a dozen gang interventionists called *Student Advocates*. They met the problem students at the bus in the morning and they stayed close to them, showing up in their neighborhood and demonstrating concern, caring and support. Within weeks of implementing this tough program, police calls to George Wythe ceased.

✱ 30 ✱

Create *Safe Street* Teams

When people think of *Safe Street* teams, the red berets always come to mind as a dedicated group of street violence interrupters with a presence in tough neighborhoods.

These are the *Guardian Angels* is a non-profit international volunteer organization of unarmed citizen crime patrollers. The *Guardian Angels* organization was founded February 13, 1979 in New York City by Curtis Sliwa and has chapters in 15 countries and 144 cities around the world.

Sliwa originally created the organization to combat widespread violence and crime on the New York City Subways. The organization originally trained members to make citizen's arrests for violent crimes. Today, they often detain criminals instead of making arrests. The organization patrols the streets and neighborhoods but also provides education programs and workshops for schools and businesses.

Creating a *Guardian Angels* patrol is a fundamentally sound way to get out on the streets and spread the message of non-violence.

The city of Boston's Youth Violence Prevention Plan was spotlighted at the Summit on Preventing Youth Violence in Washington, D.C., hosted by the Department of Justice and other federal agencies, highlighting *Safe Street Teams*.

In 2007, the Boston Police Department created *Safe Street Teams* to foster police and community engagement on a more personal level. Originally piloted in three of Boston's high-crime areas, there are now 13 teams spread throughout the city in these neighborhoods.

...there are now 13 teams spread throughout the city in these neighborhoods.

Safe Street Teams have been invaluable in building trust with the community and reducing crime in Boston's neighborhoods and it is the city's goal to increase the number of *Safe Street Teams* in this upcoming year.

The neighborhood-based *Safe Street Teams* were born out of the recognition that most of the city's violent crime is concentrated in a few, small geographic "hot-spots." And further, a research-based understanding that officers engaging in problem solving within specific hot-spot areas can reduce crime.

With the support of funds from the U.S. Bureau of Justice Assistance's Smart Policing grant initiative, the Boston Police Department collaborated with researchers from Rutgers and Harvard to evaluate the crime reduction effects of the *Safe Street Team* hot spots policing program. The research team used crime mapping, database, and statistical matching techniques to identify near-equivalent comparison areas for a rigorous quasi-experimental evaluation.

Carefully orchestrated evaluations have demonstrated that:

- *Safe Street Teams* significantly reduced violent crimes in the target hot spot areas relative to violent crime trends in the comparison hot spot areas.

- *Safe Street Teams* did not simply displace violence into areas immediately surrounding the target hot spots.

31
Camps Build Trust with Police

We learned of *Camp Awareness* from the *U.S. Conference of Mayors' Best Practices Guide*.

The Wichita Police Department partnered with the Boy Scouts of America in a unique mentorship program that matches at-risk youth boys, ages 6-11 years, who are not currently involved in any scouting programs, in a day camp program.

This approach not only helps the Boy Scout organization gain a foothold with at-risk kids, but it helps the Police Department establish a trusting relationship with a growing body of young people.

The officers and military personnel, who serve as staff, spend the first three days together participating in activities such as swimming, fishing, shooting range, field games, etc.

During this time, the officers and military personnel are dressed in civilian clothes. This time together builds relationships among the officers and campers.

The final event of the four-day camp is to reveal the professional identities of the staff.

... the negative outlook they may have had or apprehension towards police officers or soldiers is no longer valid.

When the young boys see the officers and military personnel in uniform drive into camp with lights and sirens, they realize that the men and women they have built a relationship with during the past four days are police officers and military personnel. They also realize that the negative outlook they may have had or apprehension towards police officers or soldiers is no longer valid.

The United Way of the Plains provides all funding for *Camp Awareness*.

The effectiveness of *Camp Awareness* is measured in two ways: First, they monitor the boys who join Boy Scouts after camp has completed. (They have been averaging over 60% for at least one year following camp.) The second measurement is a comprehensive survey of families to evaluate program goals.

Also in Wichita, the *Planeview Activity Camp for Kids* (*PACK*) was created in 2002 as a way to reduce juvenile crime during the summer. Since then, juvenile crimes such as vandalism, larceny and graffiti in the area are down by 18-20%.

The camp, which runs for eight weeks each summer, is the result of a survey of residents in the area who felt the children lacked positive things to do during summer break from school.

In creating *PACK*, the Wichita Police Department teamed up with the Parks Department, the neighborhood education department in the City Manager's Office, neighborhood groups and businesses.

Since that first year when 78 young people attended *PACK*, it has blossomed into a very successful project to help children who are at-risk for gang violence, and who come from families with limited means get involved in constructive and fun things each summer.

PACK was instrumental in helping the International Association of Chiefs of Police awarding the Wichita Police Department the Webber-Seavey award in 2003. In 2007, the *Planeview Activity Camp for Kids* had 135 neighborhood kids involved in the camp, with a waiting list for the rest of the kids who wanted to attend.

There were also over sixty parents in attendance at the end-of-camp party. In addition, five past *PACK* kids, who are now too old to enroll, volunteered their time to help supervise the camp attendees.

The effectiveness of the program is measured by the amount of burglaries, larcenies, vandalisms, and graffiti (common juvenile crimes) that occur within the Planeview neighborhood, during the 8-week program.

The eight-week program costs approximately $50,000 – $53,000. Costs associated with time spent by the officers is absorbed by the Wichita Police Department as a part of the departments mission under the *Community Policing* philosophy to work proactively with the community in dealing with crime.

❋ 32 ❋

Deliver Creative School Interventions in Elementary, Middle and High School

... students in second and third grade are being peer-pressured into joining gangs.

At a Sacramento Gang Violence Forum in April 2011, Mayor Kevin Johnson said there are 60 gangs and about 6,000 gang members in Sacramento County, and that students in second and third grade are being peer-pressured into joining gangs.

Sacramento Press reporter Brandon Darnell reported that the Mayor noted that the city and school districts will be working together, since the schools oversee youths for seven hours per day during the school year.

"They will combine efforts through after school programs, joint use of facilities and a renewed focus on school safety, he said, adding that benchmarks will be set up so progress can be measured," the *Sacramento Press* reported.

Darnell's report included comments by Mayor Johnson on reading level of third graders, a point he brought up at his *State of the City* address earlier this year.

"If you can read, you're not going to jail," Johnson said after mentioning that 70% of incarcerated people are illiterate and only 30% of Sacramento's students are reading at their grade level by the time they finish third grade.

In November 2010, more than 100 Oakland fifth-graders graduated from a gang prevention program, a program eagerly conducted by the Oakland Unified School District. These 100 children were in four different classes in two different elementary schools. The six-week course is called the *Gang Resistance Education and Training (G.R.E.A.T.)* program.

Law enforcement officers taught the classes and included discussions about anger management, communication skills and being a good citizen.

The national program is meant to prevent youth violence and delinquency, particularly gang participation, the school district said. It has partnered with the Boys & Girls Clubs of America and the national Association of Police Leagues.

Developed in the Phoenix area by local police officers, *G.R.E.A.T.* has been proven over time, showing that long-term investments in a child's continuing reinforcement pay dividends.

The *G.R.E.A.T.* program begins in elementary school, has a middle school program and a summertime program. The program teaches leadership skills, problem solving and helps young children understand the consequences of gang involvement. It is taught by police officers in school.

Developing positive relationships with law enforcement is a vital key to any school-based violence prevention initiative.

It has been shown by numerous studies, including University of Chicago economist James J. Heckman that skill building investments such as mentoring, community service, and literacy do pay off. It has been demonstrated that that boys from high-risk families were much less likely to commit crimes than boys not receiving such assistance.

G.R.E.A.T. has developed partnerships with nationally recognized organizations, such as the Boys & Girls Clubs of America and the National Association of *Police Athletic Leagues*. These partnerships encourage positive relationships among the community, parents, schools, and law enforcement officers.

In Belize, where the U.S. Embassy just funded *G.R.E.A.T.*, they had this to say about the program:

"The *G.R.E.A.T* program produces attitude and behavioral changes through a unique combination of skills training, cooperative learning, discussion and role playing. Students are provided with many opportunities to model and practice relevant life skills. Once students have rehearsed these skills, they will be most likely to use them in real-life situations."

The program is promoted by the Bureau of Justice Assistance of the U.S. Department of Justice.

The *Orangeburg, S.C. Times and Democrat* describes the motivational speaker and comedian "*Akintunde*" who visited Orangeburg and questioned more than 400 Orangeburg School District 3rd, 4th, 5th and 6th-graders.

An inaugural member of the *Call Me MISTER* program at Claflin University, *Akintude* has appeared on the *Oprah Show* and *South Carolina ETV* with his message of positive choice. *Call me MISTER* is a college campaign of encouraging African-American students to become elementary school teachers.

Performers say the deeper problem with rap performers is not just their message of gang life.

"They're pretty much stealing the identities of the youth by not allowing them define who they are."

"I let them know they can't be the next Obama, they can be the first 'them'."

The message of positive choice is for parents as well.

The Boys & Girls Club of Greater Sacramento partners with the Sacramento City Unified School District to target 100 at-risk children from four elementary schools by providing mentoring and after school activities.

So in January 2011, 50 students from two elementary schools in dangerous neighborhoods joined the club – in hopes they don't end up in gangs instead. The fourth- to sixth-graders will do the same activities as the other kids – plus the *Street Smart* program, where they'll hear from police and ex-gang members and learn about resolving conflicts.

The *Sacramento Bee* notes that the new after school effort is a "promising way to push back against the complacency that can creep in when there is no record number of homicides making headlines."

This is the place to break the cycle.

❈ 33 ❈
Gang Exit Centers –
Rescuing Kids from Gangs

Highlighted at the 2010 Canada-U.S. Gang Summit, *Ozzy's Garage* is a model youth mentorship program developed by Ontario Gang experts Michael Chettleburgh, Rick Osborne and Andrew Bacchus.

The *Ozzy's Garage* program is founded on the two premises that redemption is possible and that we can reach and work with some high-risk and gang-involved youth better through a non-traditional, fun and highly unique skilled trades program, as compared to a typical community-based intervention.

Their website describes this powerful program.

"With this program, youth have the once-in-a-lifetime opportunity to build a custom motorcycle chopper or 60s/70s era muscle car which, when completed, is then raffled off in benefit of a local community program or youth centre."

While the chance to build a chopper or car is a powerful drawing card, the enduring value of the program is the opportunity for youth to work alongside master mechanic, mentor and former gang member, drug addict and prison veteran Rick ("Ozzy") Osborne.

Ozzy has the opportunity to engage youth in what he calls "small C" counseling around the issues they are facing in their lives, and provide "reality-based" advice derived from his years of study in and graduation from the school of hard knocks. At the same time, youth learn marketable skills, earn the satisfaction that comes with completing a major project, and "give back" to the community they have sometimes harmed as a result of the proceeds derived from the raffle of the bike or car.

Canada's leading edge intervention initiatives also include a walk-in gang rescue center. Canada's *Breaking the Cycle* program is widely respected, and the program has been ranked by some criminologists as one of the most effective in North America.

🚂

... a safe place to go where an umbrella of services and support awaits you, even re-location.

🚂

This walk-in center is especially designed to help young people exit from a gang; a safe place to go where an umbrella of services and support awaits you, even re-location.

The *Regina Anti-Gang Services (RAGS)* project works with gang-involved Aboriginal youth and young adults living in Regina, Saskatchewan.

The primary goal of *RAGS* is to reduce criminal activities committed by young gang members. The program provides intensive support services to reduce involvement in gang life and to facilitate leaving gangs. The *RAGS* program is supported by Public Safety Canada, National Crime Prevention Centre's Youth Gang Prevention Fund and is delivered by the North Central Community Association, a not-for-profit, grass-roots agency dedicated to enhancing the quality of life of residents. The project began in October 2007 and will be in evaluated in 2011.

🌑 34 🌑
Middle Schoolers Targeted as Key Rural Strategy

The Robeson County region of North Carolina is one of the most ethnically diverse rural counties anywhere — with more than 68% of its approximately 135,000 residents being American Indian, Black and Latino.

The first major grant in the nation to tackle gangs in a rural region has been awarded here. The community team assembled quickly named their target – middle school students.

> *The community team assembled quickly named their target — middle school students.*

According to the N.C. Department of Juvenile Justice and Delinquency Prevention, the county's youth death rate of 123.6 per 100,000 people is nearly double the state's rate of 74.7, and the county's homicide rate of 23.9 per 100,000 is more than triple the state's average of 7.2 from 2004 to 2008.

That's why the county is the first rural community named a recipient of a federal $6.5 million grant from the Centers for Disease Control and Prevention. It is the nation's first rurally focused youth violence prevention center, and is being led by researchers from UNC.

Staff writer Bob Shiles of the *Robesonian* interviewed Dr. Paul Smokowski, director of the new North Carolina Academic Center for Excellence in Youth Violence Prevention and a researcher from the University of North Carolina at Chapel Hill.

"While Robeson County is unique multi-culturally, it has a lot of company when it comes to juvenile violence....the indicators of violence here look more urban than rural. This is quite interesting and dynamic."

The center, based in Lumberton, will serve all of Robeson County.

Shiles reported that similar youth violence prevention centers are in Chicago, Richmond, VA., and Flint, MI. In past funding cycles, the CDC has funded centers in Philadelphia, Memphis, and Riverside, CA.

The goal of the center is not only to determine the causes of juvenile violence in Robeson County, but to try to fix it, Smokowski commented.

The five-year project is a collaborative effort among the UNC School of Social Work, the UNC Injury Prevention Research Center, and community agencies from throughout Robeson County, including the Robeson County Health Department, the nonprofit Center for Community Action and the Public Schools of Robeson County.

To assess the impact of the center's activities, the rates of violence in Robeson County and across the state will be tracked. The *Robesonian* reported that the project team will follow 3,000 Robeson middle school students over five years and compare their development with similar students in Columbus County.

"We are targeting middle school students so that there can be positive development before problems become entrenched at a later age," Smokowski said. "We want to promote positive and successful development of middle school age students so that they go on and have bright futures."

✻ 35 ✻

Generate Amazing Results with Restorative Justice in Schools

The school-to-prison pipeline is real. Suspended students, especially those who come from poverty and gang infested neighborhoods, are likely to get into trouble without a place to go every day.

And kids given long-term suspensions, especially high school students, often turn into drop-outs, which not only severely limits their ability to get decent employment, but, according to a paper published in the *Journal of School Psychology* in 1998, makes them 26% more likely to become involved in the criminal justice system that their peers.

We must as a society re-address how we deal with punishing young people. We cannot keep putting all of the offenders in jail. It's just not working.

In January 2011, the New York City Council approved the *Student Safety Act*, which mandates that the police and education departments produce quarterly reports on school-based arrests and suspensions.

> *We must as a society re-address how we deal with punishing young people. We cannot keep putting all of the offenders in jail. It's just not working.*

The quarterly reports will likely be thick, according to Julia Dahl of *The Crime Report*.

Dahl reports that the number of student suspensions in the city has nearly doubled since the 1990s, and the number of behaviors that subject a student to suspension grew by 200%. Students with disabilities were four times more likely than their peers to receive a suspension, and black students served longer suspensions, often for "subjective" infractions like misconduct and insubordination.

New York isn't the only place where the so-called school-to-prison pipeline is swift and well oiled.

The Crime Report notes that in Texas, school police officers routinely issue Class C misdemeanor tickets, which can stay on a child's record, to students for such nonviolent infractions as leaving school grounds and disrupting class, according to a December 2010 report by the nonprofit *Texas Appleseed Project*.

"Zero-tolerance" policies came about following the 1994 federal *Gun-Free Schools Act*, which resulted in most states implementing mandatory one-year suspensions for students who bring a firearm to school.

"These 'one strike and you're out' sentences started to trickle down to less serious offenses and we saw more long-term suspensions for things like fights," *The Crime Report* noted.

Nor should we continue to kick kids out of school. School may well be their only hope for making it outside of street life.

This brings us to the subject of Restorative Justice, a movement that began in the faith community that has been gently making its way into our culture for over a decade. It's a completely different way of responding to violations of the law.

Restorative Justice is emerging in both Canada and the United States. As the nation's leadership is suddenly awakening to the fact that we have about 12 times as many people behind bars as any other nation on earth, they are beginning to re-examine incarceration. This is primarily motivated by the dramatic need for cost reduction in state and local budgets.

It's not at all new for Aboriginal populations in Canada or Native Americans, but for modern mainstream culture, this is really new.

The *St. Croix Valley Restorative Justice Program (SCVRJP)* for St. Croix and Pierce counties bridges the gap between victim and offender in an effort to focus on the harms of a crime rather than just the laws broken.

Their mission is, "to build and sustain a culture of peace and belonging utilizing Restorative Justice principles and programs in our community."

The nonprofit organization, which relies largely on public donations, will mark its 10-year anniversary in 2011.

Services offered include victim impact panels, underage consumption panels, controlled substance circles, community conferencing, victim empathy seminars, safe teen driving circles, training, workshops and presentations.

It might sound strange to have victims and offenders sit down in a group and face each other, but it seems to work.

Most offenders see themselves as victims and don't realize or understand the harm they have done to the victim and the community, organizers note.

The program seeks to support offenders while encouraging them to understand, accept and carry out their obligations by teaching responsibility and accountability.

The circle talks they use have roots deep into divergent cultures from ancient times, particularly the indigenous people in North America.

The circle creates a confidential, respectful setting where communication is structured. Trained Restorative Justice facilitators and community members are also circle members, a *SCVRJP* handout explains.

Liesl Nelson, attorney manager at the state public defender's office in Hudson that serves Pierce and St. Croix counties, said Restorative Justice programs are best as an alternative to prosecution ordered by the court rather than an add-on to probation and a jail sentence.

Nelson is supportive of the programs that place the victim and offender together. She notes that a lot of offenders really want to apologize to the victim.

Nelson said that a courtroom isn't the best forum for an offender to apologize to the victim and it always carries the stigma of whether the defendant was sincere or just doing it to influence the sentence.

In short, Restorative Justice programs have value. "We can't fine or jail our way out of bad behavior," she said.

WindyCitizen.com tells the story of Restorative Justice in Chicago, the Windy City.

From spring 2009 to summer 2010, *Alternatives, Inc.* agency's staff went into seven elementary after school and summer programs run by the YMCA of Metropolitan Chicago to teach students about conflict resolution and Restorative Justice.

The YMCA staff running the programs also received training in using Restorative Justice to resolve discipline issues. At one high school, *Alternatives* helped design a peer mediation program. The initiative cost about $90,000.

The news item noted that "At a couple of schools, it took six months before the staff was really open to the idea that we would be able to help them," says Karen Lambert, a Restorative Justice specialist at *Alternatives,* Inc. "[But] they were talking to each other and hearing success stories." Parent involvement has shored up longstanding Restorative Justice programs in Chicago, including three that are funded by the Juvenile Justice Division of Cook County courts at Brunson and Key elementary schools and Wells High.

WindyCitizen reports that Lynn Morton, a parent who helped organize the program at Brunson, says it got off the ground in 2005 as an all-volunteer effort, although parents who run it are now paid a stipend of $10 an hour through a state grant. Altogether, she says, the three programs run on about $25,000 a year.

The *Peace Center* program serves about 12 to 15 students at a time, who are referred by school administrators, teachers or parents (although some come of their own accord). Students come for about two hours once a week for 6 to 10 weeks. Boys come on one day, and girls on another.

The goal is to give children the opportunity "to feel safe and talk about what's going on in school, what's going on in the home, and getting them to see how each one of their behaviors [affects] their community, their school, their classroom," *WindyCitizen* quotes Morton. Parent volunteers are on Brunson's campus during most school days to work with current and former peace center students who get in trouble.

Suspensions can be a pipeline – leading from dropped-out straight to prison, said the Rev. Robert Biekman, of Southlawn United Methodist Church in Chicago's Avalon Park neighborhood.

Here is how the peer jury program works in Chicago:

In Chicago, the peer jury is "about creating a space where young people can be respected and be heard and be engaged in this problem solving process," said Andrew Tonachel, youth development director of *Alternatives*, Inc.

The peer jury process is student-centered and completely voluntary – from the students applying to be jurors to the students who are having their cases heard.

Peer Juries are sanctioned only for Group 1 through Group 4 inappropriate behaviors as found in the Chicago Public Schools Student Code of Conduct. Groups 5 and 6 actions automatically require administrative recourse that is not limited to suspension.

Medill Reports Chicago outlines how a peer jury hearing basically works:

During the proceedings, which are confidential, parties give an opening statement before a team of jurors where both the person accused of the wrongdoing and the victim give their sides of the story and discuss a solution.

An agreement is reached between the parties. Tonachel said the solution should be one that is specific and measurable.

The peer jury designates a student to follow up with the involved students to make sure the agreement was carried out successfully.

The Virginia Center for Restorative Justice's Sylvia Clute articulates a different and even higher level of Restorative Justice, the inclusiveness of "Unitive Justice" on her website.

"Those harmed may include not only the primary victim, but also members of the victim's family, members of the offender's family, and the community at large."

Clute describes the process.

"At the appropriate time and in a safe setting, the offender hears the victim and these other voices describe the harm from their perspectives. This furthers the offender's understanding and results in the moral learning that can motivate a desire to repair the harm and to be restored to the community."

She notes that "Unitive Justice" approaches the victim, the offender and the community as parts of a whole and no one is forced to lose.

"The victim feels heard and valued, as the offender is held accountable in ways that are meaningful and aid the victim's healing. The community is seen for what it is, the basic building block of a safe and secure nation."

✹ 36 ✹

Teach Business English, Social Skills in Elementary School

There is a theory that kids have their lifelong speech patterns hard wired before they are twelve.

So if you want to teach a kid how to speak proper English, you better get started very early. And you better make it an everyday exercise. When the at-risk kids go home in the afternoon, they speak "*Street.*"

If you have never heard of a school that has table manners classes, wears uniforms, and learns to "*Speak Green,*" learn more about the world-class school for at-risk kids in Newport News, VA. An Achievable Dream was named by *Readers Digest* as one of the top five at-risk schools in the world.

CBS News came to Newport News, VA to visit the school for at-risk children in one of America's toughest neighborhoods.

The Achievable Dream Academy is a public school that has partnered with the business and military community and developed a unique program to give kids from kindergarten through 8th grade the tools and structure they need to succeed in life. By all indications, it's working.

Achievable Dream Academy isn't like any other school, reports *The Early Show's* Melinda Murphy. For starters, each and every child is required to shake hands with school administrators before they can start their day. The kids wear uniforms.

CBS reported that school officials aren't the only ones who greet them, so do U.S. soldiers — the same soldiers who lead a morning rally, of sorts.

The children say the *Pledge of Allegiance*, get their uniforms inspected by U.S. Army volunteers from neighboring Ft. Eustis, interact with Sheriff's deputies and recite life mottos that are printed on banners hanging on the walls.

Reporter Melinda Murphy asked "So what's the point of all this?"

Director Richard Coleman says, "Our focus is to provide a character development education for all our children. Our focus is to narrow the achievement gap."

These kids are from some of the poorest neighborhoods in Newport News and almost 80% of them are from broken homes.

Myron Smith, who is in the 7th grade, says, "My mother died and my father's in jail, but I think I will do better...because I know I have to strive harder to do better so my mom will be proud."

In addition to regular subjects like math and science, these kids take classes in things like etiquette. It's all geared towards helping them in the business world.

LaBrea Bryance, a 5th grader, explains, "The gentlemen learn how to seat the ladies, and we learn how to fold our napkins and sit down properly."

Coleman says, "Those social skills are critical social skills for our children. So they need to know what the hidden rules are, so they're not eliminated before they even get in the game."

There's also an elocution class called, "*Speaking Green*" (because green is the color of money).

"We have a tendency to say 'tick' instead of 'thick,'" a teacher notes.

"We want to make sure we're correctly producing those words so people will know that we have control over the English language and that we are serious."

Coleman says, "We teach them that it's OK to speak the language in your neighborhood, but when you're in a professional environment, you need to learn to speak the appropriate language."

Achievable Dream was the brainchild of Walter Segaloff, a local businessman.

Segaloff says, "Many of the kids that I was interviewing for a position for our company were coming out of high school and, basically, they were functionally illiterate; they were not prepared."

It all started as, believe it or not, a tennis camp. And every kid there is required to play tennis. It's the only sport at the school.

Segaloff says, "I was looking for a hook, something magic. I was watching a tennis tournament one day and I said, 'Oops — that's the hook.' I wanted something that would support the character development portion of the program. Shaking hands, rules, regulations, non-violence, a lady's sport, a gentleman's sport.

Since 1992, the school has grown to a 1,000 students and now is K-12 but they've grown in more than just size.

Segaloff points out, "It's a unique program that works. And look at our results. We have literally no violence. How many schools can say that? We have a very high graduation rate. We're giving kids the foundation they need to be productive, law-abiding citizens."

And students there believe that attending this school is the chance of a lifetime.

CBS News concluded their report with an interview with sixth grader Makynzee Madden.

"Without knowledge, you'll probably be working at McDonald's saying, 'Do you want fries with that?' But if you have a nice job, a nice education, then you'll be sitting like Donald Trump and having your own multi-million dollar business."

She has pretty high goals. "Yes," she affirms. "I think without the program, I would probably be great, but now that I'm here, I will probably be extraordinary."

The school day at an Achievable Dream is 8 1/2 hours, instead of the normal 6 1/4. And the kids go to school year round. But they don't seem to mind, because they feel the hard work will pay off.

The issue of gangster speech in schools goes to the heart of the problem. Kids need to learn to speak English, not "Street." They are just imitating the radio, hip-hop and gang culture.

Allowing anything else is dooming the child to discriminatory practices in the workplace because the young person cannot speak clearly to others.

It is certainly a different issue outside of the school — students may speak any way they want to. But inside the school and classroom, we need to retard this disadvantaged behavior. It gets no one anywhere and creates peer pressure to imitate it.

37

Take Truancy Interventions to the Homes

Detroit has many problems and truancy is among them.

Detroit Free Press reporter Naomi Patton reported that city of Detroit and Detroit Public Schools officials are collaborating with federal, state and local law enforcement and community partners to combat truancy, which is listed as a first offense for nearly 80% of criminal offenders, according to the Department of Justice.

Operation Safe Passage kicked off in 2011 with a sweep that netted 63 truant students. The program is designed to reduce juvenile crime, combat truancy and replace discipline with productive activities.

Detroit Police Chief Ralph Godbee Jr. called the program "an example of what problem-oriented policing looks like — making substantive steps toward saving our youth."

Students found to be truant — instead of being ticketed for truancy — are to be mentored, assigned to community service projects or given whatever they need to enable them to return to school.

U.S. Attorney Barbara McQuade called the effort "an incredible collaboration ... so that these kids aren't simply tomorrow's criminals."

The Rev. Larry Simmons, president of the Brightmoor Pastors Alliance, was with police during the sweeps and said his group will work with the campaign to mentor students.

One of the best truancy prevention programs we have ever seen is the school nurse team at An Achievable Dream Academy in Newport News, VA.

Funded by corporate partner Riverside Health System Foundation, this two-nurse clinic serves this special population of kids from tough, poor neighborhoods.

Almost 90% of these kids come from broken homes. Almost all have at least one family member in prison. All of them know children who have been shot. They come to Achievable Dream to level the playing field and the local nonprofit hospital is helping them do just that.

They get medical care from watchful school nurses sponsored with an annual grant from Riverside Health System Foundation. Among many duties, such as helping diabetic children keep tabs on the diet and blood sugar, or helping the 10% of kids in the school who have asthma, is truancy prevention.

The prevention comes when every child knows that if they do not show up for school, there will be a knock on the door and a school nurse will be standing there wanting to know why the student is not in class.

If a student does not show up for school, and there is no excuse, the nurses go to the home and find out why. If the child is sick, the nurse is there to evaluate and assist. Truancy is almost zero at Achievable Dream. Skip school and the nurse is on your doorstep.

Even in the toughest projects, the gangsters usually look on nurses as protected people. They do not obstruct or get in their way. A nurse looking for an absent student is accepted.

Montgomery County, Maryland school officials announced a 43% drop in student truancy rates at a November 2010 meeting on gang prevention. This created some disbelief among community leaders.

But county officials working on reducing truancy said they believe their numbers are accurate. They say a slew of new policies, including identifying students at-risk of becoming habitually truant before they get to the breaking point, are working.

For the 2008–2009 school year, the county's public schools had 984 habitually truant students, or students who missed school 20% or more of the time, according to school officials.

For 2009–2010, the number dropped to 557 habitually truant students, they said.

Brenda Wilks, the director of the Department of Student Services, and Steve Neff, the director of Pupil Personnel Services, both work within the school system on establishing new policies to keep students in the classroom.

School officials said the improvement in truancy is due to a variety of factors. Primarily, whereas principals used to get monthly lists of habitually truant students, they now receive lists of all students absent 10% or more of the time.

Having this data handy allows teachers to sit down with truancy lists in the same way they would sit down with reading, math or behavioral data and decide the best approach to interventions, he said.

There's also better collaboration between teachers, school officials, counselors and the school's equivalent of social workers, willing to make house calls to work with students and parents.

✸ 38 ✸
Go With Special Efforts to Target Hard to Reach Hispanic Youth

Most communities in America have experienced a surge in Hispanic population during the last decade. The fact that many of the Latino young people are not legal immigrants has forced them to band together to prevent being preyed upon by local gangs.

An illegal immigrant is not comfortable calling the police if robbed or abused. Hence, it is important to address this special population in your violence prevention programming.

> *An illegal immigrant is not comfortable calling the police if robbed or abused.*

Richmond's *G.R.I.P.* program, considered one of the most effective in the nation, administered through the Virginia Office of the Attorney General, focused on emerging conflict between local gangs and the city's growing Hispanic population.

Local leadership reported that the city's gang problem was centered around African-American and Hispanic gangs preying on Hispanic day laborers. In addition, although the community had in place a significant number of social service providers with the capacity to address gang-related issues, many of those providers felt overwhelmed by the influx of immigrants.

Local *G.R.I.P.* leadership in Richmond cited the language barrier and the immigrants' culture of distrust of the government, especially the police, as complications to its ability to serve that population.

Initiatives such as the iconic bi-lingual *"One Stop"* neighborhood center, deep involvement by the faith community, on-site police youth advocates and the establishment of a Free Clinic in the challenged neighborhood were the keys to success.

Periodically, California's Vista Unified School District hosts free weekly classes every Thursday for parents of students attending Rancho Buena Vista High School as part of the school's *Encuentros* program for Latino boys.

The *Encuentros* program has been ongoing for over eight years to offer classes and after school programs designed to help Latino boys better define who they are, what they want out of life and how they can get it.

Each week's classroom experience is a different topic, such as gang awareness, drug prevention, communication and Internet safety. Each is designed to help parents identify, understand and prevent gang involvement.

Getting more parents involved will help encourage more success among students, said Shannon Garcia, assistant principal at Rancho Buena Vista.

The classes are held in English and Spanish from 6 to 8 p.m. Thursdays at a middle school. Baby-sitting is available.

In High Point, NC, the faith community plays a big role in addressing this special group of young people in their community.

Students recently completed a two-year program called *Amigos and Hermanos* (friends and brothers), which is designed to prevent elementary and middle school students from the influences of gangs. The program was housed at the Hispanic Center of High Point at Christ the King Catholic Church.

The program was part of the Governor's Crime Commission approach to identifying and addressing the influence of gangs on young children. It was an outreach program of the Sisters of DePaul Society. During the two years, students were educated in gang prevention, participated in role-playing seminars and community service. Parent education was an important component of the program. Officers of Guilford County Juvenile Detention Center taught *Gang Resistance, Education and Training, (G.R.E.A.T.)* The program started in July 2008 and celebrated its accomplishments with a graduation at the church.

Bi-national Health Week is emerging as a focal point across America - one of the largest mobilization efforts of federal and state government agencies, community-based organizations, and volunteers in the Americas to improve the health and well being of the underserved Latino population living in the United States and Canada.

The *Napa Valley Register* tells the story of a 20-year-old gang member who wanders onto the campus of Harvest Middle School up to no good. He attempts to climb onto the school's rooftop. He wants to impress the younger kids who are following him.

The school is closed; the administration has gone home.

The only thing standing in the way of this gang recruiter is a short, white guy — Travis Newton, who runs the Boys & Girls Club of Napa's after school programs at Harvest. Early this spring, Newton launched the Boys & Girls Club's gang prevention program. He got help from Vanessa Luna, a gang violence suppression education coordinator for the Napa County Office of Education.

Even in the upscale lifestyle of Napa, gang prevention is a serious program. As communities all over America are discovering, the Hispanic kids are well organized.

Reporter Carlos Villatoro quoted the interventionist.

"It used to be that *Sureños*, one of Napa's biggest gangs, traditionally wore blue, he said. Now the gang has abandoned blue in favor of black. "That's kind of the new uniform for *Sureños*," he said. It allows them to get around school bans on gang colors.

During his campus patrols, he had confronted gang members, witnessed fights between rivals and seen the bruised face of a student moments after being jumped into a gang.

Gang recruiters begin targeting potential members as early as elementary school, Newton said. By the time a child leaves middle school, they will have made a decision to either join or stay away.

☀ 39 ☀
Train School Board Members and "Student Advocates"

Most communities have a working relationship between the schools and police. This works best when an officer is assigned to a specific school on a regular basis.

These officers should be specifically trained in gang recognition and investigation.

These officers should be more than wandering uniforms. They should have a detailed working plan of contact and intervention with all the kids in the school who are frequently absent, struggling academically, or are known gang members.

They should meet them at the bus, get in their face and let these at-risk kids know that someone really does care about them and someone is watching them very closely.

We believe these officers should work for the local police, not the school system.

They should be in full uniform and serve as a positive role model for the kids as well as a friendly face of the law. We believe it is vital for all children to have a good relationship with a police officer so they know they are there to protect them and that they are human beings – not just a uniformed predator looking for them to make a mistake.

One of the most progressive gang intervention and prevention training efforts we have seen is in Monterey, where a panel of professionals discussed the practices underway for combating gangs in Monterey County Schools with 24 different school boards.

The school boards from 24 different school systems underwent three-hour gang training.

That's right. The school boards from 24 different school systems underwent three-hour gang training.

The training was held at the Monterey County Office of Education, in Salinas.

Salinas Police Cmdr. Bob Eggers, representing the Monterey County Joint Gang Task Force, and Daniel Villarreal, of the *Strengthening Families* program, provided school board members with information about the gang problem, how to recognize gang involvement and what is being done in the community to solve it.

❈ 40 ❈

De-Glamorize Gang Culture

The glamorization of gang culture is one of the most troublesome social developments in contemporary society. Freedom of speech is fine, but someday, developed nations will begin to protest the cashing in on the destruction of a vast generation of young people.

Look at the nexus of marketing of gangsterism and the thousands, even millions, of young people begin drawn into gang life.

Examine the present fabric of youth in America and the impact of violent lyrics, gangster clothing, gangster language and the hyping of violent behavior and guns. Look further and identify those businesses, particularly the music executives, who are making a fortune by glamorizing gangs.

Kids abide by a "no snitching" creed. Guns are cool.

And this is not just in the big cities. It has now reached and fully immersed in suburban culture.

Gangs have become a fashion statement. To walk, talk and dress like a gang member is very popular right now. They dress in urban ware. And this has one unfortunate result. It attracts the attention of real gang members. Recruitment follows.

Salina police officer A.V. Plank sees youth, both in public and at Central High School and Lakewood Middle School where he's a resource officer, dressing, acting, walking and talking like their counterparts in movies or on TV.

Salina Journal reporter David Clouston's article "Code of Silence" examines the glamorization issue, interviewing Officer Plank.

"Everyone wants to belong or fit in, and youth who do not have strong role models or have low self-esteem are looking to do just that" by dressing the part of those they see being glamorized in the media, Plank said. "By doing this, they believe it will help them blend in."

Plank is the new president of the Kansas Gang Investigators Association, a fraternal organization of law officers. The group's purpose is to combat the spread of gangs in Kansas, and provide updated gang prevention information to local pediatricians to pass on to youth and parents in the community.

We went to Washington, D.C. two years ago and asked a very high-ranking executive in the Department of Health and Human Services to consider something profound.

We asked him to re-define HHS's role in preventive health to embrace youth violence as a major cause cause of death and injury and to actually begin funding community infrastructure initiatives to tackle youth violence – not from the Justice point of view, but from a public health perspective.

He looked at us like we were from another planet.

We believe a de-glamorization of gang culture needs to come from the medical community, from the public health perspective.

Posters or slogans from school administrators or city leaders just don't carry the same weight, nor have the information machine the medical community has to sustain the messaging.

If all the pediatricians, all the public health doctors, all the federally funded healthcare clinics, all the school nurses, all the EMT's carried out the de-glamorization message – we believe it can gain traction among the young people.

Most schools are already telling the kids that gangs are bad. And gang membership is going up. It's time for a new initiative to take hold.

We have been gratified that it has begun in Boston, a community that has done terrific work in standing up to gangs and working with their youth.

Helping the kids off the streets and into positive environments for violence prevention now tops the list of priorities at the Massachusetts Department of Public Health.

The state's public health commissioner, John Auerbach, said his agency would follow the lead of Governor Deval Patrick, who in his inaugural address declared youth violence a scourge that must be reduced.

Auerbach said his agency would draw upon the violence prevention campaigns crafted by the Boston Public Health Commission, which recently released a roster of the top ten healthy and unhealthy relationship songs.

Boston.com's Elizabeth Comeau and Stephen Smith quoted Auerbach in a feature article about the new public health priority.

"Our perspective in public health is about changing the conditions at the community level with grassroots groups, as well as elected leaders," Auerbach said.

The commissioner said the emerging approach to reducing youth violence reflects a dramatic shift in the gestalt of public health.

The commissioner said the emerging approach to reducing youth violence reflects a dramatic shift in the gestalt of public health.

"When I first began doing public health work a couple of decades ago, the focus was very much on personal behavior and counseling people that they should just stop doing unhealthy things and start doing healthy things," said Auerbach, who is also president of the Association of State and Territorial Health Officers, an advocacy group representing public health agencies.

Now, he said, public health agencies attempt to address the broader social causes underlying individual behavior.

Sometimes, even the smallest victory can seem like a giant step in fighting youth violence.

In January 2011, Birmingham held a celebration. They had experienced 100 days with nobody under the age of 18 losing their life to violence.

To mark the occasion, City Councilor Jay Roberson and many young people took part in a march for unity and nonviolence starting at City Hall.

This speaks to the public de-glamorization of gangs. Mark your milestones against youth violence, no matter how small they may seem.

Roberson says the outcome of his initiative has put a positive spotlight on the city.

In an interview with Roberson, *WBRC Television* reported, "It's commendable to Birmingham to have this effort. It changes the scope of our city, makes it more willing to have events come in, have hospitality in our city."

"People feel more welcome. They feel safe. You look at developments; Birmingham is on the move and going in the right direction," he said.

Several colleges and high schools in the suburbs of Birmingham took part in the ceremony.

❋ 41 ❋

Consider Fifteen Absolutely Essential School Anti-Gang Initiatives

Throughout **No COLORS**, we suggest that communities examine the full universe of opportunities in selecting their focus and initiative in their Strategic Plan.

We look at Minneapolis as a best practices example of how to deploy the educational system to its best advantage in reducing youth violence.

Since 2006, the number of youth suspects in violent crime in Minneapolis has declined 62%, and the number of youth arrested for violent crime has declined 52%.

Minneapolis Mayor R.T. Rybak was honored as an "*After School Champion*" by the national After School Alliance in Washington, D.C. in 2011.

> *Since 2006, the number of youth suspects in violent crime in Minneapolis has declined 62%, and the number of youth arrested for violent crime has declined 52%.*

Mayor Rybak champions the *Minneapolis Promise*, engages with the *Minneapolis Youth Congress* and spearheads the Minneapolis' youth violence prevention initiative. He was one of nine state champions honored in the United States for supporting and working on behalf of after school programs:

The *Minneapolis Promise*, an innovative cluster of coordinated efforts that eliminate barriers to college for Minneapolis students. The *Minneapolis Promise* provides young people with high-quality summer jobs, privately-funded College and Career Centers in every public high school that help them plan a vision for their future, and financial assistance to attend college.

The *Minneapolis Youth Congress*, an organization of 55 teens in 8th through 12th grade from neighborhoods across Minneapolis who collaborate with elected officials to create and influence public policy that positively affect local youth.

Be inspired by this city and Mayor Rybak. And consider the following fifteen absolutely essential anti-gang initiatives we believe should be present in every school in America.

Special thanks to the Department of Justice for solid guidance on many of these fundamentals.

15 Essential Anti-Gang Initiatives
That Need To be in Your Schools

1.   *Train teachers on how to manage disruptive students.*

2.   *Provide training for parents of disruptive and delinquent youth. Review and soften school "zero tolerance" policies to reduce suspensions and expulsions. These punishments propel kids into gangs.*

3.   *Make sure that punitive sanctions target delinquent gang behaviors, not gang apparel, signs, and symbols.*

4.   *Provide tutoring and mentoring for students who are performing poorly in school.*

5.   *Increase adult supervision of students after school.*

6.   *Provide interpersonal skills training to students to help resolve conflicts.*

7.   *Hook kids up with a center for youth recreation and referrals for services, to include transportation.*

8.   *Provide one-on-one speech lessons to intensely enable every child to speak English correctly. Do not tolerate "Street" language within the walls of the school.*

9.   *Provide gang awareness training for school personnel, parents, and students.*

10. *Teach students that gangs can be dangerous.*

11. *Provide training for school resource officers in mediating conflicts.*

12. *Provide speech training for teachers who have gravitated to "Street" language in an effort to connect with the children. That is the worst thing educators can do.*

13. *Everywhere in the school, banners of affirmations of success, patriotism, diversity and friendship should greet the kids.*

14. *After school sports, music, theatre and the arts should be available at every level.*

15. *Zero tolerance for bullying. Pay special attention to monitoring school buses, where much of the bullying can occur.*

❋ 42 ❋

Challenge and Reward At-Risk Elementary and Middle School Kids Directly

This unique idea is designed for elementary and middle school kids. It gives them incentive to stay out of gangs and be a family hero.

> *It gives them incentive to stay out of gangs and be a family hero.*

Each holiday season, thanks to the Orange County, CA *Gang Reduction Intervention Partnership* (*G.R.I.P.*), turkey dinners will be delivered to at-risk youths and their families.

"We offered these kids a challenge — improve your school performance between now and Thanksgiving — and you'll receive a complete turkey meal for your family," Senior Deputy District Attorney Tracy Rinauro said.

The true impact of this is that the entire community takes part. The turkey meal is sponsored by the local Albertsons supermarket and supported by checkout counter donations.

Volunteers from Saddleback Church followed with a Thanksgiving feast that included turkey and the trimmings, pumpkin pie and a recognition certificate from the multiagency *G.R.I.P.*, honoring about 420 students from 25 Orange County elementary and middle schools.

Law enforcement officials credit the *G.R.I.P.* program for bringing about a significant change.

"Many of these kids started sobbing when we made the announcement. They'd never had the chance to give their parents or families anything, and now here was their opportunity," Rinauro says.

The key to its success, Rinauro says, is the incentive-driven model where rewards, such as the turkey dinner, do not come free. Grades are up and school violence and truancy are down in all 20 of the participating school districts, including Kinoshita Elementary School in San Juan Capistrano, CA, where school performance has gone up since the program was implemented two years ago, Principal Peggy Baerst says.

Of the 450 students who signed on at the start, 415 will complete the challenge, Rinauro said.

"One of my favorite aspects of the program is that the police officers have the opportunity to connect in a positive way with these kids and their families, like delivering the turkey dinners," she says.

And the children get to see themselves in a new light.

"These kids get to be a hero for their families, something they've not ever had the chance to do," says Brian Uyeda, pastor of Saddleback Church, a *G.R.I.P.* partner and originator of the turkey challenge idea.

❦ 43 ❦

D.A.R.E. Works –
Bring It Back. Strengthen It.

Many *Drug Abuse Resistance Education (D.A.R.E.)* programs across the nation have been felled by budget cuts in our public schools.

No COLORS co-author Bobby Kipper spent four years as a *D.A.R.E.* officer in his hometown. He was a celebrity among parents and kids alike and when these kids grew up and established themselves in the community, Bobby got stopped in malls to introduce him to their kids.

The *D.A.R.E.* program does involve expenditure of law enforcement police resources. But we have found that the results measure up as well, as well as create lasting relationships in the community.

In November 2010, the *Times-Picayune* in Louisiana reported the demise of the *D.A.R.E.* program after 13 years in Jefferson Parish public schools.

D.A.R.E. was a rite of passage for fifth graders, the newspaper reported.

It taught them everything from resisting peer pressure to making smart decisions.

But the police-led *D.A.R.E.* program fell victim to budget cuts this year — as it has across the United States — with the Jefferson Sheriff's Office pulling its *D.A.R.E* deputies out of more than 50 elementary schools."

The newspaper reported that school system and the Sheriff's Office have other programs to teach children about the dangers of drugs and alcohol.

"But *D.A.R.E.'s* demise has disappointed some parents, who think it was unique in its approach of providing children with skills to resist drugs and violence as well as opening the lines of communication between law enforcement and youth," the *Times Picayune* reported.

"You're with the same officer the entire year, and the officer gets to know the kids and the kids get to know the officer," said Fred Parker of Metairie, whose two older children went through the program but who's younger child missed out. "The kids can tell you what alcohol will do to your brain. It teaches them how to respond to bullies, how to respond to invitations related to drugs and alcohol."

Founded in Los Angeles in 1983, *D.A.R.E.* is taught in 75% of U.S. school districts and in more than 43 countries.

So, the Jefferson Parish program lost *D.A.R.E.* in a tough economic environment. The Sheriff has to choose between protecting the public and educating the children.

Any businessperson who understands cost-benefit analysis can do the math between the cost of providing *D.A.R.E.* and the cost of imprisoning one young person.

Rep. Bobby Scott (D-VA), who has been championing prevention and intervention in our nation's communities, has made this argument for over a decade.

So they gave up *D.A.R.E.* due to Sheriff's funding.

We should never boil down decisions about the future of our young people in these terms – eliminating key programs based on the volatility of the Sheriff's budget from year to year.

> *Rep. Bobby Scott (D-VA), who has been championing prevention and intervention in our nation's communities, has made this argument for over a decade.*

✸ 44 ✸
Deploy the Boys & Girls Clubs in Targeted Schools

Recent success pictures are emerging from communities where Boys & Girls Clubs are co-located at schools. Communities all over the nation are beginning to integrate this organization into the lives of their students.

The Boys & Girls Club of America places facilities in some of the toughest neighborhoods in America. So it seems odd at first that they would locate a club in or on the grounds of a school instead of in the projects. But then, after careful review, it becomes clear that the location is perfect to intercept these kids before they hit the streets after classes are over.

> *... the location is perfect to intercept these kids before they hit the streets after classes are over.*

One of the most powerful examples of community partnerships came to life in 2010 in eastern Virginia, home of a progressive and powerful Boys & Girls Clubs organization.

Led by Steve Kast, who has spent two decades building friendships and partnerships for this organization, they have achieved a model school-club interface, which is an impressive example of an entire community coming together for their at-risk kids.

"We go where we are needed the most," says Steven S. Kast, Boys & Girls Clubs of the Virginia Peninsula Chief Executive Officer.

The new 24,000 square foot club is located adjacent to Yorktown Middle School. During the fund raising and construction period, York club members met in the middle school.

The *Daily Press* reported that the original plans called for a teen center, but that changed when the York County School Division superintendent Dr. Steve Staples expressed interest in having an in-house club at the middle school.

Boys & Girls Clubs of the Virginia Peninsula partnered with York County and York County Schools to fund the addition to Yorktown Middle School. The county will give $100,000 to the facility over the next 10 years and the school division will contribute $1.1 million at the end of construction. Staples successor Dr. Eric Williams brought the project to fruition.

Contributions were also received from private organizations. Cox Communications provided $1 million and $250,000 came from Dominion Resources, Inc. and the Dominion Foundation to help fund the project.

In the end, the capital campaign raised a total of $4.3 million.

"During the campaign, we left no stone unturned," Kast said. The new club will feature a basketball court and recreation rooms. The building will also provide classroom space for York River Academy that currently meets in trailers.

Kast often wisely counsels communities to start small. Try a "little" change, he says. Try to make a "small" change at first.

At the Virginia Conference on Inclusive Communities *2011 Humanitarian Awards* event in eastern Virginia, Kast accepted the honor by encouraging everyone in the audience to just do one small thing for the at-risk kids who are carrying a load we have never had to bear.

"Imagine what a great community we would have if everyone did a little something every day for our kids," he said.

45

Lights On After School

Lights On After School is a national movement. It's a movement that has traction.

This event is designed to encourage these unoccupied buildings to remain useful after school hours, to help kids stay safe, stay off the street and develop mentoring relationships.

Over 5,000 communities signed up for the 11th annual *Lights On After School,* which was observed on October 21, 2010. The 12th annual *Lights on After School* is planned for October 20, 2011.

More than one million Americans rally each year for after school programs at 7,500+ events nationwide. Mt Rushmore will light up with the Empire State Building for *Lights On After School.* On September 28, 2010, the U.S. Senate passed a resolution in support of *Lights On After School.*

Newly elected Mayor of Chicago Rahm Emanuel ran his 2010 campaign promising a new focus on gang intervention, and his concept of a "lighted school house." We cheer Emanuel's plan. Chicago is a war zone and deep problems require deep measures. We just wish he had exercised these ideas while in the White House.

... "lighted school house."

The campaign press release outlines why to keeps the schools lit.

> *"Of the 435 murders in Chicago last year, nearly half of the victims were between the ages of 10 and 25. A majority of those and other violent crimes happen in the hours when children are not in school. Providing opportunities for youth to be engaged in educational, artistic and athletic activities will reduce the likelihood that our children will become involved in the cycle of violence that effects too many of our neighborhoods."*

Emanuel outlined his plan to keep children safe during the after school hours when youth violence is highest:

> *"By expanding after school opportunities, Rahm's plan will provide children in every community the opportunity to participate in a range of academic, artistic and athletic extra-curricular activities. Such programs have been proven to both accelerate children's academic progress and reduce violent crime.*
>
> *Access to after school programming is a win-win for our children: it is shown to both increase academic progress and reduce violence.*
>
> *While the details will be worked out with nonprofit partners, teachers and CPS officials, Rahm will require that the program meet several basic requirements:*

1. *The program must run five days a week for the entirety of the school year. It must run at least two-and-a-half hours per day.*

2. *The program must offer opportunities in three areas — academics, arts and athletics. The mix will allow all students to extend their academic learning day by an hour each day, and add on an elective in sports or cultural arts for an additional hour.*

3. *The program will be staffed through a mix of teachers and community-based nonprofit staff, and would be coordinated by the new Director of Family and Community Engagement that Rahm proposed as part of his education plan. The Director will have access to a menu of programs and professionals that would be vetted by the central office. Each school would have the flexibility to individualize its offerings based on local needs.*

4. *The program should reach the most at-risk youth and be used to incentivize parental involvement. Those parents who stick by their commitment in the parent-teacher contract will get priority spots for their children in after school programs.*

5. *Almost all CPS children are eligible for a "third meal option" — a snack or a hot meal after school — that they would receive during the after school hours. The cost for this meal is covered by the federal government."*

"*The cost of the program is estimated at $95 million per year. The majority of funding would come from current sources — for example, the $50 million received for Supplemental Education Services through Title 1 federal funding, and the current $15 million used for after school programming in a less coordinated manner."*

"*Much of the federal funding is restricted to specific types of programming, so the remaining $30 million would be raised from two sources — $5 million can be raised through school partnerships with local businesses and nonprofit organizations that want to target specific schools and communities with innovative after school programming, and $25 million from new advertising revenues that will be earmarked for enhanced educational opportunities."*

"*This would include new ads on the city's vehicle stickers, on garbage trucks, and at other public venues, like farmers' markets."*

Naturally, all this came with the disclaimer.

"*The specific approaches will be finalized as part of Rahm's broader plan to bring in outside experts to identify and prioritize potential assets where advertising would be appropriate. The team will provide both a revenue estimate and a recommended process for implementing the plan. On all of the assets, Rahm will ensure there are adequate disclaimers and limitations on the extent to which advertising will be allowed."*

❦ 46 ❦

Remove Graffiti Immediately

This may sound simple. Remove the graffiti. For gang suppression, it's important to erase graffiti as soon as it appears.

Graffiti demoralizes a neighborhood, even a whole city. It's expensive to remove and the problem never goes away. The challenge becomes a contest of wills, and a metaphor for the battle against gangs.

The *Lakeland Times* in Wisconsin reported that some experts believe the effects of graffiti are not limited to aesthetics and pocketbooks, but that it can also affect the stability of a community.

Reporter Laurel Carson wrote, "according to a 1996 report on graffiti by the Federal Bureau of Investigation, allowing graffiti to remain visible in a community sends a message that this type of behavior is acceptable to residents."

"Further, allowing graffiti in an area encourages other offenders to degrade the community with more graffiti or other acts of vandalism." Doing so makes a strong public statement against gang activities, the *Times* noted.

But it's not easy. Systems need to be set up to alert the response staff.

But it's not easy. Systems need to be set up to alert the response staff.

Paints for utility boxes, frequent canvasses for gang works of art, need to be secured for the telephone and power and cable television providers.

Someone has to make it his or her business every day to remove graffiti as soon as it is seen. The best time of day to do this is very early in the morning.

Carlson notes that a group of eight students from the Lakeland Union High School student services department in Lac du Flambeau are dedicating Saturdays to "scrub away gang-related graffiti in Lac du Flambeau."

Ms. Carlson reports that the group first hit the town water tower and propane tanks, garbage cans, utility boxes and even some houses in the downtown area.

The kids noted that "It was hard work ... It didn't come off with one spray and one wipe." ACE Hardware in Woodruff donated cleaning supplies to support the effort.

In one community we have worked with, a local commercial photographer got up every morning at first light and removed any graffiti that appeared on any public right of way. He asked for and received matching paint from the telephone company, the power company and other locations where gang signatures usually appeared.

The result of his quiet, anonymous efforts were very gratifying. As soon as the graffiti was up it was down. This must have frustrated the young artists beyond our imagination. The problem with the Good Samaritan is that eventually, this generosity runs out of steam.

In Porterville, CA, the Supervisors funded a $20,000 grant, $10,000 of which provided Terra Bella youth an opportunity to be involved in community service — focusing on graffiti abatement — and expand the Terra Bella explorer post.

In Woodburn, OR, officials offer free clean up kits for any citizen wishing to take part in the removal of this art.

According to Michele Roberts, coordinator for the *Weed and Seed* program, the campaign offers resident graffiti cleanup kits to help deal with the problem. The kits are available for checkout to anyone who lives in Woodburn, she added.

"The kit, which is offered for no charge through *Weed and Seed*, contains materials for painting over graffiti, including paintbrushes, paint rollers, wire brushes and paint," she said.

Roberts pointed to a city ordinance that requires residents to cover graffiti wherever it appears on their property.

47

Hire At-Risk Youth

In the summer of 2006, 121 employers provided jobs and an average wage of $8 an hour for over 500 youth. Evaluations showed that 96% of supervisors felt program was a success and 94% of youth said their summer job was a valuable learning experience.

The city is Minneapolis – again, a benchmark for the nation in so many ways.

Low-income 14- and 15-year-olds in Minneapolis experience the *STEP-UP* Program, offering summer jobs for 30 hours a week for nine weeks of the summer.

Students attend class one day a week to earn high school credit and can take part in a mentorship program and an optional environmental summer camp experience.

In 2006, 453 youth learned employability skills at 38 nonprofit organizations and some schools in learning-rich environments that provided them an opportunity to develop the behaviors, knowledge and skills necessary for success in employment. Wages are paid by *STEP-UP*.

The older youth *STEP-UP* Program is operated by *Achieve! Minneapolis*, in partnership with the city. The program prepares Minneapolis students ages 16-21 for employment and places them in summer jobs.

Students complete a rigorous work readiness training program certified by the Minneapolis Regional Chamber of Commerce and customized with insight from local businesses. They work 30 to 40 hours per week for private and public sector employers. The youth can also participate in workshops on finances, careers and leadership.

Boston again emerges as a benchmark for gang prevention through jobs.

Youth Options Unlimited Boston (YOU) is a citywide program that provides essential services to over 400 high-risk youth annually. Court-involved young people, ages 14-24, are referred to *YOU* for intensive case management, educational support and placement, job-readiness training through subsidized employment, and assistance with job placement.

YOU provides subsidized employment through Boston's Transitional Employment Services, which allows young people to move through three levels of employment as they improve on their skills, workplace behavior, and overall professional development.

This model enables high-risk youth to establish a positive work history and obtain the competencies required to earn and keep a job. *YOU's* model is designed to develop academic, job readiness, and occupational skills to prepare participants for their next step, whether unsubsidized employment, occupational skills training, or higher education. Participants progress through the three levels, and are compensated at $8 per hour.

In collaboration with 17 community partners, *YOU* provided 134 jobs for youth during summer 2010. The majority of youth worked in a team setting with an assigned *YOU* supervisor. Some young people who demonstrated readiness worked with community partners in individual placements that demand more maturity and experience. *YOU* career development staff conducted weekly check-ins by at the worksite.

Examples of community service projects included:

- Maintaining the landscape of various Boston Public School yards. Each team was trained once per week by a horticulturist in entry-level techniques that they used during the program.

- Working on multiple projects for local churches, including: landscaping, general maintenance, light painting, de-weeding, mulching and planting, food prep and shopping for soup kitchen, maintaining kitchen facility and thrift store.

- Cleaning and maintaining various parks in the Charles River/Esplanade area and at Constitution Beach in East Boston. Maintenance projects included removing invasive species, trail maintenance, and cleaning parks and beaches.

- Providing the Long Island Shelter with general care and maintenance of their two-and-a-half acre organic farm. The kitchen at the Long Island Shelter, which provides over one thousand meals daily, uses much of the produce cultivated at the farm.

Assisting the Boston Redevelopment Authority in demolishing and painting a 3,000-square-foot warehouse.

San Diego operates the gang prevention initiative from a formal Commission, which is all about results. In a recent report to the Commission, Jared Aaker with the San Diego Workforce Partnership described their *Hire a Youth* initiative.

This program is school-based, with youth workforce development especially targeted to gang-involved youth or those at-risk of becoming gang involved.

The core components are work readiness training, work preparation, work based activities, educational activities and youth development.

Performance outcomes are measured by placement in employment, literacy numeracy gains, and placement in post-secondary education or advanced training.

Measures achieved during the 2009-2010 period include 82% of the young people with literacy gains. San Diego placed 102 kids in the program; 48 kids had grade point average improvements and 90 achieved grade level in school. Prior to the program, 94% of these young people were at-risk of dropping out of school.

In Richmond, VA, where you really cannot see the difference between city efforts and faith-based efforts, a faith-based group operates a car wash with young people emerging from the gang lifestyle as employees. A Thrift Shop next door provides more employment, and significant revenue for the program.

Barrios Unidos in Santa Cruz generates revenues through BU Productions, a custom silk screening shop that employs the community's youth.

The story in neighborhoods all across Chicago is "No jobs. No mentors. No support network for youth," and it's a recipe for crime and violence, according to *Medill News* reporter Courtney Subramanian.

The evidence is the summer of escalated violence – including three police officers killed, a spike in fatal shootings and gang activity.

Police Supt. Jody Weis even met with gang leaders to find an answer as Chicago continues to garner national attention – most recently landing the No. 1 spot in a listing of the nation's 25 most dangerous neighborhoods.

Gov. Pat Quinn has launched efforts to curb violent crime in Illinois' urban communities, including a $50 million *Neighborhood Recovery Initiative* aimed at youth safety and stimulating small businesses located in neighborhoods with high crime rates.

Subramanian reported that Gov. Quinn said that "It is so important that we make sure every neighborhood counts." His remarks were made at the groundbreaking for the Ray and Joan Kroc Core Community Center in the West Pullman neighborhood on Chicago's Far South Side.

"Everybody in, nobody left out. Everybody's important in Illinois."

Barbara Shaw, director of the Illinois Violence Prevention Authority said a designated agency or organization from each neighborhood implements the program in each community.

The *Neighborhood Recovery Initiative* entails a youth mentoring program including school-based counseling as well as job training and access to funding for small businesses and members of the communities.

Dr. Harold Pollack, a professor at University of Chicago's School of Social Service Administration said that youth joblessness and lack of mentors poses a real problem with violence intervention programs.

"I work with kids every day and the first thing they say when they come up to me is, 'How can I get a job?'" he said.

"It's going to have a really good impact on the youth in Englewood and this will address some of the issues that create youth to impose violence on each other."

> *"I work with kids every day and the first thing they say when they come up to me is, 'How can I get a job?'" he said.*

Though much of the *Neighborhood Recovery Initiative* emphasizes youth mentoring and job training, part of the program also focuses on small business development through job training and partnering with local financial institutions for lending practices.

The financing for the $50 million project is a combination of federal and private money, including a portion from Quinn's lump sum from the General Assembly.

Every state should follow California's lead by emphasizing summer jobs for youth.

CalGRIP usually sets aside funding to give about 5,000 kids a safer summer in an effort to keep at-risk kids out of gangs. Funds are targeted to the most stressed regions. The statewide gang initiative also gets youth into job training. *CalGRIP* sets aside 200 slots in California Conservation Corps summer programs for gang-involved young adults.

In California, a nonprofit has been experimenting with ways to keep this cycle from happening. There is no more powerful program in the nation than *Homeboy Industries*, the gang intervention program founded and run by Father Gregory Boyle, a Jesuit priest. (See our Dedication to this intervention at the beginning of **No COLORS**.) *Homeboy* is all about jobs.

The seed for *Homeboy Industries* was planted 20 years ago, when Father Boyle created "Jobs for a Future." Hoping to provide an alternative to gangs, Boyle and others established an elementary school, a day care program and resources to help young people find legitimate work.

☙ 48 ❧

GPS Gang Members like High-risk Sex Offenders

In Albany, GA, the juvenile judicial system is taking full advantage of the latest advancements in monitoring technology. The county rents monitoring ankle bracelets for $7.25 per day. The bracelets can locate a person within eight feet. The tamper-proof devices also have the ability to sound a siren in the event the child tries to run away.

> ### *The bracelets can locate a person within eight feet.*

The bracelets are considerably less expensive than the $225 it costs per day to house a child at a detention center.

Taxpayers do not foot the entire cost. Parents are assessed a $100 to $300 monitoring fee when their child receives the bracelet.

California law enforcement is increasingly relying on GPS technology. Reporter Judy Joffe-Block has done extensive reporting on this development for *News21* in Berkeley.

Joffe-Block notes that law enforcement agencies across the country are using GPS technology more and more with probationers and parolees. "But nowhere in the nation is the technology more prevalent than in California, where use of GPS ankle bracelets is expanding," she reports.

The number of Californians tracked on GPS monitors increased substantially following the approval of Proposition 83, a 2006 ballot initiative also known as "*Jessica's Law*" that mandated lifetime GPS monitoring for convicted sex offenders released from prison.

Within a few years, parole authorities implemented GPS monitoring of all of the state's roughly 6,500 paroled sex offenders, the largest population tracked in the U.S. After the initiative passed, more county probation offices across the state also invested in GPS units.

Parole agents use the bracelets to monitor whether individuals are complying with home curfews, mandatory treatment programs, and staying away from restricted zones, such as a victim's home or places where children congregate. They can also use the technology to determine an individual's current location or review their movements, Joffe-Block reported.

While sex offender supervision initially drove California's GPS trend, law enforcement agencies across the state are beginning to use electronic monitoring to track other kinds of offenders and as an alternative to incarceration.

At the start of the year, the Department of Corrections and Rehabilitation began expanding its use of GPS supervision to track the most dangerous gang members on parole. About 800 gang members are tracked across the state and the department says 200 more will be added in the coming months. Stanislaus County in the Central Valley originally acquired 20 bracelets from GPS vendor B.I., Incorporated at a cost of $8.70 a day each, to comply with sex offender supervision requirements. Now the county uses the technology to help enforce a gang injunction against *Norteño* gang members in a southern Modesto neighborhood.

"It became clear to me very quickly that the technology shouldn't be limited to just sex offenders," said Stanislaus County Chief Probation Officer, Jerry Powers.

It might be better utilized for other offenders, he noted.

Since the gang injunction prevents named gang members from associating or being out past 10 p.m. in a certain Modesto neighborhood, probation officers can use GPS data to check whether probationers are compliant and send violators to jail.

Another useful tool for dealing with gang members on probation or parole is to make certain they stay away from areas off limits to them as a condition of their release.

To do this, gang investigators make direct contact with the probation or parole officer and request that the subject be restricted from areas of significant gang activity.

The probation officer then describes the area in the official conditions on file with the court and the probation or parole department. This is useful for gang members who have been served with gang injunctions. This makes it a violation of a court order and a violation of the gang member's probation or parole should they return to the area.

In California, San Bernardino County utilizes satellite tracking anklets on paroled gang members. The program targets parolees who meet specific criteria, such as being a prison gang member or part of a gang injunction. With the anklets, officials can view a parolee's location 24 hours a day and be alerted if the wearer tampers with the device or enters an exclusion zone, such as a victim's neighborhood. Law enforcement can also check whether parolees have attended mandatory drug counseling or obeyed requirements of their house arrest.

In the fall of 2010, San Diego Parole Department had deployed 54 GPS units to gang members in North and East San Diego County. In the last two months, there were no reported new prison terms for gang members monitored by GPS.

They rotate the GPS units — if the person on parole is doing well, they will rotate off.

❋ 49 ❋

Hold Regular Gang Prevention Community Meetings

Inviting the general public to community meetings about gang prevention is a fundamental part of a thoroughly thought out communications plan.

In creating the community's Strategic Plan, dozens of neighborhood meetings are suggested. But once the program moves forward, regular briefings need to continue. It takes continuous communications for the message to filter throughout the community.

The people doing the briefing should be the people who are on the front lines. Community members want to hear the information from people who are doing the work.

"We don't have any children who are expendable do we?"

"We don't have any children who are expendable do we?"

Tarboro, NC high school assistant principal Darryl Morris posed this question at a gang awareness and prevention seminar in August 2010 at Saint Stephen Missionary Baptist Church.

"One hundred sixty thousand children miss school each day because they are bullied," Morris said. "The work that has to be done starts with us."

An audience of parents, children, school officials and staff, clergy, community members and activists listened and began dialogue on the presence of and remedy to gangs in Edgecombe County.

Ashley's report noted that Tarboro Police Department's Sgt. Jesse Webb began the presentations by providing background information on gangs in general then narrowing in on the gang presence in the area.

It's usually a turf-related issue around here, according to Webb, "but it's none the less an issue."

Webb explained that while gangs in the Tarboro area are far less formal than their counterparts in large cities and on the west coast, there is definite structure.

At the community meeting, they reviewed a 15-page document containing gang knowledge that a gang member was responsible for knowing which includes codes, prayers, a pledge to the gang, an oath and a chronological history of the gang's development.

"This shows clear cut organization," he said.

In Madison, WI, the community holds free gang prevention and safety special events at a local church with entertainment, music and kids' activities.

Speakers include, the chairman of a local outreach, representatives from the YMCA, the school board, the fire department, ministers, mental health organizations, the National Guard/U.S. Army, the hospital, the police chief and more.

In Newport News, VA, Sergeant L.W. Spencer heads the Organized Crime Division /Gang Enforcement Unit. His regular community briefings are standing room only as he uses a PowerPoint to show the most recent gang signs, Internet presence and codebooks.

Parents and community leaders are mesmerized by his revealing presentation, which busts many of the myths about gangs. He shows a video produced by the Commonwealth of Virginia's Attorney General's office.

This powerful video interview tells the story of a gang member who was shot and completely paralyzed. He felt totally abandoned by his former "Brothers" who now pay no attention to him, in his wheelchair forever.

Gang units such as those in Newport News are commonplace in larger city police departments. Over half of the gang units in major cities took part in prevention programs with young gangs.

It's very powerful and very important for the head of a Gang Enforcement Unit going to public meetings and school assemblies. Attendance is always good at these public forums as those police officers closest to the gangs tell a concerned group of citizens what they are seeing and hearing.

According to an October 2010 publication by the U.S. Department of Justice on *Law Enforcement and Gangs*, 9 out of 10 gang units monitored graffiti, 93% tracked individual gang members, 93% monitored the Internet sites for communication among gang members and 91% engaged in direct patrols and performed undercover surveillance.

☀ 50 ☀
Engineer Second Chances
for Exiting Gang Members

✄

... ask each to take a hard look at their policies regarding hiring ex-offenders.

✄

A community that is serious about gang reduction will call together leading employers and ask each to take a hard look at their policies regarding hiring ex-offenders.

In California, the State Gang Coordinator develops a list of community organizations that rehabilitate and provide job training to former gang members, as a resource for businesses interested in hiring them.

California also gives a tax break to employers that provide jobs. *CalGRIP* adds "former gang member" to list of criteria allowing companies in Enterprise Zones to receive tax credits of up to $29,234 per employee. Status of "former gang member" is verified by completion of a program recognized by the gang coordinator.

The state also helps young gang members give back and move on. *CalGRIP* allocates millions in federal and state funds to support full-time *AmeriCorps Restoring Youth and Communities* positions. Reformed gang members fill these positions. They mentor youth who are currently incarcerated in Department of Juvenile Justice facilities or on parole as they get out of gang life.

Churches often are the first to step up and give former gang members a chance.

Southern Maryland Online published a story recently about one such gang member. Sitting inside the walls of a prison cell six years ago, Henry "Hank" Johnson would have seemed an unlikely candidate to mentor students or work alongside police to reduce gang violence.

But in 2004, after being released from prison after serving five years for attempted first-degree murder, Johnson got involved in a fatal gang fight that led to a role he now treasures: helping at-risk elementary school children stay out of trouble.

Johnson was offered a way out and stability through facilities work at Ebenezer AME Church in Fort Washington.

Johnson negotiated and signed a peace treaty with a former rival gang leader. On March 17, 2005, both gang leaders received a *Community Peace Building Award* from the Washington-based Search for Common Ground.

That same year Johnson and friend Jamal Spratley started a group called *Circle of H.O.P.E. (Healing Our Personal Environment)* to do mediation, mentoring and gang prevention with police and local schools.

As part of that effort, in 2007, Johnson called the principal at Forest Heights Elementary School and told her he wanted to give back to the community, to steer students away from the path he took. Principal Theresa Merrifield began selecting a group of seven to 10 students each year to join Johnson and Spratley's mentoring group.

Johnson and Spratley provide the students with positive male role models and alternatives to drugs, gangs and crimes, Merrifield said.

Johnson also works with county police to diffuse conflicts.

He still loves the streets and continues to spend a lot of time there. He started a ministry with Ebenezer AME Church where he goes out and talks to people on the streets.

The faith-based community offers new hope to young people who seek a second chance. We continue to see the dramatic impact of dedicated ministers and congregations across America.

❋ 51 ❋
Bring Civil Suits Against Gang Members

A lot of people are holding their breath and watching developments across the country as bold communities file civil lawsuits against gang members, seeking compensatory damages.

Never heard of such a thing? It's happening in Illinois.

The Chicago Tribune reports that Elgin police say gang activity in their city has dropped in recent months.

"It could be a benefit of colder weather, which often is a natural deterrent, but they suspect it may have something to do with a relatively obscure tactic that few other law enforcement agencies have embraced," the *Tribune* reports.

Elgin officials take reputed street gang members to court — not to charge them with crimes, but to sue them.

"I hate saying this because I don't want to jinx it," Elgin police Lt. Bill Wolf said, "but it has been a pretty quiet fall and winter."

Police in DuPage and Boone counties also report that they saw declines in gang activity after similar lawsuits went to court.

Still, the *Tribune* noted, critics argue that the suits can be used to unfairly target people who aren't even gang members.

The lawsuits stem from the *1993 Illinois Street Gang Terrorism Omnibus Prevention Act*, which allowed prosecutors to pursue civil cases, including monetary damages, against gang members.

In 1999, DuPage County State's Attorney Joseph Birkett was the first in Illinois to file suit against individual members of street gangs. DuPage filed the complaints against 22 reputed members of the *Satan Disciples* street gang in West Chicago.

The suits sought monetary damages, a relatively complicated endeavor, but also something interesting.

Prosecutors asked judges to bar the alleged gang members from associating with each other in public.

A judge's approval clears police to arrest gang members congregating in public and charge them with a criminal misdemeanor, which leads to a search that can turn up more serious charges. That power is, in some ways, as critical as receiving monetary damages.

The *Tribune* observed "preventing gang members from gathering often prevents them from planning and carrying out crimes."

"Monetarily, they haven't had to pay damages," said DuPage County State's Attorney Robert Berlin, who supports the gang lawsuits, "but I think it's a monetary savings for police departments because they have less criminal activity," the *Tribune* reported.

... the tactic has been effective. Cook County prosecutors have yet to use the lawsuits against reputed gang members. But police and prosecutors who have say the tactic has been effective. They say many reputed gang members fail to appear in court, which leads to an automatic order barring them from associating with others alleged to be in the gang.

DuPage County has filed suit against dozens of alleged gang members, including suits targeting the *Latin Kings* in Addison and Glendale Heights in 2006, the *Sureños* in West Chicago and Addison in 2007, and the Latin Counts in Addison in August 2010.

Boone County filed a similar set of lawsuits against 30 reputed members of the *Latin Kings* street gang in 2009.

In September 2010, the Kane County state's attorney's office filed a civil lawsuit on behalf of Elgin, naming 70 reputed *Latin King* members whose activities "have threatened injury or caused injury to the people." and imposed costs on the city for police and related resources.

🔥 **52** 🔥

Open and Program Your
Recreation Centers at Night

Because of the discipline throughout California's gang reduction strategies, results are measured on everything. When California cities repeat an initiative, it is usually a good sign that it is working.

At the October 29, 2010 Gang Commission meeting in San Diego, it was reported that the grant which funded the extended hours of recreation centers was almost at the end of the cycle.

"The grant has funded the recreational centers throughout the city with high areas of gun violence. The grant pays for the recreation centers to stay open on Friday nights from 6 p.m. to 9 p.m. and have officers present," the minutes from the meeting describe.

The 2009 statistics indicated that there was a 37% drop in gun-related crime near the three recreational centers.

They are reapplying for the same *CalGRIP* grant, but want to expand to four recreational centers, which will include two other neighborhoods with high incidences of gang violence.

If you have ever driven through a large California city on a summer night, you'll notice something quite distinctive – the ball fields and public parks are usually lit and being used late into the evening.

In LA, the Mayor's popular *Summer Night Lights (SNL)* program keeps neighborhood parks open well past normal hours, and provides activities to keep kids away from trouble. The activities serve as a recruiting tool to help make contact with troubled kids and funnel them into the appropriate prevention or intervention program.

The California Communities Gang Prevention Network highlighted LA's program in their February 2011 *Bulletin*.

"The Baldwin Village community of Los Angeles helped develop and pilot *SNL*, which was initially called *Summer of Success (SOS)*, in the summers of 2002 and 2003. Today, 24 different parks and communities participate in *SNL*."

The *Bulletin* noted that "Everyone is having a great time, eating, taking part in a recreation activity...engaging in peace." During the six weeks that *SNL* runs, communities participate in basketball games, soccer games, and tennis games. Participants are also able to attend theatre and musical performances, and play in dominoes tournaments. At the end of the summer, the 24 different *SNL* sites get together for a day of competition, food, and dancing.

SNL's 2010 statistics show that the program has "led to a 57% reduction in gang-related homicides, a 55% reduction in shots fired, and a 45% reduction in victims shot. The *SNL* also develops the community's trust in city and police employees." More importantly, community backing and participation helps develop the power and skills of citizens, reigniting the problem-solving mechanisms of the communities *SNL* supports.

Fort Collins, CO has an excellent summer youth programs. Ft. Collins is one of the most beautiful, desirable places to live in America. And they have never let their at-risk youth be forgotten there. It's a city of about 144,000 people about fifty miles north of Denver. A college town, Fort Collins was named *Money* magazine's *Best Place to Live 2006*, #2 in 2008, and #6 in 2010.

Their Summer Youth Basketball League targets low-income students that statistically face the greatest chance of engaging in at-risk behaviors such as drug abuse, unprotected sex and crime.

According to the Fort Collins school district figures, one in every five K-12 students receives free or reduced-fee lunches and 23% are being raised in single-parent households.

The Summer Basketball Program attracts boys and girls of all ethnicities 8-18. The program attracts organized teams, pick-up teams, and beginners.

Teams are divided into divisions by Recreation Department staff based on age and overall ability and are coached by adult volunteers. Teams are all males, all females or co-ed. Games are scheduled weekly throughout the summer at a local recreation center, with a season-ending tournament scheduled the last weekend in July.

For many, the league's greatest appeal is its uniqueness of bringing a diverse group of children together to gather, play, and become friends. This program allows children to interact in a positive activity without the pressure of many competitive sports — there are no try-outs, no all-star teams, and no benchwarmers.

Quite often it's the players who recruit the coach, not the other way around. The program provides leadership, volunteer and job opportunities, and life skill development and training. The program also functions as a bridge between an enjoyable low-cost sport that promotes active, healthy lifestyles and the opportunity to help kids see ways to develop into productive adults.

The Recreation Department's Summer Youth Basketball League began in 1992 as a way to help curb gang involvement among teenagers. Since then, this popular program has expanded to include all children ages 8-18, as well as a separate adult league. Although the youth/teen league is still designed to provide these kids with a way to spend their time constructively, the program's main objectives are to let kids play, improve their overall fitness, and have fun.

According to Recreation Department figures, the Summer Youth Basketball League averaged 27 teams in its first few years of existence. In 1999 that number more than doubled, attracting 67 teams and 700 participants. In 2006, the program attracted 92 teams and 1,200 participants, all on a "level playing field" to interact, compete, and learn life lessons related to teamwork, sportsmanship, and fair play.

The program fosters a community consciousness that values recreation and fitness in developing youth character. It also instills a sense of ownership and stewardship where adults and businesses feel compelled to be involved as volunteers or financial contributors.

The greatest measure of program success and effectiveness comes when past participants return to the program to officiate or to coach a new generation of players to help instill in them an attitude that promotes a positive future.

The program began with no city funding and for many years it was financed by donations, sponsorships and grants. Currently, minimal fees are charged to help offset costs, and much of the program is funded through the Recreation Department's budget. Donations and sponsorships continue to supplement the program.

The original program was created with collaboration between the Recreation Department, the Sheriff's Office, and interested citizens. The community continues to maintain its involvement with the program through donations, business sponsorships, and individuals who volunteer as coaches and officials.

The program structure should remain simple and flexible.

Organizers caution that teens do not like to be over-programmed in the summer and inflexibility will lead to disinterest on the part of the group you are trying to attract.

"It is, however, essential to maintain tough rules concerning behavior on and off the court while in the public facility and should be stringently enforced. Failure to enforce from day one will lead to disciplinary problems as the season progresses and will undermine efforts to develop and build positive character traits," organizers note.

Ft. Collins was recently named *The Happiest City in America* by a Gallup poll. Besides amazing Rocky Mountain beauty, clean air, fit people, and a strong base of small businesses – the community is well known for its community spirit. They have events almost every night when the weather is warm and they have hundreds of people continually volunteering to put these events on for everyone. This could well be the most community-spirited city in America. It is no wonder they have few problems with their youth. They don't leave them out.

> *It is no wonder they have few problems with their youth. They don't leave them out.*

The San Jose community also deploys basketball. Mark Gomez at *Mercury News* wrote about one such pickup basketball game in San Jose.

"The pickup basketball game in South San Jose was starting to heat up, and soon tension between rival players boiled over. Words were exchanged. Two young men got face-to-face. On the streets of San Jose's Edenvale neighborhood, this confrontation might have turned physical," Gomez reported.

"But inside the new multimillion-dollar basketball gymnasium at the Edenvale Community Center, conflicts among players, some of whom are gang members, are being resolved peacefully. On this recent December night, teammates jumped in and separated the opposing players until they cooled down."

The *Mercury News* reported that twice a week, a San Jose gang intervention agency opens the gym doors at the Edenvale Community Center for as many as 70 teens and young adults who live in a neighborhood that is rife with crime and youth violence.

Let's all notice that the city built a beautiful facility for this. Let's also notice that the program probably thrives on being located in an appealing new venue. Nobody wants to play basketball in a dimly lit abandoned warehouse.

By allowing noted gang intervention specialist Sonny Lara and his agency to operate the after-hours open gym, city officials are setting a benchmark for using recreation as way to prevent violence and provide alternatives to the gang lifestyle.

Well-respected gang intervention workers staff the gym. The *Firehouse Community Development Center* receives funding from the San Jose Mayor's Gang Prevention Task Force. The interventionists try to connect the players to a variety of services, such as a job-training workshop.

City officials employ similar recreation strategies in other areas considered hot spots for gang activity.

Gomez reported the support of the deeply respected Angel Rios of the city's parks and recreation department and a Gang Task Force leader.

"What we've found when we do this is crime and gang-related incidents, all the things that serve as barometers, seem to go down," said Angel Rios.

"There's something about giving something to somebody, a sense of gratitude."

Rios said the teens and young adults who play basketball at Edenvale take care of the center and agree not to wear gang colors while inside the gym.

❦ 53 ❦

Send a Strong Message to Teens That They Are Important to the Community.

At every opportunity, your community should recognize and praise youth for their important contributions to the world around us.

This is a fundamental aspect of a good prevention mentality. Kids value being praised. Any good Little League coach can tell you that. Scolding does not work. Praise is the only motivator that consistently works with kids.

Many communities have a Mayor's Youth Commission. Having such an organization is one thing. Making it become a vibrant, sought-after honor is a challenge.

We like the common sense approach and deep involvement of the entire community in El Paso.

The *Mayor's 100 Teens* program in El Paso recognizes and praises El Paso youth. Many of these young people achieved significant goals by overcoming obstacles in their lives, and often, their contributions go by unnoticed.

This program provides a forum to recognize these exemplarily students and allow them to become a positive role model to others in the community.

Many of these young people achieved significant goals by overcoming obstacles in their lives, and often, their contributions go by unnoticed.

The *Mayor's 100 Teens* program is for teens completing 9th, 10th or 11th grades who are nominated during the spring of each year by teachers, counselors, friends, clergy or family (but not their parents).

The nomination process is publicized through local media, all area schools, libraries, police regional command centers, and a variety of youth and community organizations.

The *Mayor's 100 Teens* was modeled after a similar program that has been implemented for the past nine years in Colorado Springs. The program's mission is to create a community that values teens and promotes a positive image of them. The program seeks to recognize a diverse group of high school teens who normally do not receive recognition. Other benefits of the initiative include the clear collaboration with youth-serving organizations and businesses and achieving prominent exposure for promising teenagers in the community. The end result is that it sends a strong message to teens that they are important to the community.

The teens get involved in community work and participate at different events with the Mayor.

Throughout the year, the teens are honored with a kick-off event in October hosted by the Mayor, a published yearbook profiling each honoree, attendance at local events and meetings as guests of the Mayor, formal introduction at a City Council and County Commissioners Court meetings, community parades and celebrations, a picture ID card and t-shirt, media recognition and benefits from sponsors such as free entrance to games, bowling, food, and other services.

The program is financed with private funds solicited from the business community and constituents.

In 2010, the program received approximately $10,000 in donations to finance the activities throughout the year, as well as in-kind donations from many businesses. The program does utilize an executive secretary to organize the program and coordinate all the activities for the teens.

Mayor John F. Cook arranged for a group of volunteers from the Optimist Clubs to review all nominations and make the final selection into the program.

The media generously promotes the program and features the teen events. Other city departments assist in funding activities such as the Parks and Recreation Department, who request for the teens to participate as volunteers in their special events.

State Senator Eliot Shapleigh recognizes the teens at every opportunity and utilizes them as volunteers.

✹ 54 ✹

Develop a Support Program for Parents of Gang Members

In Los Angeles, judges can now make parents of gang members go to classes.

The moms and dads were ordered to attend the class under a new California law giving judges the option of sending parents for training when their kids are convicted of gang crimes for the first time. *Associated Press* writer Thomas Watkins reported that Assemblyman Tony Mendoza, the lawmaker behind the *Parent Accountability Act,* said it is the first state law to give judges the power to order parents of gang members to school, though other court-mandated classes exist at the local level.

"A lot of parents do not know how to handle teenagers. Now more than ever, parents need a guide," Mendoza said.

The new law went into effect in January 2011 and eventually will be in place across California. Budget cuts in Sacramento meant implementation of the classes was delayed and they have been rolled out on a limited basis in the Los Angeles Unified School District.

In El Paso and Chicago, interventions are ongoing that include a training and development component for parents of kids involved with gangs.

It appears that the support offered via "how to" workshops and the group and individual mentoring/referral assistance enable them to become an empowered intervention tool as parents.

Many focus groups held around the country also have noted the suggestion of helping parents of gang members who basically are helpless to do anything about their teenager who has become a gangster.

While this is noble and definitely worthwhile, a community strategy must focus on replacing the "lost family" of the gang member with mentors and role models who care about them and their future.

Quite frankly, it's easier to provide these needed assets to kids than to try to train parents on what is right and wrong; too little, too late. Remember, we are dealing with, in some cases, multiple generations of the family belonging to the same gang. Many don't want to be educated in parenting – they were sent out on the streets when they were nine, so that's what they know.

We are not saying that working with these parents is not worthy of the time and effort. It certainly is. But this will require a deft touch.

... this will require a deft touch.

55

Create a Youth-Led
Movement Against Violence

Canada has a vibrant organization that reaches into the population of young people affected by violence and brings their strength to others in a very big way. It's now beginning to gain traction in the U.S.

This program could be a model for many communities in America. It relentlessly puts faith back into kids who have suffered violent events.

Leave Out Violence (LOVE) is an award winning, not-for-profit, grass roots youth organization that is an effective means of social change, providing hope, motivation and opportunity to thousands of young people.

LOVE was started because violence had deeply affected the life of a remarkable woman: Twinkle Rudberg.

In 1972, her husband was stabbed to death while trying to help a woman who was being attacked for her purse. To further compound the horror and senselessness of this act, the attacker was a 14-year-old boy who was both homeless and under the influence of drugs. The young boy was a runaway, who recently joined a gang. Clearly this tragedy began long before he took the life of an innocent man.

In response to this tragedy, Twinkle decided something had to be done to help troubled youth like this lost teenager. She wanted to create an organization that would identify and focus on the causes of teen violence – neglect, isolation, lack of mentorship and domestic abuse. Fourteen years ago, she created *LOVE*.

Since its inception, *LOVE* has become quite a success helping over 40,000 teens with programs from coast to coast in Canada.

The trend has found its way to the United States, where *LOVE* had an impressive launch several years ago. With the support of the Department of Education, the NYPD and other prominent New Yorkers, *LOVE* is successfully being implemented in several New York City high schools.

... teaching credible youth how to use their voices and become champions against violence.

This nonprofit organization is creating a youth-led movement against violence by teaching credible youth how to use their voices and become champions against violence.

Since *LOVE* began in 1993, these young leaders have reached hundreds of thousands of children, youth and adults reducing violence in schools, neighborhoods and homes.

Programs are designed to help youth overcome the challenge of violence in their lives and develop the skills to become local leaders against violence.

Young people who have been victims, witnesses or perpetrators of violence attend a series of weekly training sessions held in Vancouver, Toronto, Montréal and Halifax.

They learn to use their personal experiences with gangs, drugs, weapons, racism, bullying, domestic violence and self-harm to help other youth make positive choices and together build safer communities.

Through the Media Arts Program, youth learn to express themselves publicly.

Instructive programming is offered in media arts includes photography, journalism, videography and broadcasting. Through the lens of a camera, their written expressions and their voices, these young people creatively articulate the impact of violence on their lives and explore positive alternatives. Programs are offered at local community colleges or universities and are led by media and social service professionals.

Young people who have completed this graduate into leadership training, where they develop the skills, confidence and passion to become part of *LOVE's* community violence prevention team.

Based on the principles of youth engagement, *Youth Leadership Training Modules* include public speaking, producing and performing the spoken word, creating videos and public service announcements, and facilitation skills.

These young leaders work in schools and the communities to promote and encourage youth participation in violence prevention by establishing Violence Prevention Committees. They promote awareness, influencing attitudes and effecting change.

To complement this program, each year, a 5-day intensive Leadership Training Camp is held in Haliburton, Ontario. Youth leaders from across the country come together to enhance their leadership skills and bring these skills back to their communities.

Violence Prevention Committees are established in priority communities, in elementary, middle and high schools. Youth Leaders and *LOVE* Staff co-facilitate these committees, which meet regularly throughout the school year, to create projects that communicate a message of non-violence to the entire student body. The goal of these committees is to facilitate students' ownership of the violence prevention initiative in their schools and neighborhoods.

LOVE was founded with a vision of what it takes to help a young person overcome adversity and become successful, and over the years, it's making a difference.

✸ 56 ✸

Use Great Resources Well –
But Don't Over Complicate Your Plan

Your community can take advantage of outstanding resources in setting up your attack on the gang problem.

The *National Gang Center (NGC)* is one of those excellent resources.

The *NGC* is a coordinated project of three federal agencies, the Office of Justice Programs, Bureau of Justice Assistance and the *Office of Juvenile Justice and Delinquency Prevention (OJJDP)*.

The *National Gang Center* website features the latest research and news about gangs. The site also offers descriptions of evidence-based, anti-gang programs, and links to tools, databases, and other resources to assist in developing and implementing effective community-based gang prevention, intervention, and suppression strategies.

Here you will locate an analysis of the findings from nearly 15 years of data collected by the annual National Youth Gang Survey of 2,500 U.S. law enforcement agencies.

Visitors can read and download publications related to street gangs.

An online form allows communities to request training and technical assistance as they plan and implement anti-gang strategies. Users can register for a variety of anti-gang training courses.

The website also hosts a database of gang-related state legislation and municipal codes, a list of newspaper articles on nationwide gang activity, updated daily, and *GANGINFO*, an electronic mailing list for professionals working with gangs.

The challenge is to pick from this enormous library just what you need to enhance your community Strategic Plan.

It's a wealth of information that can be intimidating to someone not immersed in the subject matter. The challenge is to pick from this enormous library just what you need to enhance your community Strategic Plan.

This resource is a target-rich environment of resources to help you make good decisions. We particularly like the Strategic Planning Tool section.

The Strategic Planning Tool was developed to assist in assessing a community's gang problem and planning strategies to deal with it. Although originally created for cities participating in the *OJJDP* Gang Reduction Program, any community can use the tool.

The four interrelated components of the tool can be used separately or in sequence, depending on the user's needs.

The Planning and Implementation, Risk Factors, and Program Matrix components provide information for any community, but the Community Resource Inventory component is site-specific.

In other words, the user creates a password-protected database and populates it available local resources. If, after reading the description and the instructions and "test-driving" the tool using the demonstration community, you would like to create an inventory for your community, you simply request an account using the online account request form.

● 57 ●
Strengthen Prevention with the Arts

In almost every case we have seen across America, when the arts gets involved, the traction of the prevention program begins to take hold.

A 2007 study showed that since the enactment of *No Child Left Behind*, 30% of school districts with at least one school identified as needing improvement have decreased instruction time for arts and music.

There is a big movement gaining momentum to make music available to at-risk kids. This revolutionary new music program is known as *El Sistema*, which has moved from Venezuela to the United States and other nations.

PBS's popular talk show host Tavis Smiley raved about the program.

"Imagine a group of 4th-grade students excited to remain after school for classical music instruction. They play instruments, study Mahler's first symphony, train with their ensemble, and practice again at home," Smiley comments.

Day after day, they are dedicated to learning and playing music. But most importantly, they think it's fun. They are passionate about classical music. They can't wait to pick up their instruments again; they dream of performing in an orchestra."

The students are not child prodigies, born into well-heeled families and studying at the top music academy, Smiley continues.

"They are poor. Their parents work several jobs, and struggle to keep food on the table and shoes on their kids' feet. Their families would likely not have the means to afford new instruments for their children, let alone classical music instruction, if it were not for a community vision that considers music education a right, not a privilege," Smiley says.

The vision, the network and the program make up *El Sistema*. It began in the South American nation in the 1970s and is slowly spreading around the world.

The Venezuelan *El Sistema* model levels the musical playing field for children of all socioeconomic backgrounds by ensuring that children from low-income communities receive the same introduction to and instruction in music (and specifically classical music) that would be available to children of families with greater resources.

The emphasis within *El Sistema* is on community-based orchestra training from pre-school and early grade school, with a focus on making music fun and making the young musician passionate about music.

Many of the children begin learning classical music as early as 2 years old and continue into their teens and beyond. The program follows a national curriculum and is intense, with music instruction lasting up to four hours a day for five or six days a week.

By 2010, the program, known formally as the State Foundation for the National System of Youth and Children's Orchestras, is nationwide, has impacted more than 4 million students, includes 200 youth orchestras, 60 children's orchestras, 270 music centers and currently reaches about 400,000 young musicians.

We've seen the kids in Newport News eagerly race to the *SoundScapes* music class. This works.

Soundscapes organizers believe that children with a strong sense of self-worth, discipline and leadership skills are equipped to conquer their disadvantages and achieve their dreams. And it's funded by donations – and it's a shame the growth of this program is currently limited by what charitable support leaders can garner.

Another application of the arts is the concept demonstrated by *Voices of Youth*, a pilot program meant to engage young people who have experienced some of this gun violence by helping them to get creative about it through film.

More than 30 students from Philadelphia's Hope Charter School, Imhotep Institute Charter High School, Martin Luther King High School and New Media Technology Charter School work with the Village of Arts and Humanities and Well Productions in an eight-week after school program to develop their own documentary films about gun violence in their neighborhoods.

They chose tough neighborhoods for the focus point. Germantown and West Oak Lane neighborhoods saw a 25% increase in shootings and murders in 2010.

A strong neighborhood relationship helped. The community and school-based Northwest *Community Coalition for Youth (NCCY)* anti-crime effort proved to be a willing partner and made this the right place to begin.

The students attend at least two classes a week to learn about filmmaking. In May, their documentaries premiere in a film festival.

Isabella Fitzgerald, co-chairperson of *NCCY*, said that "It's allowing us to see what's going on in their communities, as opposed to what adults see," she said. "They can talk about the issues in a more realistic way."

There have been 20,000 victims of shootings and homicides in Philadelphia from 2001 to 2010.

For seventeen years, The Shakespeare Center of Los Angeles has implemented a summer jobs program for youth that is second to none.

Will Power to Youth (WPY) is a highly acclaimed youth development program combining academics, human relations, job training and art to create a unique summer employment opportunity for youth aged 14-19.

Los Angeles youth, many of whom attend overcrowded urban schools and come from families living at or below the poverty line, work closely with professional artists and human relations facilitators for 30 hours a week for seven weeks.

Together, they create a unique adaptation of a Shakespeare play that is relevant to, and inspired by, their personal experiences.

The website for the program notes that *WPY* "empowers youth and is designed to help participants transition into adulthood. Youth not only thrive in this creative and supportive environment, but also learn first-hand the values of teamwork, a strong work ethic, and keeping a positive attitude,"

Nationally recognized by the National Endowment for the Arts, and U.S. Department of Justice, *WPY* has been hailed for its effectiveness at addressing unemployment, youth violence, and high-school dropout rates. The 2010 *Will Power to Youth* performance schedule culminated with four performances of their original adaptation of *As You Like It*.

In Reading, PA, a graffiti-art contest is held as part of the summer *Hip Hop Summit*. The art contest is designed as a positive pro-social youth engagement effort aimed at teens from the inner city. It uses urban arts and culture to educate and illuminate prevention messages.

The theme for the 2011 contest is "*Stop the Violence*" as it relates to perhaps the most compelling youth issue in the city of Reading. There are also connections among youth violence and other safety issues, including drinking. The first 25 participants will be eligible for a $500 prize. Entrance fees of $10 each will help pay for a 4-foot by 8-foot piece of plywood for the artist to work on. All entries will become the property of A.C.O.R. Gallery of the Arts for further exhibition and promotion.

✸ 58 ✸

Cool Bus Picks Up Kids for After School Activities

Here's a project with a perfect measurement built in.

In Tulare County, CA, at-risk children began sporting a new ride when Tulare County leaders unveiled two new buses as a part of the *LOOP* Bus Program."

> *...the vehicles take at-risk children to places that provide them with after school activities, such as mentoring and gang prevention workshops.*

KMPH Fox Television said that the vehicles take at-risk children to places that provide them with after school activities, such as mentoring and gang prevention workshops.

The new buses feature comfortable seating, air conditioning, and DVD screens so they can watch programs while they ride.

KMPH TV featured a news segment about the beautiful, comfortable *LOOP* bus and its importance for at-risk families.

"The buses are important because we're taking kids off the streets," said Tulare County Supervisor Phil Cox. He noted that a lot of kids don't have transportation or a way to get to youth centers so they find something else to do, like the streets.

Cox noted that the community would rather these kids get to young centers and be with capable mentors.

Families need to do some paperwork, with all the appropriate permissions, to transport the kids. Visalia organizers need two weeks to process the applications before service can commence.

Initially, the *LOOP* operated from noon to 8 p.m. Monday through Friday and noon to 6 p.m. on Saturday during the summer. It takes about 45 minutes to complete a circuit.

It seems to be working pretty well," said Sgt. Ernie Villa of the Visalia Police Department, who is helping to coordinate the program. "There are really a lot of kids using it between the rec centers and the Boys & Girls Club."

Villa said the *LOOP* is averaging about 120 riders a day, and that number has been steady.

They use an essential formal parental consent to establish permission to pick up the children.

59

Create Interventions
for the 19- to 25-Year-Olds

When we discuss intervention, the most powerful provider in America always comes to mind. Father Gregory Boyle's *Homeboy Industries*, which in 2011 is working with over 8,000 young people looking for a way out of gang life.

It's all about jobs.

In most communities, over half of the gang members are over the age of 18. We need to remember that many of these young people may have been gang involved since elementary or middle school. They have developed street life into a pattern of existence.

Gang members coming out of jail and prison should be addressed by an active re-entry strategy in every community. We must give these people every opportunity to straighten themselves out and lead a law-abiding life.

Yet there is another population of gang members over 18 who have not been to jail. These are the young people that need to be addressed in a community-wide Strategic Plan.

Most communities' first instinct is to reach out with suppression alone. But, as we have learned, you cannot arrest yourself out of this national emergency with our youth.

Programs of the Boys & Girls Clubs and other great at-risk youth organizations do not traditionally reach this population of 19- to 25-year-old young people.

We believe that a distinct set of strategic initiatives needs to be created to target these young people.

It is a myth that gang members are in a permanent state of gang membership. People come and go out of gangs every day.

We understand that with this group of young people, all we can do is prepare the community to support them when they are ready to come home.

> *It is a myth that gang members are in a permanent state of gang membership.*

The objective of this set of initiatives should be to provide a welcoming atmosphere for these young people and to streamline access to caring mentors, jobs and relocation if necessary.

Providing services to the 19- to 25-year-old age group is "an area where communities need to bolster their resources," says Jack McDevitt, associate dean for research and graduate studies at Northeastern University.

Northeastern is research partner for the Springfield, MA program, offering technical assistance to participating sites, hosting quarterly meetings on best practices and authoring research papers and annual reports.

The Republican reports that services most appropriate for older youth include GED classes and employment preparation programs — but serving the demographic can be an uphill battle, according to McDevitt.

"The challenges you get with these kids are much more difficult. They are difficult to bond with, because so many people have reached out to them over the years and then have walked away," he said.

In many cases, these young people will test you before they trust you...

In many cases, these young people will test you before they trust you, and challenges arise as they struggle to cut ties with the friends, acquaintances and cliques that have encouraged prior delinquent behavior, McDevitt said.

A young man's journey to a job-training program, for instance, might take him past old haunts or through neighborhoods populated by former rivals, he said.

"People might still think they're in the gang life," meaning that the risk for conflict doesn't immediately fade with a few steps in the right direction, he said.

And, even when agencies attempt to offer services to a wider range of ages, there are challenges, McDevitt noted.

"Sometimes when you reach out to that (older) cohort, you're going to have some failures," McDevitt said.

"And if you have younger kids there, will other parents object to seriously gang-involved youth coming in the door?"

McDevitt explained that the kids want jobs at that point and they have unrealistic expectations about what that means. They are going to make mistakes, he said. They need a job with an employer who is not going to fire them the first time they don't show up.

McDevitt said 19- to 25-year-olds also respond well to programs that focus on raising awareness about the cost of violence to families. Research has found that the most compelling message isn't "You're going to go to jail" — instead, it's, "What will your mother, or grandmother, or little brother or little sister do while you're in jail?"

A nonprofit street intervention group working throughout eastern Virginia uses an unusual hook to reach this group of young people – free haircuts.

Imbued by a motivation only to help stop the violence, Terry Riddick sets up in front of neighborhood hang outs and offers free haircuts to all young people, taking the opportunity to spread the non-violence message.

This group is aptly called, *"Best Kept Secret — Stop the Violence."* They receive support from community activist groups, churches and private donations. Their members show up at major community gatherings, shaking hands and mixing with people from all walks of life in the community. They understand that this activity needs credibility, so they make sure the right people know who they are and can see that they are all about the right things.

Terry Riddick is the founder and President/CEO of *Best Kept Secret — Stop the Violence*. He established his organization in 2006. He and his brothers Randy and Wilson are against youth and gang violence. They have collected guns from the streets and turned them in to the police.

Rejoice that there are people like Terry and his brothers who are willing to be a part of the effort. And you have to understand they have one foot in each of two very different worlds.

They have helped ex-gang members find other positive avenues such as job corps, which gave them a positive alternative in life.

Their goal is to let them know that there are people out there that still care to see them live another day.

Terry says "this is real and not a game we have to keep this moving!" He describes *Best Kept Secret* as a faithful, committed organization with a strong impact on the youth. Their mission is to keep the youth focused on education and encourage them to always do their best.

Professional intervention is maturing, especially in Boston and in California communities. In Sacramento, Gregory King, who works with the *Always Knocking* nonprofit organization, said at an April 2011 gang forum that the *Big Homie Street Team* is a program through the nonprofit in which volunteers talk to kids on the streets and show them there are other options. *Always Knocking* is an organization focusing on ending youth and gang violence.

Yet while these interventions are powerful there is one intervention that blasts them all away – jobs deliberately made available to this population by the community. Father Gregory Boyle of *Homeboy Industries* said in a recent *PBS* interview that jobs fulfill "about 85%" of what young people need to change their lives.

... jobs fulfill "about 85%" of what young people need to change their lives.

60

Proclaim Youth Violence Prevention Week

... brings focus to the importance of anti-violence messaging in the community.

Many of the hundreds of national observances are unworthy of great effort, but *Youth Violence Prevention Week* is most worthy because observing the celebration brings focus to the importance of anti-violence messaging in the community.

It encourages planners to develop a series of meaningful events, and gets people thinking about gang prevention again.

In Minneapolis, Mayor R.T. Rybak has proclaimed the week of March 22-26 as *Minneapolis Youth Violence Prevention Week* to coordinate with *National Youth Violence Prevention Week*.

The proclamation emphasizes the extent of the problem youth violence creates in our country, as well as highlights the city of Minneapolis' work to target and prevent youth violence. Among other things, the proclamation notes that:

- Youth violence is the second leading cause of death nationwide for youth ages 10-24.

- Research is proving that youth violence is a preventable disease and that violence is a learned behavior that can be unlearned by systematically shifting social norms and community expectations of violence.

- The *Minneapolis for Action* plan has shown that public health models can be successfully applied to community violence and result in dramatic decreases in violent injury and death.

Throughout the week, there are a number of events and initiatives that folks can take part in or learn more about. Notice in the list below that Minneapolis makes learning about key programs an event. They set aside a day for it and promote access and appreciation for those initiatives on a set schedule. They include:

- 3/22: Peace Pledge and Rally: *Community Power Against Violence* (CPAV) is a grass roots collaborative of over 15 community organizations working with youth to help develop multimedia tools for at-risk youth. *CPAV* will be hosting a rally for diverse youth groups to discuss violence prevention

- 3/23: *Blueprint for Action*: Speak-Up Minneapolis/Hospital Protocol are two innovative initiatives launched by the city of Minneapolis to address weapons threats and to intervene in aftermath of gunshot injuries for juvenile victims.

- 3/24: Violence Prevention through Youth Development Resources (contact 612-807-2047 for list of featured programs).

* 3/25: Social and Emotional Learning in Schools: an initiative offered in Minneapolis public schools for parents and youth that include promotion pro-social skills such as coping with stress, anger management and impulse control, how to resolve conflict, and bully/violence prevention.

* 3/26: Family Support Programs: Project Murua/Kwannza Church has two pilot programs that reinforce parental practices, which promote development and provide alternatives to practices which are harmful or nonproductive.

61

Create a Funding Strategy and Build Neighborhood Centers

If you have studied the crime patterns in your community, you know where the problems areas are. Usually centered in rental housing or subsidized housing complexes or lower middle class neighborhoods, you can find the strongest gang influence.

When gangs cluster in these neighborhoods, a number of negative conditions may arise, including:

* A greater level of criminal activity

* A large number of neighborhood youth involved in illegal behaviors

* Widespread availability and use of firearms and drugs

* A small level of neighborhood attachment (i.e., positive feelings of belonging and being valued

Unfortunately, in most distressed neighborhoods, schools, churches, and other community agencies and institutions do not provide adequate gang prevention and intervention services.

In the worst conditions, it's a train wreck.

Where to get funding today to support community initiatives is a question on everyone's mind connected to local government.

We have seen communities struggling with gang controlled neighborhoods realize they need to provide infrastructure there, but become like a "deer in headlights" when the magnitude of the task, and the investment necessary, is examined.

One needs only to see how many communities in California have line items in their city budgets for gang prevention and intervention. They have been actively tackling gangs for two decades and state grant dollars have flowed consistently to the most desperate communities.

A number of communities in America are in serious economic trouble. Yet gang reduction must be a sustained part of the budget process. Communities are facing difficult choices. One possible solution to this issue is to plan for at least a portion of the budget surplus funding to go to a Strategic Plan to reduce gangs.

The luxury of a budget surplus would show that a community has the ability to select various special projects to invest the additional funding. The issue with unbudgeted public funding is that it generally becomes a local political issue. The immediate need must be well communicated and defended.

In most city or county budgets, there is usually noble attention paid to not exceeding the limit of spending. So much so that often, when all is said and done there is a significant amount of aggregate money left over. This is what we refer to as "surplus" funding.

From a political point of view, use of surplus funding to address gang issues may or may not be a popular suggestion. But it is not a tax increase.

The brutality or violence of the gang problem will be the determining factor.

Gang members, once united, bring a form of instant blight to a community and many have very little regard for the way a community looks.

Since surplus dollars are not budgeted, new and innovative strategies to address community problems can be in play.

Communities must have the foresight to plan beyond a onetime expenditure into the future in order for their efforts to be successful.

This form of funding to insure success over a period of time will need to be examined for a good sustainable plan going forward. Communities must have the foresight to plan beyond a onetime expenditure into the future in order for their efforts to be successful.

Gang issues do not appear overnight and in most cases will not be reduced with one-time appropriations of surplus funding. In reality if that is the only source of funding available, it would make for good use of the resources by addressing a major social issue which has the ability to become costly if not addressed.

We believe that one of the best and brightest uses of surplus funds is to deploy as capital expenditures to create neighborhood centers in the most challenged neighborhoods.

In other words, create the crucible into which a myriad of services can be brought safely into the neighborhood.

In July 2011, Charlotte, NC re-opened the *Greenville Neighborhood Center* as part of the Charlotte-Mecklenburg Police Department's *Gang of One* program, an anti-violence initiative designed to engage children in sports, the arts and other activities to prevent them from joining gangs.

The neighborhood center had closed several months back due to budget cuts but it is now a central piece to reducing crime in the area, according to *Charlotte News14*.

There are 13 uniquely designed locations throughout Orange County.

"They say it takes a village to raise a child, but you have to be able to engage from a village standpoint with that child and keep them off the street and give them some other enrichment types of opportunities," said Jeff Hood, director of youth activities.

Funded by a $339,765 grant from the North Carolina Department of Justice and Delinquency Prevention, leaders say *Gang of One* gets kids into a safe space where they can invigorate their minds and bodies.

The program also provides career training. *News14* interviewed *Gang of One* director Fran Cook.

"Because of our work with these young people, they're no longer involved in criminal activity. About 83% of our youth in the program are no longer committing criminal acts," said Cook.

The *Police Activities League* moved its administrative offices into the center, where it has launched *Summer Camp 2011*. There are currently 65 children in the program, 60% boys and 40% girls. The projects are fun, but the mission is serious: enforcement, prevention, and re-entry.

Soon, *Gang of One* will join forces with Johnson & Wales University to start a culinary arts program for the kids. It will operate as a Saturday academy, *News14* reported.

"They're just one agency," Cook said. "We hope to have others as well so the Greenville Neighborhood Center becomes once again a Neighborhood Center not just a center in a neighborhood," the *Charlotte Post* reported.

We have known communities who have identified neighborhood infrastructure as their weakness, or gap, in services but cannot seem to get their government to prioritize capital dollars to actually build (or retrofit a building) as a neighborhood center. What occurs is a tug of war about to which what part of the community the funds should be deployed.

While that argument does not disappear with the use of surplus funds, it makes it a softer negotiation. No one loses. This is the community's bonus round each year.

In our view, there is a difference between a "community center," a "recreation center" and a "neighborhood center."

We see community centers a lot. These are usually under-funded operations in central locations offering city or county-sponsored modest programming, usually closed by dark and not impacting very at-risk kids at the right times of day.

Recreational centers are more powerful. They might include swimming centers, gyms, computers, classrooms, meeting rooms and the like. We see them across the country doing good work. Or, they are giant competitive sports venues subsidized by the city serving as a nice venue for competitive athletics like swimming or basketball. They may have an outdoor pool for kids in the summer. Many charge fees. Rarely are they located in the right places.

A true neighborhood center, by our definition, is deliberately placed into a struggling neighborhood to serve as an island in the storm. The more you put into one, the more you get out of one. In Newport News, Task Force leaders are considering naming the planned centers a "*Family Centers*" to avoid the confusion around naming.

In Milwaukee, it was announced in July 2011 that they are naming their center the *Holton Youth + Family Center*, a neighborhood effort run by a coalition of social groups with participation from police and the district attorney's office, aimed at reaching children and families in two large neighborhoods.

Immediately, it should be clean and well managed by a board of citizens of the neighborhood and serve as a refuge for young people to get them off the street into a welcoming environment.

> *The idea is to bring services to the neighborhood to include de-centralization of city services.*

The idea is to bring services to the neighborhood to include de-centralization of city services.

Once built, it becomes the crucible into which you can pour services from willing providers, both faith-based, city based and non-governmental agencies.

You can seek funding from the state and federal programs that have been developed to offer communities competitive grants. These grants are rarely used for bricks and mortar. The Department of Justice Office of Justice Programs each year readies support for community initiatives in several forms, to include:

- JJDP Title II State Formula Grant;
- JJDP Title V Local Delinquency Prevention Grants
- Juvenile Accountability Block Grant
- Youth Mentoring grants
- Second Chance Act
- Byrne Criminal Justice Innovation Program

Florida discovered the power of neighborhood infrastructure years ago. Orange County has a seasoned network of neighborhood centers and other innovative program for at-risk kids, governed by a Citizens Commission for Children.

The *Citizens' Commission for Children (CCC)* serves Orange County residents by funding and monitoring the programs of a number of local service providers. The *CCC* partners with local nonprofit agencies, government and school programs, civic organizations and the faith community to bring services to help ensure Orange County citizens have access to quality services. The *CCC* consists of three primary components:

Neighborhood Centers for Families are family-friendly one-stop-shops that provide children and families with a multitude of valuable services within their communities. There are 13 uniquely designed locations throughout Orange County.

In each Neighborhood Center resides:

- Case management
- Information and referral
- Counseling
- Academic support
- Parent education
- Alternatives to school suspension
- Employability skills and job fairs
- After school and summer youth programs
- Senior activities
- Community events
- School supply, toy, clothing, and food drives
- Health information, screening and immunizations
- And much more

The *After School Zone (ASZ)* offers innovative summer and after school programs to middle school students in 26 Orange County middle schools. The *ASZ* provides a fun and safe environment to help students excel academically and choose the right path to becoming productive healthy citizens.

Curriculum in each program is uniquely structured to address the cultural diversity, interests and needs of the community, while incorporating five core areas of youth development:

The *After School Zone* provides youth with the opportunity to learn and play in a fun, challenging environment under the supervision of caring adults. In return, the youth have responded through improved grades and attendance, and reduced juvenile delinquency. With results like these, the *After School Zone* is a "win-win" for students, as well as for the Orange County community.

- Character and leadership
- Fitness and recreation
- Education and career development
- Health life skills
- The arts

The *Summer Zone* operates during the months of June and July in 23 county middle schools. For a nominal fee covering registration and field trips, children can participate in a variety of recreational activities including: arts and crafts, dance, drama, sports, swimming, and much more.

In Oceanside, CA, almost a decade ago, a neighborhood center was the first boots on the ground in a neighborhood controlled by two gangs, with territory divided by a bridge over the interstate. Kids lived in fear.

The *Crown Heights Resource Center* was cobbled together funds from the city of Oceanside with grants from the state and charities.

Reporter Brandon Lowery reported in *NC Times* that organizers and staff of the neighborhood center know it works. About 40 to 60 kids show up after school on weekdays. Up to 45 more show up every day at the group's center in the San Luis Rey neighborhood.

Research shows that, demographically and culturally, Houston is a precursor for what Texas will look like in the next 10-15 years. Texas, some believe, will be the model for what the nation looks like in the middle of the 21st century. We have much to learn from this multicultural environment.

The neighborhood centers approach that has been taken in Houston is an advanced concept that involves senior centers, schools, neighborhood centers, youth programs, medical care access, jobs training and revitalization.

Neighborhood Centers Inc. brings resources, education and connection to more than 236,000 people throughout the Texas Gulf Coast area each year.

Their literature boasts "our 59 service locations offer comprehensive community-based programs for people at every stage of life – from infants to seniors."

"We work with residents of underserved communities to help them discover the strengths and skills necessary to become productive, prosperous and self-sufficient."

Neighborhood Centers, Inc., founded in 1907 by the grandmother of former U.S. Secretary of States James A. Baker III, combines passion, commitment and an entrepreneurial philosophy to make the human dream a reality for all who are willing to work for it.

Neighborhood Centers, Inc. is the recent recipient of a $500,000 *Promise Neighborhood* grant awarded by the U.S. Department of Education, and that focuses on neighborhood transformation through the improvement of educational outcomes for children.

We love the "*Promise Neighborhood*" identifier. What an uplifting way to describe building a neighborhood center in a distressed community.

Neighborhood Centers is funded from many different directions. First, it is a *United Way* recipient. It receives federal grants, city funding, and consolidates the duplicative business operations of many other nonprofits to serve as a revenue stream.

We are seeing many communities integrating the neighborhood center, or family center, with neighborhood school buildings.

In Portland, OR, at Rosa Parks School, many elementary students go to the local Boys & Girls Club to receive homework help and take part in fun activities. It's located in the same building as the school, the result of a partnership between Portland Public Schools and the local Club.

President Obama and educational Secretary Arne Duncan have been pushing for "community schools" which offer facilities and programs outside original school hours, typically in partnership with local nonprofit or city agencies.

Research shows that for every dollar a school system spends on such partnerships, it sees a return of $4 in the value of the services the district receives.

The community school concept, sometimes called the *ELT (Extended Learning Time)* is gaining traction among educators and policymakers as a potent school improvement strategy.

Wake County Public Schools in Raleigh, NC region has partnered with four different cities to create five community centers, which have all opened in the last five years.

✸ 62 ✸
Operate a Confidential Telephone Tip Line

If you are going to do a tip line, do it right. We like what Hampton, VA is doing with their "dial 311" tip line called *Youth Connect*.

Reporter David Macaulay of the *Daily Press* on the Virginia Peninsula published an article in January 2011 about a new tip line for youth violence in the city of Hampton.

Macaulay quoted Sabrina Jones, Hampton's program manager with Youth Education and Family Services, who said the phone line is aimed at youths between ages 5-18.

"Anyone who lives in the city will be able to dial 311 from their home phone, and 727-8311 from any other phone to get help for a young person at-risk of engaging in violence, gangs or other delinquent behaviors," Jones said.

She said *Youth Connect* is focused on prevention and early intervention. Macaulay reported that young people referred more than likely have some early indicators or they may be court involved at a minimal level, but they will not be youth who have committed serious offenses.

"*Youth Connect* works to stop the cycle of violence by providing programs and services to youth who are in danger of falling on their path," Jones said in the *Daily Press* article.

When young people are referred through 311 there will be an initial meeting with their parent or guardian as well as the young person to conduct a social history and initial assessment of their needs and interests, Jones noted.

The next step is to connect the young person with a community provider who will take them in and work to fill in those gaps identified during the initial assessment.

These community providers range from mentoring organizations, to after school programs and mental health services. Organizers seek to have a wide spectrum of providers meet the varied needs of each young person who is referred. In turn, providers are asked to give updates on how the youth are progressing from month to month," Jones noted.

We know these telephone lines work if promoted. Nationally, there is a 1-800 number that organizers know is making a huge difference.

Daniel Gross, Executive Director of The *Center to Prevent Youth Violence* has a national 1-800 number that he claims has saved lives over the last decade.

... inspiring and empowering kids to speak up...

America can "prevent hundreds of deaths every year by inspiring and empowering kids to speak up about the threats of violence that, in the overwhelming majority of cases, exist before a tragedy occurs," Gross says on his website.

Gross' national tip line for young people to anonymously report weapon threats is 1-866-SPEAK-UP.

They have received more than 36,000 calls in less than 10 years, leading to the prevention of hundreds of acts of violence, Gross says.

Manitoba, Canada operates the *Project Gang-Proof Resource Line* at 1-800-691-4264, or locally at 945-4264 (Winnipeg). These resources are widely promoted throughout the anti-gang literature of the province.

The Raleigh Police Department is one of 60 partners in the *Wake County Gang Prevention Partnership*. They also have an aggressive suppression plan and a tip line 996-GANG that citizens can use to request information about gangs or police department presentations and to report gang activity. The tip line is an open information line to report concerns or learn more about gangs.

❋ 63 ❋
Develop Violent Crime Suppression Teams

Many communities have those nighttime establishments that are edgy. The wrong crowd shows up. There are always police calls. Violence erupts frequently. Beneath the surface, gang tension arises.

Everything from busy, downtown nightclubs to corner bars, bowling alleys and casinos are fair game for the *Calgary Violent Crime Suppression Teams (VCST)*.

Thus, the *Calgary Sun* describes the new team to target gang violence.

Modeled after similar ones successful in quelling chronic gang violence, including frequent gunplay in the Vancouver entertainment scene, it is now called a mainstay for Calgary police, reporter Nadia Moharin notes.

While public education and prevention are still very much part of the anti-gang strategy, suppression is a key tool, too.

Police routinely meet familiar faces in the city's bars and social settings.

But rather than sharing a beer, the encounters typically end with people, often gang members or organized criminals, told to leave.

"Since November 2009, the teams have ejected more than 200 people from establishments, the majority known criminals and/or associates," the *Sun* reported.

"That doesn't include people who just walk out when they see us," he says.

Two teams with eight officers on each venture out several nights a week.

Knock on wood, this presence has had an impact thus far. Fewer open-air shootings at lounges and bars, which put so many innocent people in peril, is in part a credit to work they do to keep potentially dangerous types out of licensed establishments citywide, the *Calgary Sun* reports.

In 2009, the Alberta government amended its gaming and liquor act to allow police to eject people from licensed establishments who they feel put public safety at-risk.

Reporter Nadia Moharin describes a confrontation.

"They start as wall-flowers, breaking into two groups and leaning up along the perimeter of the dance floor, shining small yet powerful flashlights across the crowd to see who is out for the night.

When they spot someone they want to talk to, the party-crashers are on the move.

In uniforms with 'police' emblazoned on their backs they stealthily move along back hallways adjacent to the dance floor to get to the other side and join fellow officers.

It isn't prudent or necessarily safe for police, who might garner a less-than-friendly reception from gang members and organized criminals, to blindly go into the crowd.

'The last thing you want to start is a fight in the bar,' VCST Sgt. Kelly Kliewer says.

With military precision the team snakes, single-file, through the swaying crowd.

One officer takes the lead to do the talking with the target while a nagging woman paws at his uniform.

'Don't get involved,' another officer warns.

Officers surround the constable making inquiries, standing guard, keeping a watch on the crowd.

When there are no issues, the team moves on.

... "like a pair of tweezers the team plucks the individual like a sliver from the crowd so quickly it barely attracts any attention."

When it finds someone who needs to leave, "like a pair of tweezers the team plucks the individual like a sliver from the crowd so quickly it barely attracts any attention."

The Sun noted that numerous incidents where shootings at or near public venues — including a triple slaying which killed a gang member, his associate and an innocent man two years ago — are testament to the "dangerous cocktail which can be served."

Canada has a special way of blending rapid response suppression of gangs with solid prevention efforts.

In February 2011, the Province increased Anti-Violence Intervention Strategy funding, an increase of 41 percent, to deploy rapid response teams that specialize in guns and gangs.

Since 2007, police and the government of Ontario have worked to together to deliver the program, which is successfully rooting out gangs and taking guns off the street in York.

The strategy has already contributed to several local success stories, including the removal of gang graffiti from four areas in the York area of Toronto as a result of police and the community working together during nine "clean up days" since 2008; a decline in the number of youth arrested for gang-related activity from 27 in 2008 to six in 2010; and a decline in the number of violent crimes committed on school property in York from 401 in 2008 to 211 in 2010.

❧ 64 ❧
Operate a Confidential Texting Program

From *Reuters* reporter Deborah L. Cohenin in February 2010 comes the story of entrepreneur Greg Whisenant, who created a powerful law enforcement tool following a personal encounter with a burglar in Chicago.

"To make amends, Ms. Cohenin reported, "Whisenant built an information-sharing website for the local police, which is now one of the fast-growing crime data-mapping services in the United States.

Whisenant had never been a crime activist or particularly concerned about personal safety when he began attending *Community Policing* meetings in the D.C. suburb of Arlington, VA. That experience led him to found *CrimeReports* website. This innovative site allowed police departments to register for free, essentially serving as an elaborate email system, creating a conduit for municipalities to send localized alerts to members of the general public who signed up.

CrimeReports provides comprehensive local crime-mapping data to hundreds of police departments, including cities such as San Francisco and Boston, and the entire states of Maryland and Utah.

And when visiting the site, anonymous tips can be sent directly to the participating jurisdictions.

Sign up for alerts in your target neighborhoods and view the crisis in real time.

In Toronto, citizens can contact "Trust and Text" three different ways to anonymously submit *information to Crime Stoppers programs to help the police prevent or solve crimes:*

- Talk: 1-800-222-TIPS (8477)
- Type: 222tips.com
- Text: TOR and your message to CRIMES (274637)

The Toronto program directors make you a believer by inviting respondents to visit the website that explains how this anonymous text tip system works at http://www.SMSCrimeTips.com

Another progressive application of technology is called *Tipsoft*.

You can enable your police department or Gang Intervention Unit to receive confidential text messages. Ideally, promote this in schools and especially through the PTAs.

...it was necessary to develop a secure and anonymous means of easy communication between mobile phone users and law enforcement...

"Due to the massive popularity of text messaging, we felt it was necessary to develop a secure and anonymous means of easy communication between mobile phone users and law enforcement," said Kevin Anderson, CEO of Anderson Software.

"With *TipSoft SMS*, everyday citizens have the opportunity to offer an anonymous tip when they are mobile to a variety of law enforcement agencies via a simple text message."

Short Message Service (SMS), often called text messaging, is a means of sending short messages to and from mobile phones.

Anderson encourages citizens to report information about any non-urgent illegal activity, such as unsolved cases, vandalism, theft and the sale and distribution of drugs.

TipSoft SMS can submit information to participating law enforcement agencies, schools, universities and corporations.

Many of these agencies are utilizing this application through their *Crime Stoppers* Program, which is an excellent deployment choice, although not required.

This secure application allows the citizen and the investigator to have two-way dialog while keeping the "tipster's" identity completely anonymous.

✸ 65 ✸

Create Sporting Events
Especially for At-Risk Kids

It can be a boxing club. Or it can be soccer teams or even rugby. Major League Baseball sponsors *Reviving Baseball in Inner Cities* (*RBI*), a youth outreach program designed to increase participation and interest in baseball and softball. The Cal Ripkin Baseball organization sponsors *Fields of Dreams* for urban city venues.

But one thing is certain. Around the country, community leaders are discovering that at-risk kids who have been resistant to Boys & Girls Clubs, YMCA's or other traditional interventional opportunities can be drawn into competition.

...at-risk kids who have been resistant to Boys & Girls Clubs, YMCA's or other traditional interventional opportunities can be drawn into competition.

The gang problem in northern Virginia is very real. And so are the interventions organized for young people involved in gangs. Cheryl Chumley of *Inside NOVA* told the story of the soccer club team.

"We have people from opposing gangs, from rival gangs on the (soccer club) team," said Rick Buchholz, a coordinator with the *Gang Response Intervention Team (GRIT)* to a crowd of more than 100 who turned out for a 2011 gang prevention summit. The event was sponsored by the Manassas City Police Department and attended by Rep. Frank Wolf (R-VA) and local governing officials, church and community leaders.

"We take them to tournaments, arrange for games; we go to D.C. games, practice with George Mason University's men's soccer."

Anything, he said, to show that another life was possible.

They had many challenges in giving these at-risk youth better options with their free time in Prince William County.

One tricky problem, reported Chumley, was the naming of the team.

Following great debate, they settled on *Soccer Crew 9540*.

"Coming up with the number was difficult," said Rick Buchholz, whose group is dedicated to providing community support to police for gang prevention activities.

"Numbers 13 and 81, and their mathematical equivalents, for instance, were definite 'no's', as both could be construed to signify established gangs – *MS-13* and *Hell's Angels*, with the latter's initials defined by numerical placement in the alphabet."

"They can take a number and twist it to represent their gang," Buchholz said. So *GRIT* members turned the tables and devised a creative solution with a meaningful message.

Juvenile Court Services in Manassas is located at 9540 Center Street in Manassas.

Name aside, the program – just one of several efforts to intercede in the lives of youth who have turned to gangs or are considering joining a gang – has proven successful.

A free indoor soccer league called *Futtsal* has been growing in Catholic churches in California, reported the *Santa Cruz Sentinel*.

Holy Cross Catholic Church parishioner Barbara Meister said she got involved after the bishop asked churches to take action to stop youth violence.

"We want kids to feel connected to a community where they gain recognition and develop a sense of self importance and belonging," Meister said.

In the *Sentinel* report Meister noted, "those are the same values that attract the youth to gangs but with a different objective."

Meister wants to create a space and utilize the parish where kids and parents within the community come together.

❧ 66 ❧
Bring in the Hospitals
for Powerful Interventions

A sleeping giant in gang intervention is your local hospital. These wonderful community resources are so focused on putting the wounded kids back together that many are unaware of the powerful results being seen across the nation when hospitals do get involved in more than stopping the bleeding.

Usually the first step in deeper involvement is partaking in seminars and briefings on gangs, gang behavior and protocols, such as the one held in Englewood Hospital and Medical Center in New Jersey in early 2011.

The half-day training session was part arranged as a part of a statewide violence education campaign for health professionals, sponsored by the state Parole Board's Street Gang Unit and the New Jersey Hospital Association.

A team of pros from Boston Medical Center, the Boston Public Health Commission and the Medical Foundation trains street workers in Boston. It's in their best interest — not only for the health of the community, but the reduction of violence.

The *Streetworkers* Program operates 24 hours a day through Boston Community Centers, city-funded agencies located throughout Boston (including in many middle and high schools). Thirty college-educated staff, ages 25-55, conduct gang and youth outreach activities engaging gang members in the streets and through home visits.

They advocate for gang members in the courts (when appropriate), help the probation department with supervision, mediate disputes and gang truces, and refer gang members and their families to existing government and community programs.

Streetworkers also have played a critical role in *Operation CeaseFire*, personally inviting gang members to meetings with federal, state, and local law enforcement agencies to communicate a message of zero tolerance for firearm homicides.

In a city where the streets have seen more than their share of violence, a team of people at the University of Maryland at Baltimore is making a big difference with victims of violence.

In a country where homicide remains the 15th leading cause of death and the leading cause of death among African-American males ages 15-34, the work of Dr. Carnell Cooper and his colleagues has resulted in an 83% decrease among participants in repeat hospitalizations for violent injuries, a 75% reduction in criminal activity and an 82% increase in program participants that found employment.

Since 1998, Dr. Cooper, an associate professor of surgery at the University of Maryland in Baltimore, has led a hospital-based violence intervention program that has helped more than 1,500 victims of violent crime and their families.

While still in the hospital, patients who agree to enroll in Dr. Cooper's Violence Intervention Program receive a "plan of action" based on their particular needs.

Members of the intervention team include social workers, a parole and probation agent, and physicians specializing in psychiatry, trauma, epidemiology and preventive health.

They visit with the patient throughout the hospitalization and on a regular basis after discharge, helping to provide access to services like substance abuse rehabilitation, job training and G.E.D. tutoring and offering the support necessary for successful completion of the patient's plan.

Often the outreach workers are former gunshot victims themselves. They visit the shock trauma unit, stopping at the bedsides of men suffering from gunshot and stab wounds. They ask them to join the hospital's violence prevention program.

The Baltimore program includes home visits, help with housing and education, meetings with social workers, a parole probation officer and group counseling meetings. This intervention model is being implemented across the nation.

One of the oldest and most successful hospital-based violence intervention programs is California's *Youth ALIVE! Caught in the Crossfire (CinC)*. The *CinC* model has been instituted with overwhelming success in hospitals both in Oakland and Los Angeles.

A study first published in March 2004, in the *Journal of Adolescent Health* found that violently injured Oakland youth who received services from *CinC* were 70% less likely to be arrested for any offense and 60% less likely to be involved in any criminal activity than violently injured youths in a control group. Results regarding rates of re-injury were not statistically significant.

The *California Cities Gang Prevention Network* published an outstanding analysis of what makes a hospital intervention effective.

Because of privacy laws, some measure must be taken into account when organizing such a program.

The *CCGPN* report noted, "it is crucial to have a member of the hospital staff dedicated to the program. Due to regulations put in place by the Health Insurance Portability and Accountability Act (HIPAA) of 1996 (P.L.104 -191), intervention specialists who are not hospital staff cannot simply take the initiative and contact a youth victim of violence in a hospital or trauma center.

Instead, it must be a hospital clinical worker who refers the patient to the nonprofit before they are allowed to make contact.

Because of this regulation, it is extremely important to have a hospital staff member willing to give referrals, provide information regarding case management, and meet frequently with the intervention agency's team.

"Having a dedicated hospital worker to be the point person is absolutely necessary for a hospital-based program to be successful," Deane Calhoun, the Executive Director and founder of *CinC* explained in the white paper.

"That person can be a doctor, a nurse, or a hospital social worker, as long as they really believe in the program and want it to work," Calhoun said.

The referral process must be deliberate. But even more deliberate is who does the intervention.

The California Cities white paper dealt with this issue clearly.

"Intervention specialists hold a specific background and set of experiences in order to be successful. For a youth recovering from a violent injury to make an emotional connection with their intervention specialist during a short hospital stay, it is extremely important that there is a level of trust from the beginning."

Similar life experiences create a successful interaction, according to the study.

He or she should have experience with violence — either directly as a victim or indirectly."

"For this reason, a large number of hospital-based intervention programs, including *CinC*, recruit exclusively from the communities they serve. The ideal intervention specialist will be someone who has had a similar upbringing as the target population and similar experiences. He or she should have experience with violence — either directly as a victim or indirectly."

In March 2009, *Youth ALIVE* hosted a National Symposium of Hospital-based Violence Intervention Programs. Representatives from nine programs were in attendance. Over the course of the symposium, they worked to publish a handbook of the best practices in hospital-based intervention. After that event, the programs officially formed the National Network on Hospital-based Violence Intervention Programs, a network of programs dedicated to working together to facilitate the startup process for any new hospital-based programs and to develop new best practices and more effective methods of evaluation.

In Nebraska, a local hospital in Grand Island weighed in heavily on designing a community response to the growing youth violence in the community.

"Arrests of a dozen suspected gang members shed light on a problem Grand Island has long acknowledged. But people may be surprised who's spearheading the community's gang prevention efforts. As a Catholic hospital, St. Francis Medical Center says social justice is part of its mission. Hospital leaders discussed the efforts before a legislative hearing last week, where they were praised for being part of the long-term solution."

Riverside Regional Medical Center's Trauma Center began publishing gunshot wounds in 2008 to help the Newport News, VA community to understand the true nature of the slaughter escalating in the city.

In a community with 180,000 people, over 2,400 gang members in 188 distinct gang sets were shooting a lot of young people. Previously, the local newspaper had only reported trends on murders. Most were the result of territorial disputes in gang-infested neighborhoods and the violence was widely perceived to be isolated there.

Yet gangsters were punishing each other with bullets with frightening frequency. When over 150 gunshot victims had been treated in the Trauma Center for the year, with over 30 murders, people sat up and realized they had a deeper problem than they thought.

When Riverside and the local nonprofit race relations group *People to People* began publicizing how many young people were being shot, eyes opened, and a rising tide of public concern led to the development of a comprehensive violence prevention strategy.

The hospital also provided thought leadership for the gang prevention program and assisted *People to People* in obtaining federal funding for a comprehensive plan.

In Omaha, NE, *KPTM TV* reporter Tony Smith reported in mid-February 2011 that several of the metro area medical centers are joining together to fight gang violence in a new public health approach.

The region's hospitals received a $100,000 grant from the city. Emergency rooms at Nebraska Medical Center, the Creighton University Medical Center, and the University of Nebraska Medical Center will work with a nonprofit organization, *Impact-One,* to put a stop to youth violence and help with gang intervention and prevention.

KPTM TV reported that the new joint venture supports victims during their time at the hospital and when they return back into the community. This is due in part to violence interrupters, who will work closely with the victim's family and friends.

The second part to the mission of the new partnership will involve detailed research by experts at the University of Nebraska Medical Center. The project will identify the risk factors that lead to violent behavior.

The program will be funded for one year with a re-evaluation after that time.

Some hospitals figured this out years ago and got involved. *Project Ujima*, a community project committed to helping stop the cycle of violent crimes by reducing the number of repeat victims of violence, started in 1996.

It includes the collaborative efforts of Children's Hospital of Wisconsin, the Medical College of Wisconsin and Children's Service Society of Wisconsin.

Since 1996, more than 2,000 adolescents with injuries due to violence have been treated in the Emergency Department/Trauma Center at Children's Hospital of Wisconsin. Because violent injuries are associated with psychological trauma, poor school performance, criminal detention and repeat incidents of violence, *Project Ujima* establishes a network of services that assist with physical, psychological and social recovery.

"Ujima" is the third principle of Kwanzaa and is a Ki-swahili word meaning working together to make things right.

✸ 67 ✸

Form a Prisoner Re-entry Council

This statistic is not a typographical error. According to the Department of Justice, the number of adults under correctional supervision in the United States declined by less than 1% during 2009, dropping to 7,225,800 (or 48,800 fewer offenders) at year-end 2008. This means that one in 32 adults, or about 3.1% of U.S. adult residents, were under correctional supervision at year-end 2009, down slightly from 2008.

... 70% of people released from prison commit crimes again, highlighting the need for education and prevention programs.

California Attorney General Kamala Harris spoke at a Sacramento Gang Violence Forum in April 2011, referencing the "revolving door" of the California criminal justice system, saying that the average prison sentence in California is two years, and 70% of people released from prison commit crimes again, highlighting the need for education and prevention programs.

Realizing the vital importance of a community's response to the flow of people back to the streets from incarceration, Newport News, VA Sheriff Gabe Morgan testified before the House of Representatives Appropriations Committee about the vital importance of federal support.

Juveniles released from confinement still have their likely 'prime crime years' ahead of them, and "unsuccessful transitions back into communities result in an alarmingly high recidivism rate of 55% to 75% for juvenile offenders," noted Morgan in Congressional testimony in March 2011.

Effective re-entry programs help reduce recidivism rates by providing support and resources to guide ex-offenders through a successful transition back to community life.

Morgan testified in support of funding *Multidimensional Treatment Foster Care (MTFC)*, among other initiatives.

MTFC provides services to youth and their families during and after a youth's out-of-home placement, ongoing supervision by a program case manager, and frequent contact and coordination of services with the youth's parole/probation officer, teachers, work supervisors, and other involved adults. In studies, Morgan said, *MTFC* has been shown to cut juvenile recidivism in half and saves the public an average of $89,000 for every juvenile treated.

Locally, Morgan champions G.E.D. programs and alternate punishments to incarceration for nonviolent youth offenders.

"We have to decide," Morgan said at a recent Newport News Mayor's Task Force meeting, "whether we are mad at this person or afraid of this person."

"If we are afraid of this person, we should incarcerate. If we are not, we must find other ways to punish this person."

As Morgan says, "they'll be back."

Morgan underscored the re-entry crisis in his testimony reminding Congressional leaders that "The Second Chance Act authorizes assistance to states and localities to develop and implement Strategic Plans for comprehensive efforts to enable ex-offenders to successfully reenter their communities such as: family reunification, job training, education, housing, and substance abuse and mental health services.

Today's prisoners will come home. They will be hardened and have fresh skills learned in prison, and a much stronger gang network. To not be prepared for this flow of parolees is a failure of a community's planning.

Research has shown that low-risk offenders do not respond well to intensive supervision strategies, such as incarceration and parole. What works for these populations, as evidenced in both academia and in communities, are after-care services and alternatives to incarceration.

These individuals need homes, jobs, and stability in order to stay out of prison.

The *California Cities Gang Prevention Network* April 2010 publication articulated the challenge.

"On being released from prison, parolees often find themselves in challenging situations."

"They may be without shelter or money in a harsh economy, lacking practical job skills, and burdened with the negative stigma associated with a prison record."

"To compound the situation many of them will have physical or mental health issues, and will be vulnerable to past addictions. Some may have family and friends to help, but others who have isolated themselves while incarcerated may face difficulties reuniting with loved ones."

The goal, then, is to minimize these risk factors wherever possible.

In an analysis completed by the National Council on Crime and Delinquency for the San Francisco *Re-entry Council*, interviews with local government agencies involved with the re-entry population revealed a lack of coordinated services.

Service areas overlapped in job training, but complete gaps have been revealed in other areas, such as housing.

The Re-entry Council is making efforts towards a more streamlined continuum of services through agency collaboration and community engagement.

San Diego's *Prisoner Re-entry Program* is another innovative approach to gradually transition ex-offenders into the community.

Those eligible must not have committed a violent or serious crime and must not be part of a prison gang. A community case manager works with an individual while incarcerated to develop a Life Plan and the individual is also eligible to participate in a variety of vocational and rehabilitative services. The case manager meets the individual upon release and continues to work with the offender for the next 18 months.

San Bernardino has implemented an innovative program for prisoner re-entry. In collaboration with CSU-San Bernardino and the Center for the Study of Correctional Education, the city has conducted a study regarding parolee needs and best practices.

They are also promoting the *Community Re-entry Education/Employment Service and Training (CREST)*, a coordinated effort between government agencies and private organizations to provide evidence-based programming to ensure positive outcomes for parolees. The *CREST* Service Center will be a one-stop shop for parolees for services ranging from employment to housing. Significantly, the cost of *CREST* services is less than half the price of re-incarceration.

With a sputtering economy, it is anticipated that the release of convicted criminals will pick up even more.

San Diego and San Francisco *Re-entry Councils* have joined folks that rarely got together to share information – but now meet actively to coordinate their efforts. The degree of difficulty is pretty high, but a new openness is occurring. These stakeholders all have a seat at this table:

- Police
- Probation
- Public defender
- Parole
- Workforce development
- Community organizations
- Housing authority
- Child welfare
- Public health
- Mental health

The city of Boston is also a national leader in fine-tuned Re-entry tactics. Presented at the national 2011 Justice Department summit, The *Boston Re-entry Initiative (BRI)* is clearly one of the best organized in the nation.

It was created in response to resurgence in violent crime in hotspot neighborhoods. An analysis showed that ex-offenders returning to high-crime neighborhoods from the Suffolk County House of Corrections contributed significantly to the spike in crime.

The *BRI* targets high-risk male offenders from Suffolk County House of Corrections ages 17-30 with documented histories of gang and gun violence who committed crimes in and/or will return to one of Boston's three main hotspot neighborhoods and adjacent areas. This population poses the greatest threat not only of re-offending, but also of propagating gang and gun violence upon release, as they already have criminal and incarceration histories that indicate future, more serious offenses. According to the findings of a 2009 study, *BRI* participation:

- Resulted in an estimated 30% reduction in recidivism rates of the population selected, based on their 100% likeliness to reoffend

- Resulted in a reduction in "time to recidivism" (arrest) relative to a comparison group of offenders

- Decreased the likeliness of participants to be rearrested for a violent offense relative to comparison group of offenders

Partners included:

- Boston Police Department
- Suffolk County Sheriff's Department
- Suffolk County District Attorney's Office
- United States Attorney's Office
- Massachusetts Departments of Probation, Parole, and Revenue
- Community Resources for Justice
- Youth Options Unlimited
- Boston *TenPoint* Coalition
- Whittier Street Health Center
- Dorchester Bay Economic Development Corporation

Each month, the Boston Regional Intelligence Center scrutinizes the list of offenders entering the community, looking for eligible participants. All new inmates who meet these age-based, historical, and geographical criteria are identified.

The foundation of the *BRI* is the monthly message panel. At the monthly panel, law enforcement, prosecutorial, supervisory, community, and faith-based organizations present directly to new *BRI* inmates as a united front: there are many life-changing opportunities available, but there are also swift and severe consequences for re-offending. Following assessment, an Individual Service Plan is tailored to each individual's needs with regard to employment, education, housing, treatment, benefits, and family. Case manager/mentors and the rest of the re-entry team match each inmate with appropriate offerings to address the prisoner's needs.

❦ 68 ❧
Create a Focused Strike Team for a Hardened Base of Crime

Omaha City Councilman Ben Gray told members of the Nebraska Legislature's Judiciary Committee that by knowing the streets and the various players, ex-gang members who work for one local group help keep tensions among current gangs from escalating.

The Omaha World-Herald reported that Gray's "non-City Council" job is to direct the emergency team run by the gang-intervention group *Impact One Community Connection.*

The team responds to shooting scenes around the city and heads to Omaha hospitals after shooting victims are taken to emergency rooms.

"Often," he told lawmakers, "members of rival gangs and their families and friends show up at hospitals to check on shooting victims, making for volatile situations in waiting rooms. The ex-gang members on hand can assess what's happening and help keep everyone under control," Gray said.

Impact One, which also runs a summer jobs program, was one of six groups that shared $350,000 in grant money from the state Office of Violence Prevention.

The Colorado Bureau of Investigation reports that Denver is home to 8,811 gang members affiliated with 78 gangs.

A $2.2 million federal grant is the result of nearly four years of work from a consortium of civic and religious leaders, social workers and former gang members who came together after the 2007 gangland slaying of Denver Broncos cornerback Darrent Williams, the *Denver Post* reported.

Post reporter Christopher Osher noted that a research team led by sociologist Jeffrey Butts, executive director of the research and evaluation center at John Jay College of Criminal Justice in New York, will monitor the work in Denver and in four other communities that recently received funding from the U.S. Department of Justice.

The results could help craft strategies in hard-hit cities like Detroit, where crime stubbornly refuses to ease.

> *"The whole idea is to find a way to tackle what we call a hardened base of crime."*

"The whole idea is to find a way to tackle what we call a hardened base of crime," he said.

In Denver, officials plan to use the money to tackle three neighborhoods where gang violence persists despite an overall drop in crime levels throughout the city in recent years.

According to Denver's grant application, young people living in those areas reported that they felt so besieged that "parts of their neighborhoods feel like Juarez, Mexico, in regards to the violence and tension."

Osher reported that to help break the cycle, Denver officials now plan to screen youth ages 7-14 living in the three targeted neighborhoods to determine whether they are at-risk of joining gangs. Those who are will get steered to services aimed at ensuring they become productive students instead.

The *Post* notes that the grant also will allow the city to hire two new "violence interrupters" to join the four that currently go to gang strongholds when violence flares. They are mentors, usually former gang members, tasked with urging peace when drive-by shootings start.

In Minneapolis, one important strategic intervention initiated in summer 1997 was to respond quickly and decisively to those shootings that had the potential of provoking gang retaliations.

This response was based on Boston's *Operation CeaseFire* model, which was adopted by the Law Enforcement Task Force.

Immediately after a shooting, a rapid response team consisting of police, probation officers, Federal and local prosecutors, and Federal law enforcement personnel met and located not only suspects, but also the victims' associates.

The message sent to all involved was that any hint of retaliation would evoke an aggressive response from law enforcement.

Probation officers also checked to see if these associates were under the authority of the Department of Probation and could be targeted for special attention to discourage violent acts.

The coordinated action of the response team and the subsequent swift action of prosecutors was a major turning point in stemming the violence in Minneapolis in summer 1997.

✦ 69 ✦

Work with Your State Elected
Officials. Much Can Be Done

It's long been a state government commitment in California. Notably, almost every state has funded or is in the process of funding organized support for communities hardest hit.

Massachusetts Governor Deval Patrick announced that his FY12 budget proposal would preserve, and in certain instances, boost funding for vital youth violence prevention programs.

This just does not happen unless a critical mass of community leaders makes it important. Such emphasis in times of austere state budgets is revealing. Obviously, a critical mass of state legislators must support the funding or it will not happen.

"A top priority of the Patrick-Murray Administration's second term," according to the Governor's press release, is the Governor's youth violence prevention plan — which includes recommendations from a variety of stakeholders to ensure a comprehensive solution to urban violence.

"We are engaging the full spectrum of people who work with young people – educators and law enforcement, street workers and clergy, human services providers and business leaders, victim advocates, and survivors – whoever is willing to help support and love a young person on to a positive future," said Governor Patrick. "The cycle of violence and poverty in any community is a threat to every community. It threatens our fundamental belief in opportunity for all and it must stop."

Virginia Governor Bob McDonnell listened carefully to people all over the Commonwealth of Virginia before executing a statewide organization in gang intervention based on proven research models.

We believe what Gov. McDonnell has organized is a benchmark for the nation on bringing together community strategic planning at the statewide level.

We believe what Gov. McDonnell has organized is a benchmark for the nation on bringing together community strategic planning at the statewide level.

This takes a responsive team of legislators who are all willing to drop party banners long enough to see a common path ahead to help our youth.

In the Executive order, the Governor noted that the *Virginia Fusion Center* "reports the presence of criminal street gangs throughout northern Virginia, the greater Richmond area, western Virginia, Hampton Roads and in far southwest Virginia. Offshoots of national gangs such as the *Bloods*, *Crips* and *Gangster Disciples* are active throughout the Commonwealth. In order to make

Virginia a safer place to raise a family and own or operate a business, it is essential that federal, state and local governments work together to address and reduce gangs and gang-related violence in the Commonwealth."

"Accordingly, the Commonwealth must work collaboratively along with local and federal partners, businesses, as well as community and faith-based organizations, in establishing best practices for combating gangs and reducing gang-related crime.

Gov. McDonnell thus created The Commonwealth's Gang and Violent Crime Executive Committee.

"Many localities have taken steps to address the gang problem within their communities; however, additional resources are needed to aid local governments in their fight against gangs and gang-related violence," he notes.

❊ 70 ❊

Create Special Events to Raise Funds and Awareness

There are many good reasons to have special events that benefit an anti-violence effort in the community. Such planning brings everyday people together to help support at-risk youth.

The event generates visual action, which the news media love, which informs more people about the cause. A special event also raises funds. Recruit area businesses, hospitals and civic groups to help and contribute to the cause.

The amount raised from the effort is important, but not the only measure. The expression of widespread community buy-in is an investment in public relations that pays huge dividends as your community continues to sustain the efforts in tough economic circumstances.

... an investment in public relations that pays huge dividends...

In Orangeburg, SC, the *Times and Democrat* reported that the annual *Rivers Bridge Ramble* raises money for *Orangeburg County Gang Intervention Project 20/20*. Riders in the event started at Edisto Memorial Gardens and could try a 27-mile, 66-mile or 100-mile ride.

Its theme line is *"A Race Against Gangs."* Nearly a dozen area businesses, groups and law enforcement contributed to the effort.

Proceeds from the ride go to Project *20/20* events held throughout the year, such as the gang summit in September. At the summit, more than 300 fifth- and sixth-grade students are provided with support and instructions to combat gang recruitment.

Another suggestion to communities looking to create a special event is to consider asking one of the local civic groups to hold their annual event to benefit the gang prevention effort.

Holding fundraisers in elementary schools helps involve the children and working hand in hand with the school system strengths every aspect of the program. Even bringing spare change or pennies to class can be a fun and enjoyable promotion.

We also see special concerts and music events to benefit community initiatives, casino nights, 5K runs, and raffles — with appropriate regulatory approvals.

One of the most common promotions we see is the donation of a car, a boat, a moped – by a local merchant or dealer and having that item raffled off throughout the community, providing enormous publicity and good will for the business, and in some states, a special state tax credit for the car donor.

The largest single night fundraiser in the Commonwealth of Virginia benefits a very special school for at-risk children. A black tie event drawing over 1,000 community leaders is held each fall on the Virginia Peninsula to benefit the leading local charity, *The Achievable Dream Academy*.

The *Tennis Ball*, a passion of *Achievable Dream* Founder Walter Segaloff, auctions a dozen cars, boats and motorcycles, exotic vacations, and hundreds of silent auction items every year to boost this internationally acclaimed school for at-risk children K-12.

It's been wildly successful for over a decade. The event is the most sophisticated and popular fundraiser in the region, raising over $400,000 each year. The *Tennis Ball* demonstrates what citizens and businesses will do to help at-risk kids. It's a cause people will give to. They will cheer the community's successes and they love being a part of lifting up young people from poverty and the cycle of crime.

☀ 71 ☀
Get Business Fired Up

When we review the history of gun violence reduction strategies in America, several cities' experiences rise to the top. Certainly we would highlight the communities that continue to benefit from *G.R.I.P* programs. But Minneapolis stands out for its amazing support from the business community.

This support originated over a decade ago and has blossomed into a remarkably well-focused strategy and it has had outstanding results.

The Office of Juvenile Justice and Delinquency Prevention of the Department of Justice outlines this amazing story on its website.

It's an example of what world-class business acumen can bring to the table if motivated and engaged.

Honeywell provided the leadership to create *Minnesota HEALS (Hope, Education, and Law and Safety)*, a unique public-private partnership that has developed a comprehensive violence reduction strategy.

The program is characterized by corporate commitments and public agency collaborations to reduce violent crime. Honeywell, Inc. has a long history of active involvement in philanthropic activities.

Honeywell reacted to a *New York Times* article that gave the city a new nickname, *"Murderapolis,"* reflecting a sharp rise in homicides — a jump from approximately 60 per year in 1994 to 97 in 1995 and 86 in 1996.

With its world headquarters in a neighborhood that had been overtaken by crime, Honeywell was concerned for the safety of its employees and property and for the quality of life in the surrounding neighborhood.

Honeywell's chief executive officer enlisted fellow CEO's from other socially responsible private corporations — Allina Health Systems, 3M, General Mills, and the staff of the Minnesota Business Partnership — to meet with the Governor to share their concerns about the escalating local and statewide crime rates.

After the Governor weighed in with support, Honeywell arranged a series of planning meetings. The business community, including a core group of local corporations and the Minnesota Business Partnership, contributed financial support, influence, and human resources.

Honeywell then retained an independent consultant to bring all the needed partners to the planning table and make unbiased assessments and hold local stakeholders accountable.

Minnesota HEALS is a collaboration of government, community, law enforcement, and business. Everyone strives for the goal of reducing crime and violence. Through a two-track system of law enforcement strategies and community long-term initiatives, *Minnesota HEALS* has achieved long-term results.

Two task forces were created. The Law Enforcement Task Force consisted of the key criminal justice agencies in the city and state. Its purpose was to analyze and develop a strategic response to the recent rash of homicides and shootings, and the current gang activities.

The Community Task Force, chaired by the director of a local business association, also was to develop long-range, local crime prevention activities funded wholly or in part by corporations.

In addition to these two groups, Forum and Support committees were created.

The Forum Committee is open to all members and shares information through presentations and discussions. This committee also makes recommendations to the other committees.

The Support Committee approves final actions and makes decisions on matters such as fundraising and key objectives. It consists of 19 members, including key corporate, community, and criminal justice agency representatives.

The Forum and Support Committee meetings are held monthly, usually at Honeywell, while the Law Enforcement and Community Task Forces meet as often as necessary. The Vice President for Social Responsibility at Honeywell serves as the primary resource to coordinate discussion topics and share information among members.

The *OJJDP* website notes that today, *Minnesota HEALS* has 61 member organizations.

Corporate members include Honeywell, General Mills, 3M, Allina Health Systems, and Medtronic. Local government agencies include the chiefs of police and Mayors' offices of Minneapolis and St. Paul; the Minneapolis City Council; the sheriff's offices, attorney's offices, and commissioners from Hennepin and Ramsey Counties; Metro Transit Police; Minneapolis Department of Health and Family Support; and the public schools.

State-level participants include the Minnesota Department of Public Safety, the Minnesota Department of Corrections, the University of Minnesota, and the Attorney General's office.

The Law Enforcement Task Force currently consists of 25-30 law enforcement representatives from the Minneapolis and St. Paul police departments' gang, homicide, and narcotics units; the sheriff's office; the probation department; and Federal agencies such as the FBI, DEA, ATF, and the U.S. Attorney's Office.

The Community Task Force consists of nonprofit members that represent various neighborhood coalitions and service providers and private business partnerships.

In 2011, Minneapolis saw an early surge in gang killings, as did San Jose. But the trend lines are solid. Like San Jose, viewed over time, the deep community involvement and programs designed to prevent gang membership are saving a lot of kids from gang life and failure.

✸ *72* ✸

Study *CeaseFire* as a Strategic Option

A Deputy Sheriff in Raleigh-Durham, NC has a lot to say about the evolution of gangs in his hometown.

Major P.J. Martin published a white paper entitled *The Nature of the Criminal Culture in Durham and What Law Enforcement Can Do to Suppress It.*

This fascinating white paper dives deep into the history of the gang movement in this community, reminding us that crack cocaine was not the beginning of street culture. Martin reminds us that gangs have been around in America before we were born. We are not the first adult generation to face gangs.

"Neighborhood groups of criminally inclined adolescents have roamed the streets of Durham for at least sixty years," Martin notes.

In Durham, Martin outlined the historical evolution of gangs in his community. "From the raucous liquor houses that existed in Durham in the 1890's…to a murder record in the mid-1930s when 26 people were murdered…to a thriving heroin trade that goes back at least until the 1940s… the foundation of the violence we are now experiencing has been firmly entrenched," Martin says.

But it is on our watch that we face gangs fueled by the music and merchandizing of American gangsterism.

Old timers know this. One veteran of a tough neighborhood, a self-described "organizer," is Newport News, VA's Annistine Patrick. She is the person to see if you want anything done in the tough East End. That is one of the reasons police officers come by her house to hear what she thinks about some of their initiatives. Unlike many of her neighbors, she feels the police are on the right track and are making gains against the violence.

"We have lost three generations of children," she laments.

And there are dangers associated with the suppression action represented by *CeaseFire.*

Annistine worries as much for the beat patrol officers as she does for the kids she has seen go astray into gang life.

Yet to reduce gun violence in gang-controlled neighborhoods, there are few programs that can match up with the consistent results over time of the *CeaseFire* program, first implemented in Boston in 1995.

This is a classic example of a multi-disciplinary approach to suppression.

The Boston Gun Project initiative expressly aimed at taking on a serious, large-scale crime problem: homicide victimization among youths in Boston.

Like many large cities in the United States, Boston had a problem with youth homicide. Homicide for young people ages 24 and under increased by 230%, from 22 victims in 1987 to 73 victims in 1990 — and remained high well after the peak of the epidemic. Boston experienced an average of 44 youth homicides per year between 1991 and 1995.

Sponsored by the National Institute of Justice and directed by David M. Kennedy, Anthony A. Braga, and Anne M. Piehl of Harvard University's John F. Kennedy School of Government, the *Gun Project* involved two main elements: a direct law enforcement attack on illicit firearms traffickers supplying youths with guns and an attempt to generate a strong deterrent to gang violence.

Throughout the intervention process the *CeaseFire* message was delivered repeatedly: in formal meetings with gang members, through individual police and probation contacts with gang members, through meetings with inmates of secure juvenile facilities, and through gang outreach workers. The message was a promise to gang members that violent behavior would evoke an immediate and intense response.

Although nonviolent crimes would be dealt with routinely within the criminal justice system, violence would receive the Working Group's focused enforcement actions.

Street operations began in earnest in early 1996; the first comprehensive gang crackdown began in March and the Working Group's first meeting (or "forum") with gang members was held on May 15, 1996.

A second major crackdown occurred in late August 1996, with other core activities — several forums, direct warnings to gangs, several lesser crackdowns, and gun trafficking investigations. The height of *CeaseFire* operational activity, however, occurred during 1996 and 1997.

Youth homicides in Boston decreased dramatically following the first gang forum in May 1996 and have remained low.

Careful evaluation of the effort, it was found *Operation CeaseFire* was associated with a 63% decrease in youth homicides per month, a 32% decrease in shots-fired calls for service per month, a 25% decrease in gun assaults per month, and a 44% decrease in the number of youth gun assaults per month in the highest risk district (Roxbury).

Yet, it has been found that the Boston experience could not simply be pulled off the shelf.

The type of problem Los Angeles faced evolved differently; the nature of the intervention had to be developed differently. The gangs responsible for much of the violence in Los Angeles are bigger and more entrenched than those in Boston.

In Boston, most gang members are African-American; in Los Angeles, the majority of gang members are Latino. The two cities are vastly different geographically and politically.

Los Angeles County sprawls over a huge area covering dozens of municipalities. This means it has no single point of political leverage; rather, it has a network of overlapping power centers. The implication was that bringing all stakeholders to the table is difficult in Los Angeles.

In a report issued following the implementation of *Operation CeaseFire* in Los Angeles, organizers issued a caution to other communities planning to use this model:

"Perhaps the biggest lesson learned from this project is the need to create concrete mechanisms that promote interagency collaboration. Typically, criminal justice agencies do not work together on common problems."

"Judging the performance of agency heads on how well they collaborate with their partner agencies would be a step in the right direction."

In Louisiana, quick response to gunfire and violence is the objective of New Orleans' *Solutions Not Shootings*, which approaches gun violence like a deadly disease and aims to stem its spread. According to the *Times-Picayune* reporter Katy Reckdahl, it is modeled after *CeaseFire*.

"It's not about who did it. It's about stopping the next one from happening," Reckdahl noted in her interview with Norris Henderson, who heads *Voice of the Ex-Offender* and has been involved with *Solutions Not Shootings* since its inception. They organized shooting responses, community marches and 'step in's' to keep escalation from happening.

"Stop the killing, let's start living," is the theme.

Reckdahl quoted August Collins Sr., who has helped shape the program through his employer, the *Youth Empowerment Project*, a partner in the Central City pilot. "We have a very tight focus."

"Stop the killing, let's start living."

The program's staff doesn't give tips to police, Collins said. They're not there to stop the drug trade or whatever else is going on in the neighborhood. All they want to do is stop the next shooting.

Solutions Not Shootings has the backing of *CeaseFire's* founders in Chicago. The *Times-Picayune* noted that a grant from Baptist Community Ministries is financing two program components, with financial support from the city and additional support from the Chicago Project for Violence Prevention.

In addition to shooting responses, the program will at some point this summer hire outreach workers to help the most at-risk residents change their behavior, by gaining skills, getting mental health help and, perhaps most importantly, securing jobs.

CeaseFire is being replicated all over the world. It is intervention at its highest form.

❧ 73 ❧
Mainstream At-Risk Kids
into Normal Channels

The Boys & Girls Club of Rochester, MN was among the first fifteen such clubs in the nation to implement a new program called *Gang Prevention Through Targeted Outreach*. The U.S. Department of Justice's Office of Justice Programs funds the program.

"When they hear gang-prevention they head the other way,"

"When they hear gang-prevention they head the other way," said Jodi Millerbernd, associate executive director. "The beauty of *Gang Prevention Through Targeted Outreach* is once a kid is identified as high-risk they are brought into Boys & Girls Clubs like any other kid."

The club recently hired a full-time staff person who is called the "impact coordinator for health and life skills," to implement the program and do outreach recruitment. When a kid is identified as at-risk of gang involvement because of a variety of risk factors such as low income, struggling in school and family gang involvement, they are streamlined into the normal programming with the 1,650 members.

Success is determined by monitoring the child's school truancy rates, grade progression, involvement in crime, behaviors at club, and in family environment. In Canada, this model of intervention is called Leadership Development and Ambassador Youth, and it is considered mainstreaming at its highest form.

John Sawdon, Executive Director of Breaking the Cycle — Toronto, spoke at the 2010 Canada—U.S. Gang Summit noting that intervention has been developed involving a three-week intensive personal development and case management process.

These gang members work on establishing group norms and developing self-regulation skills in order to enter a 25-week Leadership Development and Ambassador Youth Component.

John Sawdon is a leading Canadian expert in street gangs, conflict resolution, crisis intervention, trauma support, workplace safety and violence prevention. In 1983, he founded the Canadian Training Institute to provide training, research and consulting assistance in these areas to justice and human services organizations, and in 2004, established the country's most successful gang exit program, *Breaking the Cycle*, which has helped hundreds of young people from Toronto's most dangerous communities leave their street gang.

✹ 74 ✹
Create a *Season of Peace* Campaign

Season of Peace campaigns promote anti-violence. This bold messaging was first launched in Boston as a part of the area ministers' *TenPoint Coalition* to send a consistent message of peace to youth who were involved in the violence.

> ✄
> *...send a consistent message of peace to youth ...*
> ✄

The strategy involves creating a period of time during the year to declare a general ceasefire throughout the city.

In Boston, *Season of Peace* campaigns happen between Thanksgiving and New Year's Day, and during the summer months. The efforts of community members, churches, community organizations, police, probation, transportation department, schools, and youth detention facilities helped decrease violence across the city.

The media campaign uses symbols and slogans youth use in daily conversations to communicate that violence is not the answer to deal with conflict. The *Season of Peace* also features neighborhood walks, which galvanize partners to walk through troubled areas of the city to engage youth and families.

One full color storefront poster pictures a youth wearing the typical hooded sweatshirt, his face in shadows. The copy reads,

An Official
Season of Peace
November 21–January 1
END THIS YEAR WITH PEACE

The *Season of Peace* movement is a multi-media, grass roots campaign to promote peace through neighborhood walks, cookouts, and night games such as basketball, swimming, and board games at the YMCA. The summer *Season of Peace* runs July 4th through September 21st.

The *Season of Peace* was likely inspired by the 50th and 30th memorial anniversaries of Mahatma Gandhi and Dr. Martin Luther King Jr., and launched at the United Nations in 1998; this international *Season of Peace* event honors Gandhi and King's vision for an empowered, nonviolent world.

More than 400 people attended *Season of Peace* events in July 2011 as clergy launched a youth violence prevention movement in Norristown, PA and similar observances are being created all over the nation as community leaders eye "*The Boston Miracle.*"

☀ *75* ☀

Offer Life Altering Tattoo Removal

Gang-related tattoos can be a barrier to former gang members from moving forward in their lives. We encourage communities to find a worthy nonprofit willing to provide this service on a regular basis.

We have seen well-meaning physicians attempt to offer this community service, but rarely do busy physicians have time to carry this load by themselves for an extended period of time.

And quite frankly, even the most well-meaning physician isn't prepared for the personalities and behaviors of a gangland culture in the waiting room.

> *It works well when Public Health champions the cause and marshals the resources to sustain the effort.*

It works well when Public Health champions the cause and marshals the resources to sustain the effort. In Alameda County, CA *Project New Start* is offered at the Public Health Department, Monday through Friday, 9am to 5pm.

Youth Removal.org is a free tattoo removal service operated by *Phoenix House* every Saturday from 1:00pm–9:00pm by appointment. The *Phoenix House* in Dallas operates residential care for substance abuse and diagnosed mental illness. The organization has several locations around the nation.

In Los Angeles, where over 86,000 gang members exist, Father Boyle runs the world-famous *Homeboy Industries*. Though the organization has been struggling to get through the economic downturn, *Homeboy Industries* offers a venue for tattoo removal.

All the employees at *Homeboy* are former gang members and they speak the language and know how to work with these young people.

"By 1992, Father Boyle had founded *Homeboy Industries*, through which he opened *Homeboy* Bakery and extended a hopeful welcome to neighborhood gang members," reported Traci Neal in the *Catholic Digest*.

Since then, the *Catholic Digest* reported, *Homeboy's* service outreach has grown to include tattoo removal, job training and placement, case management, legal services, counseling, and more. For women, a bakery was followed by *Homegirl Café* and enterprises such as a silkscreen shop, a landscaping and maintenance branch, a retail store, and a literary magazine — "all headquartered in a gleaming new building and staffed by former gang members from all over Los Angeles County who have learned how to come together in peace." (See our dedication to Father Boyle in the *Foreword* of **No COLORS**.)

❧ 76 ❧

Call in a Warning to the Gang Leaders

With a population of around 25,000 people, Statesville, NC is large enough to have serious concerns about gangs and violence. In late 2010, the community viewed the first results of their anti-gang initiatives, and they were pleased.

The effect of early and direct intervention and suppression tactics is evident here.

Major crime in Statesville is down significantly and far more than nationally.

Earlier in the year, twenty residents facing charges from assault to robbery filed into Statesville City Hall and were essentially given their last chance.

They were told, "Play it straight or face severe consequences," the *Charlotte Observer* reported.

The "call-in" marked the official start of the Statesville/Iredell County Gang Initiative, designed on a similar and successful program in High Point, NC. The goal is to improve the quality of life in Statesville and the county and to end violent crimes involving groups and gangs.

With local, state and federal partnerships, the program targets violent groups and offers support for members who change their behavior and commit to nonviolence.

"Major crime in Statesville is down significantly, and at least six of the 20 "target individuals" at the February call-in have chosen to avail themselves of community resources and counseling rather than to pursue crime," the *Observer* reported.

The crime decrease included a 40% reduction in aggravated assaults, robberies less than half the previous year, graffiti incidents down 69%, and sexual assaults down 54%. In addition, the city is nearing the end of its second full year with no homicides.

Community leaders noted, "This is not just a law enforcement program. It's a communitywide initiative. That is clearly one of the reasons it's working so well," the *Observer* reported.

The *Pittsburgh Initiative to Reduce Crime (PIRC)* is a gang group related homicide deterrence strategy based on the *CeaseFire* strategy, championed on the city's website. It was brought to life by Mayor Luke Ravenstahl and City Councilman Rev. Ricky Burgess.

At a "call-in" session, gang group members are confronted with law enforcement, community members and social service agencies presenting a single message:

Violence is wrong, the community needs you to be a productive member, we love you, further homicides will be met with a coordinated effort to remove the offending group from the streets for a long time, and there are services available if you need help changing your lifestyle. Please share this message with your gang group buddies.

The individuals attending these call-ins represent one or more participants or members of each street gang or group in the city of Pittsburgh. In addition, they are on probation or parole, so they can be required to attend. They are instructed to take the message back to their gang group.

After these sessions, gang group members will be encouraged to voluntarily contact *PIRC* to access the social services they need.

These "call ins" have been used across the country for decades to draw a line in the sand with violent offenders and gangs. Chicago is among the many cities that have used the "call in" tactics, but in one of America's worst cities for gang violence, this tactic met some vocal criticism.

"The idea seemed simple though bold: call reputed gang leaders to a meeting with top police and federal prosecutors and deliver an ultimatum to end killings in the nation's third-largest city," *Associated Press* reporter Sophia Tareen noted.

The Chicago Gang Violence Reduction Initiative launched at "an unpublicized Aug. 17, 2010 meeting," when Weis met with parolees and reputed gang members from Chicago's west side.

Chicago Police Superintendent Jody Weis said the message was simple: "If you should resort to violence, we'll sharpen our focus on you and really, really make your lives uncomfortable. You have the ability to influence people within your sphere. You guys are in the position to stop the killing."

But Chief Weis faced criticism for holding a so-called "gang summit."

"What are we doing negotiating or having a sit-down with urban terrorists who are killing with guns and drugs on the streets?" a Chicago Alderman said. "Gangs are not to be coddled."

This is an example of a highly politicized community.

He may be well intended. But there is no time for this back seat driving by politicians. Hire a police chief with the tactical strategies the community accepts and get out of the way. Find something else to make political. Rescuing the community from gangs should not be divisive.

Everyone needs to get behind the strategy and move forward. No program will gain traction with political defiance slamming against the strategy every time the community seeks to implement a tactic.

Here's how you know your gang problem is out of control: some Chicago gang leaders actually called a news conference that week to respond to Weis, saying his comments amount to unfair harassment, the *Sun Times* reported.

❧ *77* ❧

Enforce Curfew with Sweeps

We believe the more deliberate a community makes its curfew enforcement, the more effective the *Community Policing* will be. This seems simple. A community has a curfew. Kids are not supposed to be out roaming the streets after curfew.

> *A community has a curfew. Kids are not supposed to be out roaming the streets after curfew.*

But very few communities enforce the regulations. The message this sends to young people is that laws don't matter.

In Northern Virginia, the city of Arlington has an organized Probation and Curfew Enforcement Program, which provides for after-hours curfew checks on targeted probationers and parolees.

Arlington County Police officers and a Courts probation counselor go together into the community to make checks on high-risk youth.

The parolees or probationers are less likely to engage in unacceptable behavior due to the unpredictable time of day or night this check will occur.

The program is popular with parents as it eases some of the responsibility of "reporting" their children away from them and places it on the Court.

The community leaders in New London, CT spent early 2011 debating the efficacy of the local curfew ordinance. Again, it was the tragic death of a youth that triggered the self-examination. One of the problems there could well be the ordinance itself. We don't see how police much less the youth of the community can keep it all straight.

You can be out until 10pm if you're under 16, September through June, but it changes to midnight until 5am in July and August — unless you have a parent accompanying you, or unless you're working. Or, unless it's an emergency.

Discussions have included debate on whether the city's curfew should be more strictly enforced.

Deputy Chief Marshall Segar said that while police do enforce the 1994 ordinance, they are restricted as the young person is committing only a status offense, he said, "which is conduct that is not illegal but potentially could lead to a crime."

The ticket or any other enforcement action is aimed at the parent, not the child.

The ordinance needs to be updated to include 16-year-olds, and several loopholes need to be closed, he said.

For example, *The Day* reports, "if a group of 14-year-olds is hanging out on the street and one member of the group is 16 or older, the group is in technical compliance with the ordinance."

State law allows towns to enact local ordinances, including curfews, but local ordinances must pass constitutional muster, said state Rep. Michael P. Lawlor, D-East Haven.

The Day staff writer Izaskun E. Larrañeta reported that town officials can close parks to all traffic after a certain hour, for instance, but they can run afoul of the constitutional requirement of equal treatment under the law if they try to ban certain age groups from using public spaces.

"A lot of towns have them, but when they actually try to enforce them, it's a disaster," Rep. Lawlor said.

Deputy Chief Segar said New London's ordinance is similar to one in Vernon, which was overturned by the 2nd Circuit U.S. Court of Appeals in 2003.

In that decision, the court ruled that Vernon's ordinance infringed on juveniles' rights of equal protection in that the curfew barred them from being on the streets even with parental consent.

The court said, "If a municipality wishes to single out minors as a group to curtail a constitutional freedom, then the municipality must satisfy constitutional requirements by tying their policies to special traits, vulnerabilities, and needs of minors."

The Day reported that David McGuire, an ACLU staff attorney, said the problem with curfews is that they essentially put an entire demographic on "house arrest" for the actions of a few.

Some cities have used curfews successfully for a limited time window. In August 2008, officials noted, Hartford issued a 30-day emergency curfew when the city experienced a dramatic increase in gang-related violence. *The Day* noted that Sgt. Christene Mertes, a Hartford police spokeswoman, said the city saw a dramatic decrease in youth crime while the curfew was enforced. She said the city was able to implement the curfew because it was temporary and met the constitutional requirements under the Vernon decision.

Detained juveniles cannot be in police custody for more than 12 hours, and they cannot be placed in a holding cell.

Segar said New London should decide if the use of the curfew ordinance should be incident-driven, like in Hartford, or if it should be applied year-round.

Across the continent in California, the *Orange County Register* reported how many juveniles were caught in one of the largest curfew sweeps aimed at preventing gang problems in Orange County. Officers from 18 county agencies participated in the sweep as a part of the ongoing gang prevention effort organized by the Orange County District Attorney's Office.

Curfews in Orange County begin at 10:00 p.m. or 11:00 p.m., depending on the city, and last until 5:00 a.m. the following day.

Reporter Mark Eades of the *Orange County Register* covered the news that more than 300 officers and Sheriff's deputies gathered from all over Orange County, many of whom volunteering their time, patrolled the streets of nearly every city to search for kids out too late.

By the end of the night, the parents of 51 kids discovered the reality of what their sons and daughters were doing late at night.

The parents found out when they came to a processing center set up at the Sheriff's training center in Anaheim to pick up their children.

Once there, Eades wrote, "They had to watch a video presentation about gang problems and what can lead kids to join gangs.

Then they had to listen to members of the *G.R.I.P.* team expose the truth of where their kids were found and what they were doing. After that, Orange County probation officers issued warnings.

Big surprise here — many parents were in denial.

"It takes a lot to get the parents to realize what is going on," said Robert Gustafson, police chief for the city of Orange.

> *Big surprise here —*
> *many parents were in denial.*

Instead of wringing their hands at what to do with underage curfew offenders, the City leadership in Chattanooga has come up with a solution. It came out of the debate over what to do about violence at Coolidge Park.

Their solution, according to *WDEF TV12,* is a new Youth Prevention Center.

The building, once used as police precinct, is attached to the South Chattanooga Recreation Center in St. Elmo.

"We felt like we were already leaning towards doing a youth development services division over here, relocating them, so it made sense to put the Youth Prevention Center over here," *TV12* quoted Recreation Director Greta Hayes.

The facility will be used as a holding center for violators of the city's new curfew ordinance. Kids ages 13-17 will be dropped off until their parents can pick them up.

The youngsters will have access to TV's, board games, and a computer lab.

There will also be showers and beds for children who are left there for longer than eight hours.

But if that happens, the parents could face child neglect charges.

"We just want parents to take a bigger role in their child's life," said Hayes in the *WDEF* report.

And Hayes wants to emphasize the fact that the Youth Prevention Center holds a different purpose than the Juvenile Detention Center. She noted in the news report that the children that will be coming here are not being charged with anything. "They're not criminals, they're not gang members that have gone out and shot somebody, and this is where they're being relocated to," she said.

Hayes noted that the center not only has security cameras, but will be well-staffed with trained officials. Police will be on-site at all times.

Children 12 and under who are picked up after hours will be referred to child services, and their parents could face child neglect charges.

78

Get At-Risk Kids into Outdoor Adventure, Exploration

When a young person is exposed to expeditionary adventures in the wilderness, in programs such as *Outward Bound*, amazing changes can occur quickly.

This was witnessed by co-author Bud Ramey, who spent 23 days on a multi-environment expeditionary *Outward Bound* Course in Utah with a patrol of eleven adults and young people and two amazing instructors.

"We climbed a 13,000 foot mountain, traveled the desert by the stars, spent three days in a solo in the Canyonlands and rafted white water through Cataract Canyon, Ramey said.

"We didn't see a road or a house for three weeks," he noted.

"There was a 17-year-old kid on the patrol who had lost his way in his home and school life. At first, this kid was lost, distrustful, bad tempered, even combative with the group's expedition."

"It was amazing to see him awaken to life, to possibilities and to hug his tearful father at the conclusion of the course. He learned about the value of relationships, about attitude, spirit and that everyone has struggles at times."

Ramey noted that the breakthrough occurred when he achieved something personal — conquered a fear — and established a new self-confidence and pride he had never before felt.

> *"It was as if a light had been turned on within this kid."*

"It was as if a light had been turned on within this kid."

The outdoor experience fails to come up on most city dweller's radar screen, but it can be a powerful intervention if the young person can be sponsored to cover the expenses. *Outward Bound* is a program with hundreds of expeditions, as is the *National Outdoor Leadership School*. Each has many options for course locale.

The *Outward Bound* program summarizes the message to at-risk youth and troubled teens: "Today is the day. To make positive choices. To embrace my potential. To realize I can change my path."

The *Outward Bound* program speaks to parents: "You find yourself trying to look at the world through your teen's eyes. You see a rocky and unsettling road from adolescence to adulthood, filled with potholes, perils and teen-age pitfalls. You want to lend a hand. We can help."

The *National Outdoor Leadership School (NOLS)* offers courses for people ages 14 and up ranging from a long weekend to a full college semester, for which many schools award college credit.

Yet it does not have to be a long high adventure expedition. It can be the wonderful opportunities offered by *Boy Scouts, Girl Scouts, 4-H*, the YMCA, YWCA or Foundations that fund opportunities nearby for kids to gain outdoor skills.

In the Charlotte, NC area, The *North Face Explore Fund* administered by *The Outdoor Foundation*, finds, engages and provides funding for new partners that help further the mission of inspiring the next generation of explorers and conservationists. They help kids discover nature's playground.

McClintock Outdoors Club not only utilizes the outdoors as a natural remedy to urban social issues, but also as a classroom for supplemental middle school science and math curriculums.

"Issues such as the 400% increase in Charlotte gang activity during the last seven years, and the rise of childhood obesity to 20%, are being addressed head-on as kids find active, constructive and creative ways to express themselves naturally," notes their website.

❋ *79* ❋

Create Robust Summer Activities, Jobs for At-Risk Kids

Few communities in America offer a more robust series of summer programs for youth than Las Vegas. *Project 5000 Kids Summer Work Experience (P5K)* seeks out community-minded businesses and motivated students to take part in the Summer Work Experience program. *P5K* recruits businesses to grant 4 to 8 week summer internship opportunities to students ages 16-21.

MyNews3 Las Vegas publishes a website listing of all youth summer programs. In describing *P5K*, editors note, "there is a direct correlation between meaningful work experiences, relevant academics and graduation from high school. Connecting our youth to the workplace at an early age can positively impact the community by encouraging them to graduate high school and strive for post-secondary success; supporting our collective future by recruiting the next workforce just as they are making important decisions about their careers."

> *...there is a direct correlation between meaningful work experiences, relevant academics and graduation from high school.*

The program is offered to businesses and students in the Clark, Lincoln and Nye Counties of Southern Nevada. Internships offered are both paid and unpaid. *P5K* screens youth participants, gauging their fields of interest then works with each business to develop the intern program and match youth to the culture and needs of the employer.

California understands the investment. In 2010, the state provided $7.6 million in summer jobs for potential offenders to stay off the streets.

In Tennessee, the city of Chattanooga, Hamilton County, the school system, local foundations, faith and community-based organizations have invested more than $360,000 as the response to Mayor Littlefield's *Summer Youth Program (SYP)*.

School resource officers, school principals, coaches and the chief of public housing police provide lists of names of at-risk youth ages 13-18 who have been in trouble in the past or who are known to be gang-associated.

The 13- to 15-year-olds are referred to training programs that offer job readiness training, money management and stipends for successful completion.

The 16- to 18-year-olds are contacted by the *Summer Youth Program* Placement Coordinator to attend an interview process, with a parent if under 18 years, and are coached on attire, preparing character reference lists and manner of conduct.

The County Department of Education, City Parks, Recreation and Public Works Departments schedule group interviews.

In addition, interns are hired in the Mayor's Office, the Chattanooga Office of Multicultural Affairs, General Services, Information Technology and the Chattanooga Area Chamber of Commerce. Youth are paid as temporary, part-time employees — $6.25 to $8.50 per hour — during the seven-week program.

Make summers important with your community's business leaders. Get a Summer Jobs program motivated among the business community.

The *Beloved Community Summer Jobs Program (BCSJP)* is one of the largest employers of youth in Providence, RI. The initiative keeps kids off the streets by providing jobs for youth ages 14-19. The Institute for the Study and Practice of Nonviolence is the primary motivator.

"With your help, this summer, The Institute has hired 80 youth," their website comments.

The young people who participate in the summer jobs program learn job skills, gain work experience, and are connected with positive role models.

"Because of donors and volunteers like you, they gain valuable knowledge through nonviolence and life skills training, which will serve them well throughout their lives. More importantly, their self-esteem skyrockets in direct correlation to their weekly paycheck. And when you feel good about yourself, you are far less likely to join a gang, deal drugs or steal cars."

The organization's website quotes one young person: "The Summer Jobs Program helped me to understand why fighting and violence isn't the thing for me, because it's a waste of time and I don't have time to waste."

Holland is a small community near Grand Rapids, MI. The Holland Gang Reduction Committee has a tremendous focus on summer distractions for youth. One recent summer, they organized 73 park events on 38 nights at Moran Park, Rosa Parks Green and Kollen Park. Twelve area churches sponsored the park gatherings, providing games, food and other activities on Friday, Saturday and Sunday nights.

Community leaders in Arlington, VA funded $100,000 from the city for increased gang enforcement during the summer. The summer anti-gang initiative focused on education and community involvement, targeting youngsters, parents and the community. The campaign begins in June and lasts until school starts. Organizers praised the significant results in fewer acts of violence and congratulated "the combined efforts of the Police Department's gang unit, along with patrol officers, the Hot Spot Enforcement Assistance Team units, initiatives at the Boys & Girls Clubs and the Arlington school district," the *Star-Telegram* reported.

80

Insist On a Planned Budget for Gang Prevention Strategy

The first question city or county executives will be asking of the gang reduction effort, at the earliest possible moment, is where are we going to find funding for all these initiatives laid out in the Strategic Plan?

The answer is not complicated. We must find funding – by re-purposing existing programs, by shifting resources, by partnering with major community organizations, by grant seeking.

> *The two options that are not on the table are to leave the plan unfunded or to increase local taxes to fund it. Forget both of those completely.*

The two options that are not on the table are to leave the plan unfunded or to increase local taxes to fund it. Forget both of those completely.

One mentality we must discard is that gang reduction is viewed as a "program."

In tight budget times, "programs" are the first to be cut. For this reason we must move in the direction of defining our efforts as a strategy and not a program.

The real success of gang prevention is clearly within the ability to understand that results are built in to the way we identify gaps and fill them with the necessary services. The budget issue comes in when we start new programs and services but we simply have to change our service delivery.

Communities are quick to point to a lack of funding when in reality, funds have been budgeted for services that have not been evaluated and may clearly be ineffective. Re-think everything. Re-purpose services. De-centralize. Take it to the neighborhoods.

The road to reducing gangs should become a way to do business and not just a temporary program. For local government, it becomes too easy not to remain in their comfort zone, failing to shift gears in their style of providing services.

At some point in this process, you may be faced with staring down entrenched city staff, who have known no other way of doing business and who openly resent the community input to their field of expertise.

Be gentle, seek their cooperation and understanding. Or ask them to find another occupation.

Many believe that simply providing kids a place to go will help eliminate teens making bad choices such as using drugs or joining gangs. It's not so much where they go; it's who is there for them.

Sadly, many communities mistakenly point to existing recreation centers, assuming that their job is done. Why aren't the street kids going there? Kids will not join gangs because they will somehow find their way there, only to find an admission fee or unavailable facilities because they showed up at the wrong time.

Buildings do not reduce gangs, but services do. A community should weigh the value of opening local schools after hours for recreational and athletic purposes with great mentors, coaches and competitions and other services.

Budget planners need to be directed toward addressing the greatest risk factors that contribute to the gang lifestyle.

It is essential to establish what best practice models a community can use to insure that their funding will go to a proven, evaluated effort.

One major reason why communities fail to budget for gang reduction is that many cities have learned to depend on federal and state grant funding to provide the necessary resources to address the problem. This position is what is entitled W.O.G. or "waiting on government."

The reality is that efforts without local support tend to come and go depending on the funding.

The federal government is focusing on the most dreadful communities, those entirely under the control of gangsters, and working hard at remedies. Just hope you aren't so far down the road that you need to get on this priority list. If you are, embrace it. The Justice Department is all about investing in programs that are effective.

For most communities, the ability to leverage federal funding is a way to either add to or start a local effort, but it is not a way to build a gang reduction program for sustainability.

A local government that will not plan for providing to address the gang issue is not serious about attacking the problem. The reality is that you get what you pay for. So a lack of local investment could be interpreted to mean that a community is not going to be invested in an organized strategy to reduce gang involvement.

California has learned that communities that have acknowledged a problem with gangs must invest resources into their plan that will reduce them.

"*Youth Alive!*" is a Catholic Charities effort, receiving strong local support for its interventions. This organization provides boots on the ground for the city's outreach to support families of homicide victims and prevent retaliation in Oakland hospitals. The program tracks street outreach workers' daily location and activities and workers file incident reports. In 2009, the outreach effort received $777,000 in city funding.

It's not just California that invests state funding into their challenged regions. The state grants can be an incentive to plan and implement a violence prevention program, such as the $600,000

North Carolina Governor's Crime Commission grant issued to Rockingham County's Gang & Forensic Unit, which is near Greensboro.

The prevention program is partnering with Rockingham County Youth Services and Goodwill Industries.

Gardner, NC Police Chief Thomas Moss is on the Governor's Commission, which distributed $4.7 million to combat the 14,500 gang members in the state.

A unique funding stream is being nurtured in Tacoma, WA thanks to the progressive thinking of the Greater Tacoma Community Foundation.

They have empowered Youth Board members, ages 16-24. The program recognizes young people as experts on youth violence and gives them the authority to hand out grant money to make that violence go away.

"This year, they'll hand out $20,000, but the foundation's long-term plan is to support the program with a $5 million endowment, giving the board $250,000 to disburse each year," *News Tribune* writer Rob Carson noted.

Carson described one member of the Youth Board, a 20-year-old visual artist and teacher at an education-centered Tacoma nonprofit organization that involves hip-hop musicians, dancers and other artists.

That board member said that this method "cuts out the middleman" by going straight to young people for answers.

☀ 81 ☀

Nurture Growth of Neighborhood
Crime Watch Programs

A neighborhood network, or a *Crime Watch* program, attempts to provide local law enforcement with additional eyes and ears to watch out for all types of criminal activity and promote neighborhood security.

Community crime watches can address all types of crime, but their primary focus is typically residential burglary and other crimes around the home, such as larceny and vandalism. Their presence can also help deter criminals.

A neighborhood network in Takoma Park, MD grew to over 125 email addresses in an eight-block area when the neighborhood was listed as a "hot spot." Over 30 volunteers were recruited immediately to serve on the patrol, which has waxed and waned as time passes and the perceived level of threat has gone up and down.

"The sense of crisis passed after a few months and patrols dwindled. However, the email list has continued to grow among my neighbors to about 125 people in an eight-block radius. I recently used the list to try and reactivate the patrol and within 24 hours we had 20 volunteers. We get more volunteers every week," the website creator reports.

"Maybe you don't have time to knock on someone's door, but because this is easy (emailing neighbors) and doesn't take much time and people are invested. It's a matter of convenience and ease. Caring for each other, mobilizing, and increasing participation and communication are just some of the fruits of neighborhood networking," the networker said.

For a formal *Crime Watch* program, the first step is to identify key leaders, people who are concerned about crime in the neighborhood and organize a meeting of these individuals to discuss safety.

The police can be invited to a neighborhood meeting to discuss community safety, and volunteers can be solicited to serve as block watch leaders.

The neighborhood could be organized by streets or by blocks. Block leaders can be assigned to serve as points of contact.

A communication network can be organized to pass along information about crime and security to residents.

We love what the city of New Braunfels, TX provides from their police department. They publish an excellent *Neighborhood Crime Watch TOOL KIT: A Guide to Starting, Organizing & Maintaining Your Neighborhood Crime Watch.*

The police will be pleased to provide training on recognizing and reporting suspicious activity and on home and neighborhood security. The watch may expand to "citizen" foot or car patrols. The watch can provide a variety of safety and security information to residents.

Local media aid watch groups by publicizing recruitment drives and successes in crime prevention through citizen involvement. Involving seniors and youth will also make the program more comprehensive.

Since 1981, the National Association of Town Watch has promoted the *Neighborhood Watch* concept.

This organization has encouraged community groups throughout the United States to pool resources in crime prevention efforts, shared crime prevention information with thousands of local organizations, and coordinated *National Night Out*, an annual August event where communities demonstrate their desire for peaceful neighborhoods through parties, cookouts, and crime prevention fairs.

In today's fast-paced and busy world, attending community meetings or volunteering can prove challenging. People search for new ways to volunteer and help. Ideas range from starting an online community newsletter to posting information on any unusual or suspicious activities taking place in the neighborhood.

Every neighborhood deserves a strong *Crime Watch* program that can be ramped up very quickly using Internet technology. Almost immediately, people step forward to organize neighborhood associations, plan events and meetings. The most important suggestion we have is to relax and make the effort social and easy, not invasive or pressured.

Every neighborhood deserves a strong **Crime Watch** *program*

❖ *82* ❖

Set Up Family Days
and Neighborhood Nights

Fifty years ago, neighborhoods were different.

People knew each other well. They visited frequently. They borrowed a cup of sugar or brought over food when someone was sick. Many attended the neighborhood church or synagogue. The local 12-year-old delivered the morning newspaper. The milkman set fresh bottles on the porch. The postman knew everyone by first name.

Older kids tutored younger kids. Ball fields emerged in open lots with pick-up games commonplace in the summer. People walked to the store. Rode bikes. Maybe some folks absent-mindedly forgot to lock the house.

Twenty-first century living is quite different in all but the most idyllic communities in America and Canada.

We believe one of the strongest actions citizens can make is to take back their neighborhood. We believe in the creation of neighborhood centers to serve as a focal point, an island in the storm.

But before we get to that advanced stage of development, the neighbors need to begin with activities that bring a lot of people back onto the street at once, and frequently.

This can begin with the churches assuming this role, holding robust neighborhood events regularly and openly.

One of the most intriguing concepts for neighborhood-specific interventions we have found is in Seattle.

The Seattle Youth Violence Prevention Initiative focuses on reducing and preventing youth violence in three Neighborhood Networks: Central Seattle, SE Seattle and SW Seattle. These Neighborhood Networks serve currently more than 1,100 young people. Each of the Networks has a lead agency that coordinates youth referrals to services.

While Seattle has experienced some of the lowest overall crime rates in years, the number of juvenile violent crime incidents continues to be a critical community issue.

The city launched the initiative in July 2009 to dramatically change how the city deals with youth violence. Seattle is tackling the issue of youth violence with a comprehensive approach that incorporates evidenced-based strategies along with home grown programs.

The goals of the initiative are to achieve a 50% reduction in juvenile court referrals for violence and a 50% reduction in suspensions and expulsions from selected middle schools due to violence-related incidents.

Community groups are encouraged to seek rather interesting grants.

The grants cannot be for ongoing events! They can only be non-permanent events.

This is very interesting.

Actively working on these events are all kinds of Seattle neighborhood-based groups, community-based organizations, and grassroots organizations. They actively engage diverse community members and are significantly composed of people who live or work in Central, SE or SW Seattle can help create robust neighborhood quality of life with a matching grant.

Neighborhood community-building projects involving youth are encouraged. Encouraged are innovative and outside-the-box projects or events, especially projects that are gender specific, focus on court-involved youth, middle school youth who have a history of truancy issues and suspensions, or other underserved, vulnerable youth populations.

Also frequently funded are culturally specific projects or events for a racial or ethnic group, especially African-American, East African, SE Asian, Latino, or Pacific Islander youth. These projects must involve building understanding of the specific culture with the larger community.

83

Explain the Situation in Detail to Your Citizens

The letter reprinted below says it all. This is a benchmark communication between city leadership and its constituency.

Novato, CA is reeling from the shock of youth violence and its City Council and City Manager Michael Frank, backed by a strong City Council, is posting a tell-it-like-it-is situational analysis for the community on its website.

Highlighted is the cooperation between neighboring jurisdictions and other agencies.

"January 4, 2011

Dear Novato Community:

As you may have heard, a gang-related shooting occurred in Novato just after midnight on Sunday, January 2. Two adult victims were shot in the parking lot of the Hamilton Marketplace while seated inside a vehicle. Both victims suffered serious injuries. This incident appears to be gang-related. The Novato Police Department currently has one suspect in custody and we are confident that our investigation will lead to additional arrests.

Such actions in our community are unacceptable. As a community, Novato holds dear its safe and small town character. As your city government, we are committed to working to maintain these community values. Our Novato Police Department has been increasing its efforts in gang intervention and investigation during the past year. Unfortunately, gang activity is on the rise in the region and will require greater resources and efforts in the future. The purpose of this communication is to provide the community with some background, local and regional perspectives, and current efforts underway.

General Gang Membership in Bay Area and North Bay

In the Bay Area, there are a number of different gangs and membership is mainly based on ethnic and racial identity. Over the past 10 years, the North Bay has experienced a considerable growth in its gang population due to the developing trend of gang member migration to our region. This upsurge in the gang population has resulted in an escalation in the region's criminal activity.

In the North Bay, the majority of gang members is Hispanic and is affiliated with either the Norteño or Sureño street gangs. Caucasian gang membership has also been on the rise in the North Bay, and there has been a proliferation of both outlaw motorcycle gangs along with white supremacists. These gangs are affiliated with associated prison gangs throughout California and the West Coast.

Local Gang Presence -- Novato, Marin County and Sonoma County

There are more than 75 documented gangs in Marin, Sonoma, Napa and Mendocino counties.

It is estimated that there are thousands of gang members living in the North Bay Area. There are more than 75 documented gangs in Marin, Sonoma, Napa and Mendocino counties. While there is no official count of gang members in Marin County, we estimate that there are several hundred gang members living in Marin's communities. Although Marin County has experienced serious incidents of criminal gang activity during the past 20 years, the county has documented a very small percentage of cases in comparison to the surrounding counties. Novato is certainly not immune from this criminal activity and we have experienced occasional incidents of violent gang activity; however, our community has avoided entrenched gang membership.

Unfortunately, this trend began to change in 2010, when we experienced an increase in cases of violent gang activity between San Rafael and Novato. During 2010, Novato experienced a handful of violent assaults involving gang members. The Police Department has also documented an increase in cases involving gang members in possession of various weapons, including firearms. To date, the violence has essentially been confined to gang versus gang activity. Sadly, it is clear that both Sureño and Norteño gang members are attempting to gain a foothold in Marin County, specifically Novato and San Rafael.

Current Efforts Underway

Members of the Novato Police Department meet regularly with allied law enforcement agencies and the District Attorney's office to share gang intelligence and develop enforcement strategies to address gang activity. We worked very closely with both the Marin County Sheriff's Department and the San Rafael Police Department this past year to identify and prosecute gang members responsible for the violent gang activity mentioned above. We are also working with the California Department of Justice and the Federal Bureau of Investigation. Our Marin County law enforcement agencies have also worked with the County Major Crimes Task Force and the County Parole and Probation Departments to conduct parole, probation and gang enforcement activities. We have submitted a request to the FBI to join an area-wide task force (Safe Streets Task Force) focusing on criminal gang activities.

The Novato Police Department continues to work with community groups and school districts in an effort to address gang membership and gang activity. We recently joined an ad-hoc gang prevention working group to develop strategies to address gang-related issues. The task force includes the County School Superintendent, the Novato Unified School District Superintendent, San Rafael School Superintendent, Novato PD, San Rafael PD, and the Marin County Sheriff's Department. This group discussed a variety of model prevention programs and also agreed to launch a Gang Awareness and Identification Training Program that will be taught county-wide to school district personnel. A planning committee has been established to design the training program. Additional training programs and gang prevention strategies were discussed for future consideration.

City Priority – Gang Intervention

In addition to the current efforts of the Police Department, we want to assure the community that preventing the expansion of gang activity is a top priority for the City. One of the City Council's Strategic Plan Goals is to, "Improve Safety and Build Community Connections" and one of the strategic objectives is to, "Increase public safety through prevention and intervention." A number of Strategic Plan action items specifically have gang prevention in mind, including the potential creation of a neighborhood enhancement team to work proactively on neighborhood crime issues. In addition, City staff will be working closely with the School District to explore programs that support gang prevention and youth development/investment.

In addition, the newly passed sale tax increase, Measure F, specifically mentions gang prevention as a priority for funding. As we move through the budget process, we will be refining the work plan items of the Strategic Plan, as well as looking at various options to support gang suppression, intervention, and prevention.

Next Steps and More Information

The City Council, with leadership from the Police Department and the Parks, Recreation and Community Services Department, will be looking at various models and best practices for how to maintain our quality of life and prevent gangs from infiltrating our community. The City will continue to work with our local community groups and allied law enforcement agencies to develop both short and long-term strategies to address continuing criminal activity associated with local street gangs.

For More Information

If you want to stay informed on further City efforts on gang prevention and intervention, please connect with us through any or all of the avenues below. We will be providing more information and seeking input as we move forward.

Visit the City's website*. Staff constantly updates the website with top stories and current news. The website is: http://www.cityofnovato.org/. On the website, subscribe to the City's "Our Town" monthly newsletter*

Sign up for electronic notifications *(E-Notifiers). Specifically, sign up for the "Police" and "GeneralCity News" subscription lists. This link is: http://www.cityofnovato.org/index. aspx?page=640*

Become a fan of the City's Facebook page and follow the City on Twitter. *The City's Facebook page can be viewed at: http://www.facebook.com/home.php?#!/OurTownNovato and our Twitter account can be accessed at www.twitter.com and searching for "TweetNovato."*

The City Council and staff believe that as a community working together, we can leverage our past accomplishments and find new solutions to actively meet the challenge of stopping gangs from gaining a foothold in Novato.

If you have further questions, comments or suggestions, please contact us at city@novato. org or 415-899-8900. Thank you.

Sincerely,

Michael Frank, City Manager and Joseph Kreins, Police Chief

Posted on the Novato city website Posted: 8:43 pm PDT August 24, 2010

☀ 84 ☀

Quit Imprisoning Nonviolent Offenders

People all over the world are examining their incarceration policies and the cost of imprisonment. In the United Kingdom, Justice Secretary Ken Clarke sparked fury from both the Left and Right after unveiling plans to go soft on crime.

Mr. Clarke said he wants to send fewer people to jail.

He proposed more fines and community sentences and greater use of Restorative Justice, where offenders apologize to victims.

All victims of crime should have the right to meet the offender in a move that could save at least £185 million over two years, campaigners said.

A *Victim Support* report found that if only 40% of the 75,000 victims of burglary, robbery and violence took up the offer of meeting the offender, the cost savings to the criminal justice system through lower reconviction rates would be at least £185 million over two years.

In Vermont, hard economic times, combined with Vermont's *"Challenges for Change"* initiative, have placed the policies of jailing low-level offenders under scrutiny.

… keeping people in jail is very expensive.

Vermont Public Radio host Deborah Luskin noted that what is clear is that keeping people in jail is very expensive.

"What's also become evident is that Vermont has a highly successful alternate, cheaper, and more effective means of dealing with nonviolent offenders called Restorative Justice, administered through local Community Justice Centers and independent Reparative Boards," Luskin noted.

Luskin's *NPR* program also highlighted a very important part of Restorative Justice.

Community Justice Centers provide *Circles of Support and Accountability* for people newly released from prison. These *COSAs*, as they're called, are comprised of citizen-volunteers who start meeting with offenders while they're still inside, help arrange housing and employment, and provide support in negotiating life on the outside. They meet weekly, and help people re-enter civil life.

Restorative Youth Conferencing, introduced in Northern Ireland five years ago, provides good results. Reconviction rates among young offenders involved in Restorative Justice are relatively low and youth conferencing in Northern Ireland has been accompanied by lower use of custody. Approval ratings among victims and all those involved are high.

Offenders in Restorative Justice do not consider it an "easy" option. Young offenders themselves acknowledge just how tough it has been to have to face up to the harm and misery they have caused their victims, their families and the community.

In Concord, MA, more than 95 trained volunteers from 10 surrounding communities are divided into six blended groups. Teenagers can volunteer because the program sees it as beneficial in the restoring process, especially in juvenile cases. Volunteers participate in a day and a half of training and are paired up with an experienced volunteer, as they get involved.

The advocacy organization Communities for Restorative Justice uses the theme line "responds to crime in ways that heal, hold accountable and put right."

Restorative Justice is an approach whose time has come, and the results, when professionally managed, speak for themselves.

As a nation, we must look at non-violent crime and re-evaluate sentencing offenders to jail. It simply is not having the desired result.

✸ 85 ✸

Work Closely with Neighboring Jurisdictions

California Attorney General Kamala Harris spoke at a Sacramento Gang Violence Forum in April 2011, noting that the attack on gang violence needs to be orchestrated regionally.

... the attack on gang violence needs to be orchestrated regionally.

Sacramento Press reporter Brandon Darnell reported that the state's top law enforcement officer likened the gang violence problem to a public health problem like an epidemic: the best way to prevent it is through inoculations and early treatment, but by the time it is being dealt with in the emergency room, it's too late, and too expensive.

Harris said combating gang violence should be dealt with regionally.

"Crime and gang violence doesn't stop at city lines," Johnson said. "It goes across multiple jurisdictions."

In fact, working regionally is absolutely mandated in mature interventional communities.

The *California Cities Gang Prevention Network* is the most organized and sophisticated violence prevention network in America. Part of their mission is to work together, realizing that gangs have no city lines.

Their funding requires that communities "establish or improve a collaboration in each city that appropriately blends prevention, intervention, and suppression, and that involves city leaders and community stakeholders."

"Teams from each city will meet regularly over the next three years to improve collaborative approaches, learn from other cities, document effective practice, and promulgate lessons learned for local, state, and national consumption."

As a national first, the initiative aims to reduce violence and victimization, help entire communities in California, and provide lessons learned to the rest of the nation.

Following a crime summit in Salinas, federal state and neighboring law enforcement agencies combined resources for *Operation Knockout*, a partnership credited for significantly reducing gang violence, including homicides.

The team in Oakland held a summit for all participants in the gang interventions there. Among the participants in the summit are the federal Bureau of Alcohol, Tobacco, Firearms and Explosives, the federal Drug Enforcement Agency, the FBI, the U.S. Department of Justice, the Alameda County District Attorney's Office and the Alameda County Sheriff's Office.

Street outreach workers, crisis response groups, and adult and juvenile re-entry service providers also participated.

By taking a $362,639 grant, the four California communities of Greenfield, Soledad, Gonzales and King City committed to working together in addressing and reducing gang violence through education, prevention, suppression and intervention efforts. The formation of the *Four Cities for Peace Plan (4C4P)* is an effort to address the ongoing gang violence. Soledad Police Chief Eric Sills said the partnership is particularly important now, when law enforcement budgets are slimmer due to the recession.

The Californian reported that as 20 law enforcement agencies partnered in sweeps, dozens of volunteers passed out more than 800 peace fliers. The effort targets at-risk youth and the toughest gang members.

Many communities reach out for federal assistance when they can no longer deal with the issues effectively using local networking and resources. One such community is the city of Newburgh, NY.

This community experienced the gang problem spiraling out of control as drug problems overwhelmed the city. The cycle of violence that always comes with gangs and drugs had quite simply become unacceptable.

The U.S. Attorney Prect Bharara for the South District of New York responded with a process that indicted 60 members and associates of Newburgh *Bloods* and 18 Newburgh *Latin Kings* for crack, cocaine and heroin.

❋ 86 ❋

Know At-Risk Kids by Name

The city of Minneapolis has done a very concise job of cleanly articulating their violence prevention goals.

… focus on knowing the youth personally, by name…

Their *Blueprint for Action*, designed to prevent youth violence, approaches the problem from a public health perspective. Formally launched in January 2008, the *Blueprint* has four main goals, all focus on knowing the youth personally, by name, and dealing with these young people one person at a time:

- Place a trusted adult in the life of every child
- Intervene at the first sign of risk
- Restore youth who have been in the juvenile justice system
- Unlearn the culture of violence

This program has received national recognition from the National League of Cities.

Juvenile-related homicides were at the lowest levels in 2009 since 2001. Violent crime in the Fourth precinct (which includes four neighborhoods in the *Blueprint*) decreased 35% from 2007.

In Ontario in January 2011, the active identification of specific at-risk kids was deployed with two grants each geared toward identifying and helping youth in Northumberland who might be prone to violence.

A little more than $48,000 came in the form of a provincial grant given to local police and school boards and just over $118,000 in Ontario Trillium Foundation funding was awarded to two agencies working with at-risk youth and families covering ages 12-25.

Both groups have engaged the participation of scores of community agencies that will assist in the individual programs.

Organizers had confidence that the identifying protocol will hopefully address the kids they see "falling through" the system.

Bermuda understands the nature of "knowing the children at at-risk."

In December 2010, Former Police Commissioner Jonathan Smith was in the news noting that the gang culture "is becoming engrained in Bermudian society."

He encouraged Government to pursue a major cross-Ministry initiative aimed at both identifying at-risk young people and preventing them from drifting into crime.

"We have one significant advantage in Bermuda over the research done elsewhere. Every high-risk boy between, for example, the ages of 8-10, and younger, is known by first name, last name and nickname. We know where each boy goes to school, we know which junior football team he might be on, where he lives and many of these boys will already be 'known to the system' somewhere and exist in the database of one Ministry or another. It's my view that we must execute, with laser precision, suitable prevention programmes to deliberately target those families and individuals at the highest risk and then measure the success of that intervention over time."

❦ 87 ❦

Promote Your Initiatives Using Websites and Social Media

Social media is key to engaging young people in America and it has a seat at the table when communications are planned regarding violence prevention activity.

Websites, of course, are now a fundamental piece of any planned communications effort.

Spokane, WA launched the first comprehensive and in-depth gang prevention and intervention website in the Northwest in July 2011. Officials said it is to encourage neighbors to prevent, report, and get involved in the anti-gang effort, *WREM 2 News* reported.

The website developed by the Greater Spokane Substance Abuse Council and the Spokane Violent Crime Gang Enforcement Team. It can be found at www.stopspokanegangs.org.

The website is intended to educate Spokane County residents about the gang presence in the area, gang indicators, common criminal activities, the dangers of joining gangs, and the various prevention and intervention efforts being undertaken.

People can also submit anonymous tips to local law enforcement. Those sending in crime tips are then given a tip number to track the status of their tip.

People can also submit anonymous tips...

Just before New Year's Eve 2010, Santa Monica City Hall officials launched a "youth violence prevention" portal on the city's website, part of an effort to better inform the public about programs geared toward at-risk minors in Santa Monica.

The *Youth Resource Team (YRT)* seeks to keep youth safe and support healthy development from infancy through adulthood through the collaborative work of the city of Santa Monica, education and nonprofit agencies, neighborhood organizations, governmental partners, business, and faith communities.

The *Santa Monica Daily Press* quoted Julie Rusk, human services manager, who said "We're very excited about santamonicayouth.net and envision it as an important tool for sharing with the public the current work of the *YRT* and ways the community can get involved."

The portal provides details on upcoming *YRT* meetings and information relevant to the efforts in youth violence prevention in Santa Monica. The site also contains links to a wide range of reports on the topic.

A beautifully designed website for the community of Yakima, WA gives viewers the opportunity to report crime, offer an anonymous tip, learn more or volunteer to help say no to gangs. The site can be seen at http://yakimacounty.saynotogangs.com/default.aspx

This website is targeting families, offers advice, opportunities to volunteer, surveys and confidential tips. There are extensive links to police, crime watch, and dozens of related sites.

In Houston, a unique website has been birthed with a very specific purpose.

The StopHoustonGangs.org website encourages anonymous tips and gang members and leaders.

The Multi-Agency Gang Task Force, an FBI-led partnership that encompasses 14 other agencies, including the Houston Police, the Texas Department of Criminal Justice, and the Bureau of Alcohol, Tobacco and Firearms. This task force seeks to identify members and leaders of violent street gangs and target them for law enforcement.

The site heightens the awareness of the public in what is going on as regard gangs in the community and enlists their help in reporting.

As of late October 2010, organizers were boasting 30,000 hits, 80 tips and ten arrests. It was developed as a cost effective alternative to the initial notion of a 1-800 telephone line.

The core concept is to solicit the citizens to help make Houston a safer place.

One blogger left a cautionary message on the site:

"How are you going to stop the gang bangers from using your site to set you up or go after rival gangs?"

A possible concern, but the end result, in our opinion, is that after all is said and done – this will result in gang suppression.

The *Las Vegas Sun* covered a story in November 2010 of unique new "apps" that can help an at-risk kid in crisis.

Turning Point Experience, a Las Vegas-based nonprofit organization, is dedicated to helping students avoid destructive influences in their lives.

This group has been working with the Southern Nevada Community Gang Task Force to produce that tool, a comprehensive iPhone application designed to educate adults about the top 20 issues teens face and provide them with the resources for finding help.

Destructive Issues debuted in fall 2010, free to those with an iPhone or iPod. It's a one-stop-shop for information and resources about teen issues, the first of its kind in the world, developers said.

Other applications are under development.

The *Sun* reports that a second app will be geared toward teens with a more user-friendly approach: Avatars illustrating the consequences of good and bad decisions students face.

An app called *S.P.I.R.I.T.* will be released third, specifically designed as a tool for law enforcement officials and chaplains. At a gang task force meeting in October, developers called *S.P.I.R.I.T.*, the acronym for Suppression, Prevention, Intervention, Referral Intelligence Tool, a "game-changer for communities to connect the dots."

"What we have is the group wanting to help and the kids needing help, and this is what will connect them," they said.

✹ **88** ✹

Expand the Role of Police
with *Community Policing*

Solid community strategic planning defines a new approach that law enforcement will be asked to take as the community adjusts to shifting priorities.

Most communities re-think their law enforcement approach because, quite simply, youth violence and gang growth require a re-examination of best practices and tactics.

Traditionally, law enforcement has led the way for providing the energy to deal with gangs in most communities. In the past, police leadership has accepted the accountability of the results. But new questions need to come from community leadership.

For example, a great deal of energy is spent by dedicated law enforcement officers in gathering and disseminating intelligence on street gangs. But the larger issue is how law enforcement efforts can assist in actually reducing the gang problem in the community.

For years, policing in America has demonstrated a strategic change from simply responding to incidents, to addressing problems through community-based strategies.

This takes shape as police officers take on the posture of policing through building close ties to the community and implementing greater strategies to prevent or intervene in the problem. This style of service delivery has been titled *Community Policing*.

While *Community Policing* is not new to the law enforcement arena, the emphasis on deploying it to deal with the gang problem in most communities is new.

Building trusting relationships in the community is an important aspect of reducing gangs.

We see many communities with superb gang intervention teams but no *Police Athletic League*, or other formal way to incorporate prevention and intervention into their efforts.

When police officers actually become stakeholders in their communities, they begin to look beyond avenues of enforcement. They view their role as more of a public safety practitioner than strictly a tool for enforcement.

> *They view their role as more of a public safety practitioner than strictly a tool for enforcement.*

This becomes necessary in the gang reduction process. To simply target gang members for arrest and conviction, while necessary, does very little in the overall effort of preventing and reducing the growth of gang membership.

Time after time, we hear dedicated and gifted chiefs of police formally declaring that "we will never arrest our way out of the gang issue in America."

While enforcement has served as our primary means for controlling gangs, we have experienced exponential growth in gangs everywhere.

Community Policing is not a soft approach on policing gangs.

The creativity that exists within the gang culture demands for more creative policing to address the problem. The *Community Policing* method of gang reduction begins with the involvement of law enforcement in the strategic planning process.

This process connects law enforcement with other community service providers such as social services, faith-based organizations and community nonprofits. It establishes a relationship beyond enforcement and provides a community application to the issue.

A determined program of prevention is the hallmark of today's *Community Policing* actions.

These include sponsoring sports leagues through the *Police Athletic League*, conducting summer camps for at-risk kids, and teaching classes such as *D.A.R.E* or *G.R.E.A.T.*

In addition, school resource officers are playing a lead role in preventing gangs. If your schools do not have these trained, vital public servants in place, make it happen.

Schools or *Police Athletic Leagues* are the perfect place to begin personal relationships with the youth of the community. Once officers identify a person at-risk for gang involvement, they can mentor and nudge them to the proper community intervention efforts.

This new level of involvement has another benefit. Local police officers gain a great deal of intelligence through building relationships with local citizens with an emphasis on gang members.

This helps to address a community's "No Snitch" issue. The intelligence that can be gained by law enforcement by forming relationships with young people will only enhance public safety in the community.

A *Community Policing* strategy enhances a community's re-entry process by providing information to law enforcement on the location of released offenders. Once officers working a neighborhood pinpoint the location of convicted gang members, it becomes easier to identify what impact they may have on the overall community.

An outstanding resource to consider on *Community Policing* is the U.S. Conference of Mayors' *Best Practices of Community Policing 2006.*

✸ 89 ✸

Deploy Prosecutors in the Neighborhoods with *Community Prosecution*

Just as experts in law enforcement are recognizing the benefits of *Community Policing* in reducing the incidence of crime and improving the quality of life, the notion of *Community Prosecution* is gaining traction across the country as an approach to law enforcement.

Community Prosecution is founded on the idea that prosecutors have a responsibility not only to prosecute cases, but also to solve public safety problems, prevent crime and improve public confidence in the justice system.

Basically, prosecutors operate in a given neighborhood sector rather than from a centralized, impersonal office.

Community Prosecution is organized for three core reasons.

- To create new and lasting partnerships with the community in order to improve quality of life;
- To implement a proactive, problem-solving approach to crime;
- To improve the relationship and partnership with law enforcement and public and private agencies;

Prosecutors who have re-organized their work life in such a manner have been gratified by their new role and feel that they are better addressing the needs of the community.

Around the country, prosecutors are setting up shop in neighborhood offices and collaborating with others (including residents, community groups and other government agencies) in the development of problem-solving initiatives.

In many cases, community stakeholders actually help to set the crime-fighting agenda and participate in the solutions. Definitions of success are changing as well.

The Department of Justice outlines seven key dimensions that characterize *Community Prosecution* initiatives. These dimensions are

- The target problems
- The geographic target area
- The role of the community
- The content of the response to community problems
- Organizational changes within the prosecutor's office

- Case processing adaptations
- Inter-agency collaboration
- Partnerships relating to the initiative

The Justice Department notes that any willing county can develop a community prosecution program to address the needs of the residents.

Community Prosecution is organized in Albany, NY by establishing four satellite sites of the District Attorney's office in the city's most challenged neighborhoods.

These *Community Prosecution Offices (CPOs)* are staffed with a Community Prosecution Coordinator, an Assistant District Attorney, a Probation Officer and a Community Representative.

The *CPOs* interact with the community at the neighborhood level to recruit volunteers and to identify and solve problems that contribute to crime and pose hazards to public order and safety.

They provide the neighborhood-based structure around which specific Community Prosecution initiatives will be built. They are intended to be co-occupied by representatives of other governmental agencies that may wish to partner to maximize resources and problem-solving results.

The *CPOs* in Albany have some key objectives:

- Maximize potential for successful reintegration of re-entering prison inmates.
- Keep middle school kids out of drug distribution.
- Make public safety services more responsive to the needs and concerns of our aging population.
- Foster the development of a strengthened and expanded infrastructure of *Neighborhood Watch* organizations.
- Expand the Community Accountability Board Program to more venues throughout the county."

The Albany organizers note that there is another clear benefit.

"Unprecedented numbers of prison inmates are being released into our communities. Research has found that two-thirds of them will re-offend within three years of release. When they get home, they are on their own. In a *Community Prosecution* county, the prosecutor assumes responsibility for making the county as crime-free as possible," they note.

"Being a prosecutor in the 21st century isn't just about trying cases and asking for the maximum sentence," he said. "It's about preventing crime. It's about working with the community." District Attorney Seth Williams noted in a *Daily News* interview in the fall of 2010.

The move in Philadelphia follows the lead of U.S. Attorney General Eric Holder, who launched a *Community Prosecution* plan for Washington, D.C., when he was that city's U.S. Attorney battling drug wars.

Community Prosecution in Philadelphia will mark the first time the majority of the city's assistant district attorneys will be assigned cases by geographic area. Organizers note that the initiative allows prosecutors to work more closely and efficiently with the same police officers, detectives, clergy members and community activists to better spot crime trends and prosecute criminals.

The Daily News reported that "the vast majority of the 75,000 cases handled each year, such as armed robberies, home invasions and attempted murders, will now flow through their community division. Each division will hear its criminal cases on a designated floor, and prosecutors will stay with their cases from start to finish.

✸ 90 ✸

Call for Injunctions Against Specific Gangs

New powers to tackle gang culture began in January 2011 in Great Britain where gang injunctions could ban suspected members from wearing distinctive colours or entering rival territory, according to *The Guardian*.

Gang injunctions will aim to break down gang culture and also give civil courts the power to ban people from going out in public with dogs that have been used as weapons, *The Guardian* reported.

Under the powers, police and local authorities will be able to apply for the injunctions, which will be issued by a county court and last up to two years, for adults who have been proven to have engaged in, encouraged or assisted gang-related violence.

In the U.S., the ACLU's posture on injunctions argues that these kinds of laws "make the problem worse." Yet reports from Los Angeles County show that crime levels dropped by up to 10% in neighborhoods benefitting from a similar law.

A survey of San Bernardino residents showed "positive evidence of short-term effects, including less gang presence, fewer reports of gang intimidation, and less fear of confrontation with gang members."

In San Antonio, gang members subjected to the law "were charged with almost 50% fewer crimes in the 20 months after the injunction issued."

In other words, the law provided an incentive for gang members to cease some of their criminal activities, the AG's office cites in their press release.

The ACLU, ever vigilant to protect citizen's rights, reacted negatively.

"Our conversations with community members from California found that faced with an injunction, gang members simply pick up and move to new territory, resulting in the spread, rather than the curtailment, of gang blight."

In 2010, Oakland became the third city in the San Francisco Bay Area to implement injunctions against a specific set of violent street gangs.

It is a civil order in the manner of a restraining order," *CBS Channel 5 TV San Francisco* reported.

"It allows a city attorney or a district attorney to bring an injunction against a group of individuals who have conspired to commit crimes or otherwise terrorize innocent people in a community."

The law was upheld as constitutional by the California Supreme Court in 1997. In Oakland's system, the objective is to prove that the individual is part of the criminal organization. John says that in many cases the persons of interest "self identify" via *Facebook*, *YouTube*, and other ways.

Because Oakland's gang injunction system calls for in-court identification of suspects using judge, jury, and law, it takes the issue of determining precisely who is part of a gang out of the hands of the Oakland Police.

But the injunction actions have splintered the community. Debates have been vicious.

After six hours of heated, often rancorous debate over Oakland's gang injunction strategy, the City Council moved to continue with the city's controversial anti-crime strategy by one vote shortly after midnight in May 2011.

But the injunction actions have splintered the community.

Crosscurrents reporter Ali Winston described the fractious debate's conclusion.

"As the council neared their vote, more than a dozen uniformed OPD officers spread out on both levels of the council chamber and outside the hall to ward off any potential disturbances. Following the 4-3 decision, the room was silent save for one blurted expletive. Injunction opponents then filed out quietly."

The injunction is a meaningful tool for the Oakland Police Department, comparable to a restraining order against an abusive domestic violence offender. By definition, officials argue, "gangs and street gangs commit crimes." The injunctions, if enforced, could "protect lives of bystanders and gang members themselves."

Gang injunctions limit illegal guns and drugs, stop assaults and robberies, prevent recruitment of younger gang members and create a curfew.

Opponents of the Oakland injunctions included Sagnicthe Salazar who advocated for the Chicano residents who already felt harassed and profiled.

"Anybody's presence in one of these zones gets you halfway to being a gang member," he said. The injunctions, he added, affect not just the 40 people on the list, but Fruitvale's (east Oakland) 40,000 residents.

"It's up to City Council to decide if this is bad policy," he concluded.

Also undeniable is the fact that he gang injunctions have divided Oakland along economic and class lines. Visalia is a community with a significant history of strategic planning and a solid plan of prevention and intervention activities. This California community had to lean heavily on suppression in 2010 to respond to a horribly violent trend.

At the beginning of 2010, gangs brought fear into the lives of those who saw clashes nearly every day on city streets, the *Visalia Times-Delta* reported at year's end.

Four gang murders by May brought the problem to the forefront for city officials and even California lawmakers.

Before the year was half over, Visalia Police Chief Colleen Mestas knew something had to be done.

A cooperative effort between California's Attorney General Jerry Brown and Visalia police led to the largest gang sweep to ever hit Visalia.

More than 50 top-ranking *Norteño* gang members were arrested in one sweep of Tulare County. *Operation Street Sweeper* was conducted at the end of October, the *Times-Delta* summarized in a year-end review article.

Visalia police employed the newly installed gang injunctions to restrict gang activity and sought further gang injunctions to increase the net.

When it became clear that newer gang members were not being affected, the District Attorney's Office and Sheriff's Department announced new injunctions in April.

"Local departments, especially the Visalia Police Department, conducted repeated aggressive sweeps, rounding up violators of injunctions and parole and putting them off the streets, at least for a time," the *Times-Delta* said.

The strategy of "disturb and disrupt" quelled the violence, and what had been predicted as a violent summer didn't happen.

Then *Operation Street Sweeper* got a boost in October when a combined operation of federal, state and local law enforcement made 50 arrests, including some in prison, in seeking to dismantle a gang network known as *Nuestra Familia.*

Visalia has 1,184 validated gang members, but the number affiliated with gangs exceeds 3,000, police officials said in the reports.

❦ 91 ❦

Don't Let Gangs Take Over Your Shopping Mall

It's an emotional topic with teenagers. Good kids love to rendezvous at the mall. So do kids who wear colors.

In many cases, this can escalate into a situation where larger groups of teenagers with baggy pants and colors are moving through the mall, leaving a wake of discomfort among shoppers. It's not too long until the mall begins to fail.

... teenagers with baggy pants and colors are moving through the mall, leaving a wake of discomfort among shoppers.

Yet, getting tough with mall regulations can be met with resistance.

In Asheville, NC, a curfew policy begun in 1993 at Asheville Mall required that teens under 16 have a parent with them after 6 p.m. on Saturdays. The mall also posted rules that included a ban on bandannas (viewed as gang emblems) and on groups of more than four teens at a time. A series of fights and one gun incident prompted the crackdown - one that "restored a sense of order," notes reporter Patty Rhule of *USA Weekend* Magazine.

"But some Asheville teens believed the limits went over the line."

Jasmine McCoy, 18, and her friends in the Buncombe County Youth Organizing Project, distributed fliers and held meetings during school lunch periods, seeking others with concerns about mall policies. In summer 2010, the youth group persuaded the mall to drop its no-bandanna policy and ease the restriction on teens congregating.

Asheville's students mirror the views expressed in the USA Weekend Teens & Freedom Survey: Most teens nationwide said they should be allowed to go to the mall without a parent at age 13.

USA Weekend Magazine notes that across the country, mall management increasingly thinks otherwise. Asheville Mall was among the first to impose a curfew to quell the growing problem of unruly teenagers, but it is hardly alone.

- In 1994, Macon, GA mall required teens 16 and older to carry ID cards; a parent must accompany those under 16.

- In 1995, Patrick Henry Mall in Newport News, VA enforced a weekend teen curfew for eight weeks that mall management says put an end to complaints about rowdy teen behavior.

And in the fall of 2010, the nation's largest shopping center, the Mall of America in Bloomington, MN, made headlines when it instituted a 6 p.m. weekend curfew for un-chaperoned teens.

A huge gang fight involving 200-300 people shut down Raleigh's Triangle Town Center mall in 2008. The fight began inside the mall before it spread outside. Raleigh PD, Sheriff's deputies, and State Troopers responded and eventually restored order. A fifteen-point Youth Escort Policy resulted.

There is an even better way – attract the kids to the Mall with a teen center.

For the past four years the Niles Teen Center in Niles, IL has called Golf Mill Shopping Center home. This year the partnership between the two has earned national recognition as a finalist in the International Council of Shopping Centers "*MAXI Award*" for cause-related marketing.

Each year an award is given to the shopping center that is found to have the best interaction with a charity. Other subcategories of the award given are for best social media campaign, best public-relations department and more.

"The Niles Teen Center's partnership with Golf Mill was recognized because of their close ongoing partnership," said Mark Williams, director of the Niles Teen Center.

The Niles Teen Center is an after school program for sixth- through 12th-grade students in local junior high and high schools. It's a place for teenagers to hang out after school, work on homework, play video games and bond with one another.

The Teen Center started about 10 years ago as a grassroots organization of teenagers getting together after school at the Niles Park District building, but after the village of Niles took over the program in 2007; it was moved to its new home in Golf Mill.

Williams said the mall was the perfect place for the center to be because teenagers and shopping malls go hand-in-hand.

Besides serving as a place away from home for teenagers to go to, the center also provides social-work services to teenagers and their families, family therapy, suicide-prevention services and peer-to-peer networking.

☀ *92* ☀

Check your State Gang Statutes – Prosecute Gang Recruitment

A Florida gang census released in late 2010 by the Attorney General Bill McCollum shows the state has 1,403 documented gangs with 56,200 members, associates and suspected members.

For the first time, it includes gang statistics from across the state. The goal, McCollum said, is to have a baseline to measure the results of efforts to fight gang activity.

The *Bloods* came in at No. 2 among the top 20 gang names most frequently listed by local law enforcement agencies. The top name: the *Crips*, the archenemies of the *Bloods*.

In the same time period that the totality of the problem was defined in Florida, an interesting development occurred when a teen who sought to recruit gang members for his gang got slapped with a charge soliciting street gang members.

Soliciting gang membership is a rare charge in Hernando County. The same is true for Pasco County, where the Sheriff's Office said officials there couldn't recall ever charging someone under the statute.

In this case, the boys involved had two ways to join the gang, and "neither option would be a cakewalk," according to *St. Petersburg Times* news writer Tony Marrero.

A 14-year-old Spring Hill boy approached at least three other teens at Fox Chapel Middle School earlier this month, told them he was member of the *Bloods* and that if they wanted to join, they could either be "beat in" or commit a crime, according to a Hernando County arrest affidavit released Tuesday.

> *... they could either be "beat in" or commit a crime.*

A "beat in" is just what it sounds like: take some lickings, and you're a member.

At least one of the teens accepted the offer, opting to do the crime instead of taking a beating, affidavits show.

Marrero reported that the boy who offered and the boy who accepted were both arrested later on charges of burglary after admitting to breaking into a vacant home on Tree Haven Drive in Spring Hill and causing about $1,000 worth of damage by painting the word "BLOOD" on the carpet, affidavits show.

"Three students signed sworn written statements stating that the 14-year-old tried to recruit them to the gang, and the teen admitted his recruiting efforts when interviewed by Detective David

Kortman, a gang specialist at the Hernando Sheriff's Office. He was booked at Hernando County Jail …and released to his parents," the *St. Petersburg Times* said.

It is a third-degree felony in Florida to "intentionally cause, encourage, solicit, or recruit another person to join a criminal street gang that requires as a condition of membership … the commission of any crime," according to the statute. The felony is classified under the state's Criminal Street Gang Prevention Act of 1996.

The charge is so rare because it's hard to prove, he said. Witnesses are often too scared or too loyal to cooperate. The juveniles in this case were facing charges themselves and talked, officials said. Gang legislation varies significantly in every state. The measures most frequently seen in many states are those that deal with increased enhanced sentencing for gang activities, drive-by shootings, graffiti, gang activity and forfeiture and gang member recruitment.

93

Cultural Targeting of Parenting Classes Creates Support Groups

It is quite likely that an analysis of your community will result in a gap in services and a call for more parenting classes as early pregnancy is clearly connected with gang behavior.

The *Center for Disease Control and Prevention (CDC)* in Atlanta has a wealth of information available on the strategies that should be considered when providing parenting classes to low income families.

The *CDC* reminds us that violence is a learned behavior. The values, attitudes, and interpersonal skills acquired early in life play a key role in the development of violent behavior.

Because a person's violent or nonviolent tendencies may be set in early childhood, preschool- and elementary school-age children are often thought to be ideal participants in interventions that promote nonviolent values and enhance conflict-resolution skills.

Based on careful documentation and research the *CDC* urges us to consider the cultural and demographic context of the young parents you seek to educate on parenting.

"When selecting your intended participants, consider their location, age, life circumstances, ethnicity or race, and needs," the Atlanta center notes.

We are encouraged to try to select a group of people who live near each other and are alike in key characteristics. By targeting a group that is fairly homogeneous, we can better tailor materials and activities so they are more meaningful to participants.

Selecting a homogeneous group increases the likelihood that participants will form support groups and friendships that extend beyond the environment of the intervention.

... select a group of people who live near each other and are alike...

You can also meet the needs of your participants more effectively when participants are alike. Wood and Baker (1999) developed a questionnaire to examine parent preferences, behaviors, and beliefs toward school-based parent-education programs among 395 low-income, culturally diverse parents from two elementary schools.

Results indicated that parents of low socioeconomic status wanted to participate in parent-education events, but they were less likely than parents with higher levels of education to attend events at school.

The effectiveness of parenting interventions seems to increase exponentially when children are very young, before antisocial or aggressive behaviors are fully developed.

By the time a child reaches adolescence, both the child and the parents are following well-established patterns and are more resistant to long-term change.

And a 14-year-old boy relies much less on his family and is much more susceptible to external influences than a 7-year-old boy.

The earlier in a child's life a parent-based intervention begins, the greater the likelihood it will be effective.

With this fact in mind, we may want to consider targeting parents who are expecting a child. Previous research suggests that intervening with a mother during the latter part of pregnancy and continuing with intervention activities during the first few years of her child's life can significantly reduce the risk of conduct disorder and violence.

✸ 94 ✸

Consider the Judicial Innovation of
Community Courts

The success of *Drug Courts* in America has encouraged other forms of judicial innovation. Experience is demonstrating that they strengthen a neighborhood and provide stronger rehabilitation measures for wayward youth.

The first *Community Court* in the U.S. was the Midtown Community Court, launched in 1993 in New York City. Over 40 community courts, inspired by this experience, are currently in operation or planning around the country.

Aubrey Fox, Director of Special Projects Center for Court Innovation notes that new and innovative *Community Courts* "are building on the drug court model, expanding the reach of problem-solving principles beyond specialized courtrooms and making a significant contribution to the fight against substance abuse."

Community Courts are neighborhood-focused courts that use the power of the justice system to address local problems, including drug possession, shoplifting, vandalism, and assault.

Aubrey Fox explains in her white paper on *Community Courts* that like *Drug Courts*, many *Community Courts* provide addicted defendants judicially monitored drug treatment.

But, she explains, they typically handle a broader caseload. Many manage all misdemeanors in a given neighborhood. Many use of a broader array of sanctions such as community impact panels.

> *Community Courts strive to create new relationships with outside stakeholders such as residents, merchants, churches, and schools.*

Community Courts strive to create new relationships with outside stakeholders such as residents, merchants, churches, and schools.

In supervising individuals mandated to long-term interventions, whether drug treatment, mental health counseling, or something else, the *Red Hook Community Justice Center* operates much like a drug court.

Red Hook utilizes ongoing judicial monitoring, information-sharing, frequent drug testing, and a combination of sanctions and incentives — to motivate behavior change. Just like *Drug Courts*.

This is also true in the courtroom, where the judge uses a mix of short-term sanctions and incentives to encourage compliance, such as a few days of jail for an offender who continually tests positive for illegal drugs, or a round of applause for someone who has successfully completed their mandate and turned their life around.

Red Hook's award-winning design also plays a role: unlike traditional courtrooms, where the judge looks down at defendants from a raised bench, at Red Hook the bench is at eye level.

Aubrey Fox explains that *Red Hook* differs from the drug court model is some crucial ways.

"It has a broader caseload." Many of the offenders at *Red Hook* are not drug-addicted. Its community location allows it to get involved in a range of crime prevention activities that are beyond the scope of the typical drug court, she notes.

And The *Red Hook Community Justice Center* operates several positive youth development programs, including a youth court, which trains local teenagers to serve as judges and attorneys handling real-life cases involving their peers, a thriving youth baseball league, and a summer youth photography project in which local students are given technical training and the opportunity to display their photographs in the Justice Center itself.

Finally, the Justice Center helped create a neighborhood organization, *Friends of Coffey Park*, which transformed Red Hook's central park from a drug hot spot to a public space enjoyed by all local residents.

Red Hook's approach of using problem-solving and prevention strategies has had an impact on the streets and in the minds of local residents.

The local precinct is now the safest in Brooklyn. And in a door-to-door survey of more than 600 local residents, 94% said they approved of the community court in their neighborhood.

Aubrey Fox also highlights the Orange County Community Court in Florida as a good example of how a community court can complement local *Drug Courts*.

"A unique experiment, the *Community Court* brings under one roof a number of specialized court dockets that would typically be scattered over several courtrooms. This includes an adult drug court, a mental health court, a driving-under-the-influence court, a veteran's court, a domestic violence court, and a homeless court," her white paper describes.

"The *Community Court* is housed in a renovated former department store located less than a mile from Orange County's centralized courthouse.

Each docket meets on different days of the week; for the homeless court, the presiding judge makes regular trips to local homeless shelters to hear low-level misdemeanor cases involving outstanding warrants.

The *Community Court* enrolls participants through mandates, through referrals from other judges and attorneys or on a walk-in basis.

Typical of this court's approach to reform is the veteran's court, which started in November 2008 after an Iraq war veteran seen in court a few weeks earlier died of a drug overdose."

Based on the model of the Buffalo Veterans Court (the first such court, established in January 2008), the court works closely with the Department of Veterans Affairs, which has assigned a full-time case manager to the project.

In addition to the Veterans Court, Lindley also operates an innovative Outreach Court, designed to address the unique issues posed by individuals who are homeless.

In the Outreach Court, individuals are sentenced to drug rehabilitation or parenting classes as an alternative to a fine. In addition, the judge conducts Outreach Court in homeless shelters, where residents are encouraged to bring warrants to the court's attention.

On-site social services include GED classes and educational workshops, available to local residents on a walk-in basis. The Justice Center also operated two innovative public health programs involving young people.

Community Courts owe a great debt to *Drug Courts*, which have provided model practices, political support, and an example of criminal justice innovation that works.

Every community should look more closely at *Community Courts* to learn lessons about engaging the community, investing in prevention, working with non-traditional offenders, and moving beyond traditional settings.

🎇 95 🎇

Attack Poverty's Impact on Young People with a Youth Enrichment Zone

Many professionals who have devoted their careers to studying what is causing the plague of youth violence in America and Canada agree that the root cause is clearly poverty.

In Harlem, they have attacked poverty's impact on young people.

"Our goal is ambitious. Break the cycle of generational poverty in Central Harlem and change the odds for the whole community."

> *Break the cycle of generational poverty ...*

The *Harlem Children's Zone (HCZ)* has created a unique, and uniquely successful, service that supports children from birth through college graduation, and creates a critical mass of engaged adults who understand what it takes to ensure a child succeeds. The model is working.

In 2000, *HCZ* tested a new paradigm on a single block in Harlem, providing extensive services to address the various problems families faced. Over the last decade the Project has grown to encompass 97 blocks, serving more than 14,000 adults and children each year.

These unprecedented results have proven remarkably effective in helping children succeed in school, raise their test scores, and get through college.

Their poverty-fighting paradigm is now a model for communities across the country and around the world. It has provided a wealth of evidence for effective strategies as these communities evolve.

In its role as the premier laboratory in this great national experiment to combat poverty, the *Harlem Children's Zone* is indispensable. *HCZ* advocates proclaim that poverty is the root of this national crisis with our youth. Studying what has gone right in Harlem is an important consideration for every community immersed in the problems associated with concentrations of poor citizens.

HCZ is assisting communities across the nation with planning. They have created the Practitioners Institute, which shares information about their work with others. Their goal is to help communities so they can identify their resources and needs, then organize a coordinated, interdisciplinary strategy.

When an organization has such success with any broad-reaching measure, it is a necessity to get organized to handle the continuous flow of inquiry. They have done this well at *HCZ*. A community delegation can attend either a three-hour or three-day workshop. The Practitioners Institute has worked with more than 70 groups across the United States, from Florida to California, and with delegations from 24 countries, from Indonesia to Romania.

One of the many communities beginning to lift the essence of *Harlem Children's Zone* into their at-risk population is Wilmington, NC.

Mayor Bill Saffo created the *Blue Ribbon Commission on Youth Violence* in 2008 as a way to respond to community concerns about increasing youth violence in New Hanover County.

A major initiative of the Commission is the formation of the *Youth Enrichment Zone (YEZ)*.

The Cape Fear Community College Newsletter noted that the *Zone* is modeled after the Harlem Children's Zone; the *YEZ* is a targeted area of crime, poverty and violence within the community.

"Through coordinated efforts, this long-term project is aimed at increasing the availability of after school, summer, educational, life skills, parenting and violence prevention programs," the College noted.

96

Share, Communicate, Cooperate with Regional Gang Summits

We believe in carefully arranging regular summits among key players in a jurisdiction as well as a regional summit whereby neighboring cities or towns or counties get together to improve communications and cooperative efforts.

Gangs have a way of not limiting themselves to city or county limits or state lines.

Gangs have a way of not limiting themselves to city or county limits or state lines.

In Prince George, British Columbia, key players met for two days in the fall of 2010 about how to combat gangs in the region.

The Anti-Gang Summit took place at a local hotel, providing an agenda that included why youth are drawn to gangs and crime, and what can be done to minimize the risk of youth taking that path.

Organized in the wake of the broad daylight shooting of a young man, the two day event also featured the release of an analysis called *"Kids 'N Crime: Economic Aspects of the Development and Prevention of Criminality among Children."*

That report says the long-term future probabilities of a person following a life of crime or a positive path are determined during pregnancy and the ages from birth to five years.

Also in fall 2010, several agencies came together in Oakland to develop their common strategies to fight gang violence in the city.

The city of Oakland, the Oakland Police Department and the U.S. Department of Justice and other agencies participated.

"The summit comes in the wake of the layoff of 80 police officers and a month after Police Chief Anthony Batts pledged to ask for federal help in reducing violent crime in the city."

❧ 97 ❧

House Calls

The Swiss intervene very personally, going to the homes of troubled kids.

House calls are the latest ammunition in the fight against youth violence in the city of Zurich.

> *... visiting juvenile offenders at home to make their families aware of the severity of the problem.*

As part of a two-year pilot project, youth advocacy workers and police have been visiting juvenile offenders at home to make their families aware of the severity of the problem. Often, parents fail to realize that what their child described as a harmless scuffle may have resulted in a trip to hospital for the victim. Lack of information means the families sometimes play down the crimes, cover them up or simply tolerate them.

This is what the home visits aim to tackle, thereby nipping potential criminal careers in the bud. "The home visit is about sending a signal and being sure that the parents are aware of the incident," said Hansueli Gürber, senior youth advocate of the city of Zurich. It seems to be working.

Gürber told *Swissinfo.ch* most of the juvenile offenders have maintained clean records since the house call.

Such house calls are already common in the Netherlands. Gürber says there are three key aspects to this approach: the direct involvement of families in solving problems; preventing improperly informed parents from shielding their children from the authorities; and closer cooperation between the police and youth advocacy workers.

Information and education about the scope of a criminal offense and its consequences is a "constructive contribution" for the prevention of youth violence, says Gürber. He stresses that most parents appreciate the service, even after initial skepticism. So far only one family has rejected the request for a home visit, he says.

Depending on the case, social workers have already contacted the parents, or it may be that the young person has already served a sentence.

Other Swiss cities appear to be waiting for the results of Zurich's two-year pilot phase.

☙ 98 ❧

Confront Gangs with a Trained Ministers Ride-Along Campaign

The idea of local clergy becoming patrol partners with area police has been carefully tried around the country over the years. This initiative found solid traction in the early 1990's when both Virginia Beach, VA and Daytona Beach, FL were learning to manage large groups of college kids and Greek celebrants swarming into their community for Spring Break. Because many of the partiers were primarily African-American, there were racial overtones to the handling of the disruption.

Virginia Beach police officials found that the Daytona Beach Police Ministers Association served as a buffer and liaison between the police and the community. The association is comprised of area chaplains, both black and white, who represent many faiths.

Ministers ride with police officers throughout the year, but increased their presence during special events such as spring break and college homecomings.

In Daytona, the ministers were trained and sensitized to the rigors of law enforcement and are trained to spot crowd "leaders." As they mingle with groups of young people, they explain what the police are doing and why.

A similar association was created in Virginia Beach in 1990 with assistance from the Daytona Beach program coordinator. Minister training has focused on crowd control, communication skills, basic self-defense, police radio operation, patrol regulations and procedures, counseling, coping with failure, human relations skills, and relating to military personnel.

Volunteer chaplains working between June and September proved to be a valuable police resource, and some chaplains continue working with the police year round.

Chaplains have provided a calming influence and have reduced anxiety during potentially violent situations. In the process, they have fostered a sense of good will between the police, the community, and visitors to the Virginia Beach resort area.

> *Chaplains have provided a calming influence ...*

Houston Chronicle reporter Cynthia Leonor Garza describes how a Bible rests on the Rev. Jose R. Fuentes' lap as he rides in Houston Police Department officer Nina Garcia's patrol car.

Garcia is racing to a convenience store robbery report.

"Fuentes, a pastor at Iglesia Hispana Pentecostes Salem, and a band of more than four dozen "brothers" from area churches are part of the area's program that links police, clergy, apartment managers and city officials with the goal of combating gangs," the *Chronicle* reported.

Police "do what they have to do and we do what we have to do," Fuentes said. "What the law cannot do, but now we can, is to start with God's plan."

Pastors do ride-alongs with police to work as a buffer by offering consolation or emotional and spiritual support to crime or accident victims. Bi-lingual, they also are able to break down any communication barriers.

The *Houston Chronicle* reported that the Fondren-Gulfton area had more homicides and robberies than any other part of the city with four slayings and 107 robbery reports in a single month.

Pastors and police who patrol the area said problems at the complexes include vandalism, robberies, domestic violence, gangs and drugs.

The ministers have been given extensive training. The program began out of Houston Police Division's Fondren Patrol Division, with mostly black and white ministers. Ms. Garza notes that it was targeting specific apartment complexes.

The program recruited pastors who lead the numerous storefront churches in Gulfton, an area with many immigrants from Latin America and Africa.

More than 50 pastors have gone through extensive training, including crisis and gang intervention with plans to do at least 10 hours of police ride-alongs per month.

Program organizers are recruiting couples or individuals to live in the complexes, rent-free, and then organize community events at the complexes.

Many ministerial associations in communities around America organize themselves, undergo training and conduct regular ride-alongs to familiarize themselves with the community challenges.

This is a wonderful first step for ministers by evolving into true street interventionists and making a huge difference in the community.

❧ 99 ❧

Walking School Bus Creates Safer Neighborhoods

In Christchurch, New Zealand, a clever initiative is having significant impact on safer neighborhoods.

The *Walking School Bus* is a group of families living in a neighbourhood who form a walking group to take children in their area to and from school.

Parents or caregivers take turns as "drivers," walking along a set route to and from school, collecting children from designated "bus stops" along the way.

Younger children wear fluorescent jackets or sashes so they are more visible on the streets.

The Christchurch City Council website promotes the initiative.

The *Walking School Bus* operates whenever its suits the families involved. Buses may operate daily or only a couple of days a week.

Some buses may operate every morning and every afternoon taking children to school and from school. Other buses may operate only in the mornings or only in the afternoons or a combination of mornings and afternoons.

The proud promotion of this unique project underscores the value.

"The number of children in a walking school bus depends upon the number of families involved in the neighbourhood. The Council recommends that one adult supervise a maximum of eight children. Many *Walking School Bus* supervisors believe that ratio should be one adult to five or six children, particularly if the bus crosses busy roads or includes young (5- and 6-year-old) children.

The city website explains the process. The *Walking School Bus* has "a set route with pick-up and drop-off points, like bus stops, along the route. The children wait at these points for the walking school bus in the morning or are dropped off at these points in the afternoon. Parents can accompany their children to these pick-up points or wait for them there in the afternoon. The *Walking School Bus* route, with its pick-up and drop-off points, is determined by the families participating."

The benefits are numerous. A *Walking School Bus* can do more than reclaim a neighborhood:

- Provide exercise to improve children's physical health, memory and concentration
- Encourage children to be independent and responsible while being part of a team
- Assist children with learning road safety in a practical and supervised situation
- Encourage families in the neighbourhood to get to know one another

- Save parents' money by not using their vehicle

- Save parents' time when there aren't "driving" the bus

- Reduce traffic congestion around the school and adjoining roads

- Improve the environment for children by reducing vehicle pollution around the school

School officials provide all the tools and the local PTA's generally put together the routes. The key to success is often a keen parent willing to take on the role of the *Walking School Bus* Programme Coordinator.

The first step is to survey parents and caregivers to determine interest in establishing walking school buses.

The city council encourages it with free stuff:

- Fluorescent safety wear for walking school bus drivers and passengers to make the *Walking School Bus* visible to motorists

- Rain gear so that the bus can run even when it is wet

- Fridge magnet contact lists, so that families won't lose contact details for one another

- Leaflets for residents along the walking school bus route

The *California Cities Gang Prevention Network (CCGPN)* reports in its February 2011 Bulletin that Flagstaff Parks and Recreation, the city's Mayor, local businesses, and concerned parents and teachers have created a *Walking School Bus* program there.

... parents and children at Thomas Elementary School "were afraid of walking to school."

The *CCGPN Bulletin* reported that before implementing the program, parents and children at Thomas Elementary School "were afraid of walking to school."

Bushmaster Park, notorious for its criminal activity, was on Thomas Elementary School's boundary and on the walking route of some families. To encourage families and children to walk to school, many individuals and groups came together to create the Bushmaster Neighborhood Committee.

The committee led efforts to reclaim and increase the safety of Bushmaster Park and to establish a *Walking School Bus* program. Park reclamation and safety efforts by the committee included banning the sale of 40-ounce glass bottles of alcohol around the park, an increase in park patrolling, and, finally, establishing a route around the park.

✺ **100** ✺
Honor the Heroes –
Create *Peace Prize* for Interventionists

The California Wellness Foundation each year announces the California Peace Prize Honorees, whereby community leaders each receive $25,000 cash awards for violence prevention work.

In 2010, very special awards were presented in Los Angeles.

Aquil Basheer received the *Peace Prize*. A renowned gang intervention practitioner, he uses his street experience to educate youth and professionals that regularly deal with gang violence in Los Angeles.

Perla Flores received the *Peace Prize*. She develops partnerships that provide local services to sexual assault victims from underserved communities in Morgan Hill and surrounding areas.

Sammy Nunez received the *Peace Prize*. A former gang member, he now works to turn around the lives of at-risk youth, particularly young fathers, in Stockton.

On October 19, 2010 The California Wellness Foundation honored these three community leaders with its 18th annual *California Peace Prize* at a ceremony in Los Angeles. In recognition of their efforts to prevent violence and promote peace, the honorees will each receive a cash award of $25,000.

If a community values a behavior, the community should hold it up in the spotlight for everyone to see and applaud. Gang intervention is a great example of an initiative filled with daily heroes, and the need for recognition speaks to the values of the community.

> *If a community values a behavior, the community should hold it up in the spotlight for everyone to see and applaud.*

"These honorees have helped youth and families devastated by violence and provided essential leadership in organizations that work to make our communities better," said Gary L. Yates, president and CEO of the foundation. "They represent thousands of unsung heroes dedicated to improving the health and well-being of California's youth."

It can also be an organization so honored.

The Florida Gang Investigators Association chose to honor PanZOu Project, Inc. with their President's Award for Gang Prevention in August 2010. PanZOu is a screen printing and embroidery shop dedicated to reducing youth violence by donating all profits to charity.

Make this important work. Honor those that risk it all to save the kids.

Endnotes

Dedication

Leonard Witt, Fighting Gang Violence with Research and Empirical Evidence, June 9, 2011, http://jjie.org/fighting-gangs-research-empirical-evidence/16445.

Part One

Gangs don't just show up in a community. They are allowed to grow there.

The Problem

National Gang Center, http://www.nationalgangcenter.gov.

The Day, NL youth violence plan needs focus, December 26, 2010.

KATU TV, Mayor looking for a few good volunteers to stand up against gangs, June 20, 2011, http://northportland.katu.com/news/community-spirit/mayor-looking-few-good-volunteers-stand-against-gangs/441298.

The Denial

Governor Arnold Schwarzenegger, Press Release, Office of the Governor, State of California Governor Schwarzenegger Announces Initiative to Combat Gang Violence, May 25, 2007, http://www.vpc.org/studies/cayouth.pdf.

PRNewswire-USNewswire, Study Compares Rates of Homicide Victimization for Californians Ages 10 to 24 by County, Race, Ethnicity, Weapon Used, Circumstance, and Location, Jan. 31, 2011.

World Vision Headquarters, Press Release, "New Study: Almost Seven out of Ten Americans Agree: Gang Violence among Youth Increasing Because of Current Economy," June 10, 2010, http://www.worldvision.org/content.nsf/about/20100610-YEP-youth-survey.

Urban Institute Justice Policy Center, Families Left Behind: The Hidden Costs of Incarceration and Re-entry, rev. 2005.

Just How Bad Can This Get?

Tico Times, "Guatemala City Grapples with Gang Terrorism," April 15, 2011, http://www.ticotimes.net/News/Top-Story/Guatemala-City-grapples-with-gang-terrorism__.

James Mills, The Underground Empire: Where Crime and Governments Embrace, (Garden City NY: Doubleday, 1986), 1165 pages.

Neil Puffett, Children & Young People Now, " Met reveals rise in serious youth violence," January 19, 2011, http://www.cypnow.co.uk/news/ByDiscipline/Youth-Justice/1050245/Met-reveals-rise-serious-youth-violence/.

Nick Meo, In Amsterdam Telegraph.co.uk, December 29, 2008.

Paola Totaro, Sydney Morning Herald, Fear and loathing in the city of rage, http://www.smh.com.au/world/fear-and-loathing-in-the-city-of-rage-20110610-1fwxq.html.

Families Left Behind: The Hidden Costs of Incarceration and Re-entry, Urban Institute Justice Policy Center, rev. 2005). June 11, 2011.

How Are Communities Responding?

Jack Calhoun, The California Cities Gang Prevention Network, Success Depends on Mayors' Leadership, http://ci.santa-rosa.ca.us/doclib/Documents/The%20California%20Cities%20Gang%20Prevention%20Network%20Success%20Depends%20on%20Mayors.pdf.

Mara H. Gottfried, Group's gang prevention efforts in St. Paul, November 21, 2010, http://www.twincities.com/.

Matt Fleischer, WitnessLA.Com, http://witnessla.com/gangs/2010/admin/follow-the-gang-money-part-ii-the-interventionists-by-matt-fleischer/.

Rocky Mount Telegram, "Edgecombe Nash, N.C. Gang Assessment," June 5, 2010, Rockymounttelegram.com.

What Is Working

City of San Jose, CA website, http://www.sanjoseca.gov/clerk/CommitteeAgenda/PSFSS/20110616/PS20110616d1.pdfEligible Services List.

City of San Jose, CA website, http://www.sanjoseca.gov/clerk/
Agenda/20110621/20110621_0249.pdf.

Tracey Kaplan, Sean Webby and Mark Gomez, Mercury News, San Jose's 20 homicides in 2010
lowest in 10 years, January 2, 2011, http://www.orovillemr.com/ci_16983897?source=rss_viewed.

Delmarvanow.com, $324K Grant Keeps Safe Streets Going, http://www.delmarvanow.com/
apps/pbcs.dll/article?AID=2011107070372.

Tom Emswiller, Committed, Collaborative and Community-based: An Overview of Gang and
Youth Violence Prevention in San Jose, CA.

Office of the Attorney General, Commonwealth of Virginia, http://www.oag.state.va.us/key_
issues/gangs/gangs_G.R.I.P._program.html.

People to People, Ten Years 1992-2002 Liberty, Equality, Diversity - The Struggle of Democracy
in America Hits Home, Excerpt from Dr. Samuel Proctor's Speech to People to People, October
31, 1995.

Jack Calhoun, Success Depends on Mayors' Leadership, The California Cities Gang Prevention
Network http://www.westerncity.com/Western-City/October-2009/The-California-Cities-Gang-
Prevention-Network-Success-Depends-on-Mayors-rsquo-Leadership/.

Tim Craig and Mike DeBonis, Washington Post, Confusion Over Possible Peaceoholics Contract,
D.C. Wire, August 17, 2010, http://voices.washingtonpost.com/dc/2010/08/confusion_over_
possible_peaceo.html.

Matthew Fleischer, Witness LA, Follow the Gang Money, August 16, 2010, http://witnessla.com/
gangs/2010/admin/follow-the-gang-money-part-1-by-matthew-fleischer/.

Part Two

100 Ways to Stop Gangs from Taking Away Your Community

1- Proclaim a New Social Norm: Citizens Set the Strategy – Executive Summary

Governor Arnold Schwarzenegger, Press Release, Office of the Governor, State of California May
25, 2007, Governor Schwarzenegger Announces Initiative to Combat Gang Violence.

2- Put a Halt to Community Denial

The United States Department of Justice Office of Public Affairs, Federal Agencies Host National
Forum on Youth Violence Prevention, October 5, 2010, http://www.justice.gov/opa/pr/2010/
October/10-ag-1120.html.

3- Develop Overall Community Ownership of the Plan

http://www.uncg.edu/csr/pdfs/ojjdpguilfordcountygangassessment_finalversion3_with_appendices.pdf.

MyFox8, Report: More Than 1,300 Gang Members in Guilford Co., December 10, 2010, http://northhighpoint.myfox8.com/category/story-categories/crime.

4- View the Seeds of the Problem

http://www.nationalgangcenter.gov/Content/Documents/Assessment-Guide/Assessment-Guide.pdf.

Juvenile Justice Bulletin 9, Office of Justice Programs, Office of Juvenile Justice and Delinquency Prevention, Washington, DC.

Howell, 2009, p. 151. Sage Publications, Inc. 10 Juvenile Justice Bulletin.

5- Pick a Civic Group Champion

California Cities Gang Reduction Network Strategy paper, http://www.nic.org.

6- Empower Your Mayor to Lead or Elect a New One Who Will

J. Robert Flores, Best Practices to Address Community Gang Problems, OJJDP (2007).

Jack Calhoun, The Network, Success Depends on Mayors' Leadership, http://www.westerncity.com/Western-City/October-2009/The-California-Cities-Gang-Prevention-Network-Success-Depends-on-Mayors-rsquo-Leadership/.

7- Reach Deep into the Community for Your Plan

http://www.CCGPN.org/.

Jack Calhoun, The California Cities Gang Prevention Network, Success Depends on Mayors' Leadership, http://www.westerncity.com/Western-City/October-2009/The-California-Cities-Gang-Prevention-Network-Success-Depends-on-Mayors-rsquo-Leadership/.

8- Separate, Empower the Operational Council

9- Focus on the Worst Problems First

The Boston Strategy to Prevent Youth Violence, Gun Buy Back, http://www.sasnet.com/bostonstrategy/story/05_actions.html.

FindYouthInfo.gov, www.findyouthinfo.gov/youthviolence.

California Cities Gang Prevention Network, www.CCGPN.org.

10- Create the Vision

The California Cities Gang Prevention Network Strategy Paper, Implementing a Citywide Gang Violence Reduction Strategy, Three Promising Examples, http://www.nlc.org.

11- Tear Down the Walls - Relationships Matter

12- Fund Measured Programs That Work

Gabriel A. Morgan, Sr., Sheriff Newport News City Sheriff's Office, Testimony to U.S. House of Representatives, Committee on Appropriations, Subcommittee on Commerce, Justice, Science, and Related Agencies Hearing on FY 2012 Appropriations March 11, 2011.

Ryan Howes, In Therapy: A User's Guide to Psychotherapy, The Definition of Insanity is... Perseverance vs. Perseveration, July 27, 2009, http://www.psychologytoday.com/blog/in-therapy.

City of San Jose, San Jose Council Agenda 06-21-11, http://www.sanjoseca.gov/clerk/Agenda/20110621/20110621_0249.pdf.

13- Expect Resistance After Years of Heads Buried in the Sand

Post-Bulletin, Twenty Years of Street Gangs in Rochester: A Timeline, January 29, 2011, archives http://www.postbulletin.com/news/stories/display.php?id=1443161.

14- Harness Faith-Based Organizations

Sunita Vijayan, The Californian, http://www.thecalifornian.com/article/20110414/NEWS01/104140313Local News.

California Cities Gang Prevention Network, Developing a Successful Street Outreach Program: Recommendations and Lessons Learned, http://www.*CCGPN*.org/Publications/Street%20Outreach%20Final%2010.20.09.pdf.

http://www.boston*tenpoint*.org/programs.php.

http://www.seopressreleases.com/after school-program-develops-mind-character/8823.

http://www.aetv.com/the-peacemaker/index.jsp.

http://www.*CCGPN*.org/Publications/Street%20Outreach%20Final%2010.20.09.pdf.

ABCTV7, June 7, 2010, http://law.rightpundits.com.

Youth Alive! http://www.youthalive.org.

15- Set Clear Goals from 10,000 Feet

City of Minneapolis, Blueprint for Action, http://www.ci.minneapolis.mn.us/dhfs/yv.asp.

FindYouthInfo.com, www.findyouthinfo.gov/youthviolence.

California Cities Gang Prevention Network, www.*CCGPN*.org.

16- Measurement Is Everything - Indicators to Steer By

Jack Calhoun, Western City magazine, http://www.westerncity.com/Western-City/October-2009/
The-California-Cities-Gang-Prevention-Network-Success-Depends-on-Mayors-rsquo-Leadership/.

17- Assure an Independent Audit

18- Conduct Baseline Survey of Student Perceptions

Virginia Bridges, *Durham News*, Students say gangs in school a problem http://www.
thedurhamnews.com/2011/02/16/205628/students-say-gangs-in-school-a.html.

http://www2.independenttribune.com/news/2010/oct/22/council-hears-cabarrus-gang-
assessment-ar-473607/.

Jessica Groover, Prevention Council hears Cabarrus gang assessment, October 22, 2010 Concord
NC.

http://www.pnj.com/article/20101222/NEWS01/101222005/McCollum-releases-gang-study.

19- Make Sure the News Media Understands

Calgary Herald, http://www.calgaryherald.com/news/Ganging+gangs/3950177/story.
html#ixzz17eAf86Aa.

20- Train Community Leaders as well as the Providers

Christopher N. Osher, *Denver and the West,* Denver Post, December 3, 2010, Denverpost.com.

21- Communicate Aggressively, Continuously

Will Jason, Marin Independent Journal, Novato officials take aim at gang activity January 17,
2011, http://www.marinij.com/marinnews/ci_17019273.

22- Partner with Your Local University

Matthew Fleischer, Follow the Gang Money: Part One: Are LA's Gang Prevention Strategies
Excluding the Kids Who Most Need Our Help? http://witnessla.com/gangs/2010/admin/follow-
the-gang-money-part-1-by-matthew-fleischer/.

Los Angeles *Community Policing* website, http://www.lacp.org/2010-Articles-Main/081810-
CriticalLook-MayorsGang-ReductionProg.

Julia Reynolds, Monterey County, The Herald New ways to cope with gangs: Officials eye
gathering data, prisoner outreach, Herald Salinas Bureau, http://www.montereyherald.com/local/
ci_16303140?nclick_check=1.

23- Reconnect Community and Schools

Annual Report 2004-2005, Celebrating 25 years of Service to the Baton Rouge Community,
http://icare.ebrschools.org.

The United States Conference of Mayors, Best Practices Guide on At-Risk Youth and High School Drop Out Prevention, by the Conference of Mayors r\Research/Education Foundation, http://www.usmayors.org/bestpractices/ary08.pdf.

24- Publish a Gang Awareness Resource to the Community
Province of Manitoba, Manitoba Justice, Project Gang-Proof, April 2007, http://www.gov.mb.ca/justice/safe/gangproof/index.html.

25- Expand After School Activities, *Police Athletic League*
Police Athletic League of Las Vegas, http://www.snpal.com/.

Megan Rolland, The Oklahoman, December 3, 2010, http://newsok.com/okc-gang-prevention-group-keeps-kids-out-of-trouble-and-in-school/article/3520122#ixzz17McdLoEw.

26- Seed Each High School with Student Leaders Trained in Mediation, Inclusiveness, Race Relations, Non-Violence
Jennifer Feals, Seacoast Online, January 17, 2011, http://m.seacoastonline.com/apps/pbcs.dll/article?aid=/20110117/NEWS/101170323&template=wapart.

AMNEW CASTLE.

27- Let the Kids Design Stop Bullying Programs
Time Magazine, http://www.time.com/time/magazine/article/0,9171,2024210,00.html.

University of Cambridge Research News, New Ways to Reduce Bullying and Youth Violence, July 6, 2011, http://www.cam.ac.uk/research/news/new-ways-to-reduce-bullying-and-youth-violence/.

Samieh Shalash, Black Out Bullying' week emphasizing being kind to others, Daily Press, December 15, 2010, sshalash@dailypress.com.

Virginia Center for Inclusive Communities, http://www.inclusiveva.org/.

GABGS Street Gang Awareness for Families and Communities, Province of Manitoba, Canada, Third Edition.

Julie Gray, The Huffington Post, http://www.huffingtonpost.com/julie-gray/bullies-it-takes-a-villag_b_763485.html.

Sara Bernard, 5Apps that Could Help to Stop Cyberbullying, December 10, 2010, Flickr: The Daring Librarian.

http://www.cfchildren.org/programs/str/overview/The *Steps to Respect* program, http://www.product-finder.net/cfchildren/Steps-to-Respect-Complete-School-Program.asp.

28- Small School Efforts Pay Dividends
Julie Gray, http:// www.twitter.com/Julie_Gray.

April Thompson, WREG TV, Memphis City Schools Program Targets, January 3, 2011.

Amanda Bellanger/KTAR, Sandra Haros/KTAR, and Kevin Tripp/KTAR, *WREG-TV* Bullying a concern for schools, politicians, October 25, 2010.

29- Deflect Violence with Non-confrontational Conversations

Yonkers Peace Keeper will patrol streets, lohud.com, http://www.lohud.com/article/20110630/ NEWS02/106300383/Yonkers-Peace-Keepers-will-patrol-streets-try-defuse-conflicts?odyssey =mod%7Cnewswell%7Ctext%7CNews%7Cp

Annie Sweeney, Chicago Tribune Unit visits high schools for nonconfrontational conversations October 15, 2010, http://articles.chicagotribune.com/2010-10-15/news/ct-met-gang-interventions-20101015_1_student-council-gang-officers-troubled-teens.

30- Create *Safe Street* Teams

Jen Maconochie, Boston Police Department, http://www.cityofboston.gov.

Anthony A. Braga, and Brenda Bond, Policing Crime and Disorder Hot Spots: A Randomized Controlled Trial, American Society of Criminology, 46 (3): 577-578.

Find Youth Info.Gov, http://www.findyouthinfo.gov/youthviolence.

California Cities Gang Prevention Network, http://www.CCGPN.org.

31- Camps Build Trust with Police

The *United States Conference of Mayors* Best Practices Guide on At-Risk Youth and High School Drop Out Prevention, by the Conference of Mayors \Research/Education Foundation supported by the U.S. Department of Justice and the Bill and Melinda Gates Foundation grants http://www. usmayors.org/bestpractices/ary08.pdf.

32- *Deliver* Creative School Interventions in Elementary, Middle and High School

Brandon Darnell, Sacramento Press, Attorney General Addresses gang problem in Sacramento, April 19, 2011, http://www.sacramentopress.com/headline/49371/Attorney_General_addresses_ gang_problem.

Bay City News, November 19, 2010.

El Guardian, http://www.guardian.bz/all-news/59-other-news/2757-launch-of-gang-resistance-education-training-great-program-belize.

Tristan Tuckett, 660 News, Calgary, Canada New gang reduction strategy to be announced Dec 06, 2010 Police and the province plan to take a new approach in the fight against gangs.

The Times and Democrat, http://www.thetandd.com/lifestyles/article_d3c13dfd-30a3-52d0-bab2-ae8360d833de.htm.

Foon Rhee, The Sacramento Bee, http://www.sacbee.com/2011/01/17/3329049/head-of-sacramento-boys-girls.html#ixzz1BOaXDvbT January 17, 2011.

Foon Rhee, The Sacramento Bee, January 30, 2011.

Julie Gray on Twitter: www.twitter.com/Julie_Gray.

April Thompson, *WREG TV*, Memphis City Schools Program Targets, January 3, 2011. http://www.wreg.com.

Amanda Bellanger/KTAR, Sandra Haros/KTAR, Kevin Tripp/KTAR, *WREG-TV*, Bullying a concern for schools, politicians, October 25, 2010, http://www.wreg.com.

G.R.E.A.T. program website, http://www.great-online.org.

33- Gang Exit Centers – Rescuing Kids from Gangs

Astwood Criminal and Social Justice Strategists website, http://www.astwood.ca/ozzysgarage.html.

Public Safety Canada, National Crime Prevention Centre, https://www.publicsafety.gc.ca/prg/cp/ml/index-eng.aspx.

Heather Polischuk, Leader-Post, RAGS rescues Regina youths from gangs, February 28, 2011.

http://www.leaderpost.com/news/RAGS+rescues+Regina+youths+from+gangs/4357309/story.html#ixzz1FHd7zmO6Robesonian.com.

http://www.robesonian.com/pages/full_story/push?article-New+center+takes+on+youth+crime+in+county%20&id=11664167&instance=home_news_lead

Canadian Training Institute website, http://www.cantraining.org/.

34- Middle Schoolers Targeted as Key Rural Strategy

Bob Shiles, The Robesonian, New center takes on youth crime in county, heartlandpublications.com.

35- Generate Amazing Results with Restorative Justice in Schools

Julia Dahl, The Crime Report The Talking Cure: Keeping Kids Out of the Juvenile Justice System, February 16, 2011.

http://www.salina.com/News/Story/New-Stop-Snitching-feature-for-Sunday-111210.

Saint Croix Valley Restorative Justice, http://www.scvrjp.org/.

http://www.windycitizen.com/chicago/2010/12/22/high-hopes-campaign-launch?cs=latest.

http://www.windycitizen.com, November 28, 2010.

http://www.myfoxchicago.com/dpp/news/elections/miguel-del-valle-chicago-mayor-issue-stance-on-education-20110125.

Bravetta Hassell, Medill Reports Chicago, CPS discipline rule changes have brought down suspensions – but not enough, critics say, February 17, 2011, http://news.medill.northwestern. edu/chicago/news.aspx?id=178951.

VCRJ website, http:www.vcrj.org.

Sylvia Clute, Genuine Justice: The Virginia Center for Restorative Justice, January 13, 2011, http://www.genuinejustice.com/.

Sylvia Clute, Beyond Vengeance, Beyond Duality, Hampton Roads. June 16, 2010, http:// www.alternet.org/story/147199/utter_failure%3B_it%27s_time_to_rethink_the_prison_ system?page=entire.

36- Teach Business English, Social Skills in Elementary School

Achievable Dream Academy website, http://www.achievabledream.org/site/ PageServer?pagename=dream_program.

CBS News, http://www.cbsnews.com/stories/2005/01/13/earlyshow/contributors/ melindamurphy/main666637.shtml?CMP=ILC-SearchStories.

37- Take Truancy Interventions to the Homes

Maryland, Montgomery County's student truancy rate called into question, November 17, 2010, http://www.Gazette.net.

FindYouthInfo.com, www.findyouthinfo.gov/youthviolence.

California Cities Gang Prevention Network, visit www.CCGPN.org.

38- Go with Special Efforts to Target Hard to Reach Hispanic Youth

North County Times, - The Californian. http://www.nctimes.com/.

High Point Enterprise, Local gangs can say "adios" to more than 150 students who recently graduated from a gang prevention program in High Point, July 11, 2010. www.hpe.com.

Bi-National Health Week website, http://binationalhealthweek.org/.

Carlos Villatoro, Napa Valley Register, June 20, 2010, http://napavalleyregister.com/news/local/ article_b93dcb62-7c19-11df-8bf6-001cc4c002e0.html.

39- Train School Board Members and "Student Advocates"

http://www.streetgangs.com/news/102610_monterey_educators_on_gangs.

40- De-Glamorize Gang Culture

David Clouston, Salina Journal, Code of Silence, November 21, 2010, http://www. Salina.com.

Elizabeth Comeau, Stephen Smith, Violence prevention named top public health priority, January 14, 2011, http://www.boston.com/news/health/blog/2011/01/violence_preven.html.

WBRC Television, Birmingham celebrates 100 days without youth violence deaths January 17, 2011, http://www.myfoxal.com/Global/story.asp?S=1385432.

41- Consider Fifteen Absolutely Essential School Anti-Gang Initiatives

Leif Knutson, FOX 9 News, Mpls Mayor Rybak Named After school Champion in Washington http://www.myfoxtwincities.com/dpp/news/Rybak-Named-After school-Champion-in-Washington-may-17-2011#ixzz1Mf2Jo9EI hington-may-17-2011#ixzz1Mf1SSanE.

Juvenile Justice Bulletin, December 2010, http://www.ncjrs.gov/pdffiles1/ojjdp/231116.pdfA.

42- Challenge and Reward At-Risk Elementary and Middle School Kids Directly

Orange County District Attorney Press Release http://orangecountyda.com/home/index.asp?page=8&recordid=2060&returnurl=index.asp%3Fpage%3D8.

43- D.A.R.E. Works - Bring It Back. Strengthen It.

Barri Bronston, Times-Picayune, Tuesday, November 30, 2010, bbronston@timespicayune.com.

44- Deploy the Boys & Girls Clubs in Targeted Schools

Denise Madrid, The Porterville Recorder, Local nonprofits awarded $20K in grant funds, December 8, 2010, http://www.recorderonline.com/articles/county-47318-grant-tulare.html.

Cara R. Anthony, The Daily Press, The Boys & Girls Clubs of the Virginia Peninsula's newest facility set to open in York County, http://articles.dailypress.com/2010-06-26/news/dp-nws-maki ngadifference-0627-20100626_1_girls-clubs-new-club-junior-staff-member.

45- Lights On After School

Lynn Sweet, ChicagoforRahm.com, Announces Plan to Expand After school Opportunities and Keep Our Children Safe, January 4, 2011, http://www.chicagoforrahm.com/news/press-releases/rahm-emanuel-announces-plan-to-expand-after school-opportunities-and-keep-our-children-safe.

46- Remove Graffiti Immediately

Laurel Carson, The Lakeland Times, UHS group makes mark on gang-related graffiti Group hopes efforts will continue, http://www.lakelandtimes.com/main.asp?SectionID=9&SubSectionID=9&ArticleID=11973.

Rachel Cavanaugh, Woodburn Independent (Oregon), Cleanup kits available for graffiti http://www.woodburnindependent.com/news/2011/January/20/Local.News/cleanup.kits.available.for.graffiti/news.aspx.

47- Hire At-Risk Youth

City of Minneapolis, http://www.ci.minneapolis.mn.us/cped/stepup.asp.

FindYouthInfo.com, www.findyouthinfo.gov/youthviolence.

California Cities Gang Prevention Network, www.CCGPN.org.

City of San Diego, http://www.sandiego.gov/gangcommission/pdf/minutes91610.pdf.

http://www.barriosunidos.net/buproductions.htm.

Courtney Subramanian, Medill News, Gang-infested neighborhoods to receive $50 million shot in the arm, October 7, 2010, http://news.medill.northwestern.edu/chicago/news. aspx?id=170081 Story Retrieval Date: January 23, 2011.

http://www.scpr.org/news/2010/09/14/homeboy-industries-la-county-partner-risk-youth-pr/.

http://reference-and-education.foroneworld.com/2011/01/08/watch-toronto-gangs.

48- GPS Gang Members like High-risk Sex Offenders

Mike Manzoni, Mysouthwestga.com, Gang task force meets, discusses juvenile crime, June 23, 2011, http://www.mysouthwestga.com/news/story.aspx?id=633137ALBANY.

Jude Joffe-Block, Berkeley News, California leads the country in GPS supervision http://berkeley. news21.com/behindbars/parole/tracked/.

http://www.lawofficer.com/article/tactics-and-weapons/alternatives-incarceration.

http://www.lawofficer.com/article/tactics-and-   weapons/alternatives-incarceration.

49- Hold Regular Gang Prevention Community Meetings

Jamica Ashley, Tarboro News, August 18, 2010, Public input makes a difference - Seminar focus on gang awareness, prevention.

U.S. Department of Justice on Law Enforcement and Gangs, October 2010, http://www.ncjrs. gov/yviolence/youthgangs.html.

50- Engineer Second Chances for Exiting Gang Members

http://www.ezpolicyblog.com/CalGRIP/.

Tami Le, Southern Maryland Online, December 14, 2010, http://somd.com/news/ headlines/2010/12951.shtml.

51- Bring Civil Suits against Gang Members

Chicago Tribune, Suing gang members works, police and prosecutors say http://www.chicagotribune.com/news/local/ct-met-street-gang-lawsui ts-0118-20110117,0,1316406.story.

52- Open and Program Your Recreation Centers at Night

City of San Diego, http://www.sandiego.gov/gangcommission/pdf/oct2010minutes.pdf.

California Cities Gang Prevention Network, http://www.*CCGPN*.org/Publications/CA%20 Cities%20Bulletin%2021.pdf.

Mark Gomez, Mercury News, Nighttime basketball at San Jose community center provides alternative to gang life, December 19, 2010.

53- Send a Strong Message to Teens That They Are Important to the Community

City of El Paso, http://www.ci.el-paso.tx.us/mayor/teens.asp.

54- Develop a Support Program for Parents of Gang Members

Thomas Watkins, Associated Press, Parents of gang members sent to classes, December 12, 2010, http://www.azcentral.com/news/articles/2010/12/12/20101212-Gang-parents-attend-classes-ON. html.

http://www.care2.com/causes/education/blog/gang-moms-and-dads-ordered-to-parenting-classes/.

55- Create a Youth-Led Movement against Violence

http://www.leaveoutviolence.org/en/programs/.

http://www.leaveoutviolence-us.org/about.htm.

56- Use Great Resources Well – But Don't Over Complicate Your Plan

National Gang Center website, http://www.nationalgangcenter.gov/SPT/Planning-Implementation.

Index to Site Content, National Gang Center, http://www.nationalgangcenter.gov/Site-Index.

57- Strengthen Prevention with the Arts

Public Broadcasting Service, http://www.pbs.org/wnet/tavissmiley/reports/2010/12/el-sistema-from-venezuela-to-the-united-states.html.

Yara Simón, NewsWorks, http://www.newsworks.org/index.php/flexicontent/item/14132-us-attorney-kicks-of-gun-violence-education-pilot-in-west-oak-lane/.

Shakespeare Center website, http://www.shakespearecenter.org/index.asp?PageTypeId=3&PageDet ailId=131&PageSectionId=4.

Ed Terrell, *BCTV*.Org, Stop the violence' is theme for graffiti art contest in Reading, June 21, 2011, http://www.bctv.org/citizen_reports/article_5019141e-9c31-11e0-99fe-001cc4c03286. html.

58- Cool Bus Picks Up Kids for After school Activities

Visalia Times Delta, http://www.visaliatimesdelta.com/article/20070716/NEWS01/707160315/
Is-the-Loop-bus-working-Just-about-everyone-says-ye.

59- Create Interventions for the 19- to 25-Year-Olds

Greg Saulmon, The Republican, Springfield receives $500K for violence prevention in latest award
through Sen. Charles E. Shannon Community Safety Initiative, January 16, 2010.

Best Kept Secret, http://www.linkedin.com/pub/best-kept-secret-stop-the-violence/17/356/9a1.

Brandon Darnell, Sacramento Press, Attorney General addresses gang problem in Sacramento,
April 19, 2011, http://www.sacramentopress.com/headline/49371/Attorney_General_addresses_
gang_problem.

60- Proclaim Youth Violence Prevention Week

http://www.ci.minneapolis.mn.us/news/20100323YouthViolencePrevention.asp.

61- Deploy Budget Surplus to Build Neighborhood Centers

OJJDP Bulletin, Overview of Gang Prevention Research, December 14, 2010 http://www.ojjdp.
gov/enews/10juvjust/101221.html.

Charlotte News, Gang Prevention Program Opens, http://charlotte.news14.com/content/top_
stories/642570/gang-prevention-program-opens-in-charlotte.

Sommer Brokaw, Charlotte Post, June 30, 2011, Greenville Center re-opens to house agencies,
http://www.thecharlottepost.com/index.php?src=news&srctype=detail&category=News&ref
no=3755.

OrangeCountyFL.net, http://www.orangecountyfl.net/YourLocalGovernment/
CountyDepartments/FamilyServices/CitizensCommissionforChildren/tabid/2392/Default. aspx.

Brandon Lowery, NCTimes, Police, Community give kids alternative to gangs, February 6, 2011,
http://www.nctimes.com/news/local/oceanside/3d76d102-c1db-5f49-98a8-7788e37f33f4.html
Sunday.

Neighborhood Centers, Inc. website, http://www.neighborhood-centers.org/en-us/default.aspx.

http://www.pps.k12.or.us/schools-c/profiles/profile_out.php?id=.

Tom Tolan, Milwaukee Wisconsin Journal Sentinel, July 11, 2100, http://www.jsonline.com/
news/milwaukee/125276514.html.

 http://www.districtadministration.com/viewarticle.aspx?articleid=2384.

Jodie Reyna, Reedley Exponent, Boys & Girls Club closer to reality, November 4, 2010, http://
www.reedleyexponent.com.

62- Operate a Confidential Telephone Tip line

David Macaulay, The Daily Press, January 19, 2011, http://articles.dailypress.com/2011-01-19/news/dp-nws-youth-violence-20110119_1_youth-violence-providers-phone-line

http://www.huffingtonpost.com/daniel-gross/gun-violence-prevention-b_b_814052.html.

Press Release, Public Affairs Department, city of Raleigh, NC, June 14, 2010.

63- Develop Violent Crime Suppression Teams

Nadia Moharib, Calgary Sun, Police hound criminals from city nightspots January 8, 2011. http://newsystocks.com/news/3923836.

64- Operate a Confidential Texting Program

Deborah L. Cohen, Reuters.com, Entrepreneur closes door on criminals, February 17, 2010, http://reut.rs/fLiYv1.

http://www.SMSCrimeTips.com.

65- Create Sporting Events Especially for At-Risk Kids

Cheryl Chumley, Inside NOVA, January 18, 2011, http://www2.insidenova.com/news/2011/jan/18/gang-prevention-summit-exposes-problems-facing-off-ar-782467/.

Santa Cruz Sentinel, November 28, 2010.

66- Bring in the Hospitals for Powerful Interventions

Bob Groves, The Records, How to spot a gang member, February 11, 2009, http://www.northjersey.com/

http://www.ojjdp.gov/pubs/gun_violence/profile58.html.

Pauline W Chen, New York Times, MD Breaking the Cycle of Violence, January 13, 2011, http://www.nytimes.com/2011/01/13/health/13chen.html?emc=eta1.

Angela Wolf, Jack Calhoun, Hunter Smith, Linh Vuong, Vanessa Hisert, The California Cities Gang Prevention Network, December 2009 Bulletin.

Youth Alive! http://www.youthalive.org/cinc/#results.

Judith Bonderman, U.S. Department of Justice, Office for Victims of Crime, Working with Victims of Gun Violence, Washington, D.C., 2001.

Sara Geake, NCN9 Nebraska Central News, Hospital Leads GI Gang Prevention, http://www.1011now.com/home/headlines/Hearing_Addresses_Gang_Prevention_107003058.html Grand Island, November 9, 2010.

Tony Smith, KPTM TV, Metro Area Medical Centers Fighting against Gang Violence http://www.kptm.com/Global/story.asp?S=14029033.

67- Form a Prisoner Re-entry Council

Office of Justice Programs, Weekly News Brief, Office of Justice Programs, http://bjs.ojp.usdoj.gov.

Brandon Darnell, Sacramento Press, Attorney General addresses gang problem in Sacramento, April 19, 2011, http://www.sacramentopress.com/headline/49371/Attorney_General_addresses_gang_problem.

Gabriel A. Morgan, Sr., Sheriff, Newport News City Sheriff's Office, Testimony to U.S. House of Representatives, Committee on Appropriations, Subcommittee on Commerce, Justice, Science, and Related Agencies Hearing on FY 2012 Appropriations, March 11, 2011.

California Cities Gang Prevention Network, Bulletin, April 2010.

Re-entry Council of the city of San Francisco, http://sfre-entry.com/.

The Crest Center website, http://www.crestcenter.org/.

Anthony A. Braga, Anne M. Piehl, and David Hureau, California Cities Gang Prevention Network, Findings from an external evaluation completed in 2008 by Controlling Violent Offenders Released to the Community: An Evaluation of the Boston Re-entry Initiative, 2008. www.CCGPN.org.

FindYouthInfo.com, National Forum on Youth Violence Prevention, www.findyouthinfo.gov/youthviolence.

68- Create a Focused Strike Team for a Hardened Base of Crime

Bob Glissman, Omaha World Herald, October 30, 2010, http://www.owh.com/.

Christopher N Osher, The Denver Post, $2.2 million federal grant to help Denver combat gang violence, December 16, 2010, http://www.denverpost.com/news/ci_16765373#ixzz17MW7H3Ey.

Minnesota HEALS (Hope, Education, and Law and Safety) - Minneapolis and St. Paul, MN. http://www.ojjdp.gov/pubs/gun_violence/profile07.html.

69- Work with Your State Elected Officials. Much Can Be Done

GovMonitor, Governor of Massachusetts, Massachusetts Invests $4.4 Million to Fight Youth Violence, January 25, 2011, http://www.thegovmonitor.com/world_news/united_states/massachusetts-invests-4-4-million-to-fight-youth-violence-45332.html.

Commonwealth of Virginia, http://www.governor.virginia.gov/Issues/ExecutiveOrders/pdf/EO_28.pdf.

70- Create Special Events to Raise Funds and Awareness

Orangeburg, S.C. Times and Democrat, November 17, 2010, http://www.thetandd.com/news/local/article_8796a626-f1e2-11df-a43e-001cc4c03286.html.

Achievable Dream Academy website, http://www.achievabledream.org/site/PageServer.

71- Get Business Fired Up

Minnesota HEALS (Hope, Education, and Law and Safety) - Minneapolis and St. Paul, MN, http://www.ojjdp.gov/pubs/gun_violence/profile07.html.

72- Study CeaseFire as a Strategic Option

City of Durham, NC website, http://pac2durham.org/minutes/january-2010-minutes.

Wikipedia, CeaseFire, http://en.wikipedia.org/wiki/Operation_.

David M. Kennedy, Anthony A. Braga, Anne M. Piehl, Elin J. Waring, Reducing Gun Violence: The Boston Gun Project's CeaseFire Operation , Measuring the Impact of CeaseFire Operation, September 2001, NCJ 188741.

U.S. Department of Justice, Research Report, http://www.ncjrs.gov/pdffiles1/nij/188741.pdf.

George Tita, K. Jack Riley, and Peter Greenwood, From Boston to Boyle Heights: The Process and Prospects of a 'Pulling Levers' Strategy in a Los Angeles Barrio.

Scott H. Decker, Policing Gangs and Youth Violence, ed., Belmont, CA: Wadsworth- Thomson Learning, 2003: 102–130.

George Tita, K. Jack Riley, Greg Ridgeway, Clifford Grammich, Allan Abrahamse, and Peter W. Greenwood, Reducing Gun Violence: Results from an Intervention in East Los Angeles, Santa Monica, CA: RAND Corporation, 2003.

National Institute of Justice, Research Report: Reducing Gun Violence - Operation in Los Angeles, February 2005, http://www.ncjrs.gov/pdffiles1/nij/192378.pdf.

Tio Hardiman, February 10, 2011, http://www.huffingtonpost.com/tio-hardiman/-success-beyond-_b_821380.html.

Katy Reckdahl, The Times-Picayune NOLA.com, New program is designed to stop the cycle of gun violence in New Orleans, April 03, 2011, http://blog.nola.com/crime_impact/print. html?entry=/2011/04/new_program_is_designed_to_sto.html.

73- Mainstream At-Risk Kids into Normal Channels

Christina Killion Valdez, The Post-Bulletin, Many groups work to combat gangs in Rochester Jan 31, 2011, http://www.gangsummit.com/speakers.html.

The 2010 Canada-U.S. Gang Summit, http://www.gangsummit.com/Assets/Gang_Summit_Brochure.pdf.

74- Create a Season of Peace Campaign

TenPoint Coalition website, http://www.bostontenpoint.org/programs.php.

More than 400 people attended "Season of Peace" events over the weekend as clergy launch a youth violence prevention movement in Norristown.

The Times Herald, Norristown Ministerium Hosts Season of Peace Event June 25-26, http://timesherald.com/articles/2011/06/23/news/doc4e03afd854c7b297565727.txt.

75- Offer Life Altering Tattoo Removal

The Youth Removal Project, www.youthremoval.org.

Traci Neal, Catholic Digest, Giving Gang Members a Reason to Hope, http://www.catholicdigest.com/articles/people/q_and_a/2010/08-31/giving-gang-members-a-reason-to-hope.

76- Call in a Warning to the Gang Leaders

Dave Vieser, Charlotte Observer, First Results of Gang Initiative, November 21, 2010, http://www.charlotteobserver.com/2010/11/21/1849240/first-results-of-gang-initiative.html#ixzz162Q1PN7v.

City of Pittsburgh, http://www.city.pittsburgh.pa.us/mayor.

David M. Kennedy, http://www.jjay.cuny.edu/departments/criminal_justice/faculty.php?key=%5Bemail%5D='dakennedy%40jjay.cuny.edu'.

Sophia Tareen, Associated Press, Chicago police chief criticized for 'gang summit,' September 2, 2010, http://www.chicagodefender.com/article-8661-chicago-police-warn-gang-leaders-to-stop-violence.html.

77- Enforce Curfew with Sweeps

City of Arlington, VA, http://www.arlingtonva.us/departments/JuvenileDomesticRelations/JuvenileDomesticRelationsProgramsServices.aspx.

Izaskun E. Larrañeta, The Day, Curfew only one tool against teen violence, January 1, 2011, http://www.theday.com/apps/pbcs.dll/article?AID=/20110101/NWS01/301019957/1070/BIZ03&template=printart.

Mark Eades, O.C. Register, Curfew sweep nets dozens of teens, November 19, 2010 http://www.ocregister.com/articles/kids-276782-parents-orange.html?pic=1.

Pat Curtis, Crime & Courts, Politics & Government, Police say parental involvement key to stopping gang activity, June 25, 2010, http://www.radioiowa.com/author.pcurtis.

CBS6 Albany, http://www.cbs6albany.com/news/konev-1279222-police-avenue.html.

WDEF TV12 Chattanooga, An Inside Look at the New Youth Prevention Center, March 31, 2011, http://wdef.com/news/an_inside_look_at_the_new_youth_prevention_center/03/2011.

78- Get At-Risk Kids into Outdoor Adventure, Exploration

http://www.planetexplore.com/partner_view.php?p=354 F.

79- Create Robust Summer Activities, Jobs for At-Risk Kids

Times Free Press, http://www.timesfreepress.com/news/2007/jun/18/Summer-youth-programs-unite/.

Holland Sentinel, http://www.hollandsentinel.com/news/x711739153/Boredom-factor-in-gang-involvement.

Las Vegas Metropolitan Police Department Website, www.lvmpd.com.

Elizabeth Zavala, Star-Telegram, Track results, shaping strategy as needs and issues shift. Summertime gang-related shootings dropped 50%, July 22, 2010, http://www.star-telegram.com/2010/07/22/2355641/arlington-gang-related-shooting.html.

80- Insist On a Planned Budget for Gang Prevention Strategy

Dana Arquilla, digtriad.com, Rockingham County Fights Back Gang Activity, July 14, 2010, http://www.digtriad.com/news/local/story.aspx?storyid=145204&catid=57.

Rob Carson, The News Tribune, Tour Hits Hot Spots for Tacoma Gang Crime, Philanthropy board of young people aims to halt violence, http://www.thenewstribune.com/2011/01/09/v-printerfriendly/1494901/tour-hits-hot-spots-for-gang-crime.html.

81- Nurture Growth of Neighborhood Crime Watch Programs

National Crime Prevention Council, Strategy-Starting Neighborhood Watch groups.http://www.ncpc.org/topics/preparedness/strategies/strategy-starting-neighborhood-watch-groups.

National Crime Prevention Council, Strategies, http://www.ncpc.org/topics/preparedness/strategies.

National Town Watch, http://www.nationaltownwatch.org/.

82- Set Up Family Days and Neighborhood Nights

www.seattle.gov/neighborhoods/education/.../FAQs.pdf.

Atlanticville, http://atlanticville.gmnews.com/news/2010-08-12/Front_Page/Pallone_bill_aims_to_curtail_gang_violence.html.

83- *Explain the Situation in Detail to Your Citizens*

Novato City Website, August 24, 2010, http://www.ci.novato.ca.us/.

84- Quit Imprisoning Nonviolent Offenders

http://www.restorativejustice.org/editions/2006/april06/gormallyarticle.

Molly Loughman, The Concord Journal, August 18, 2010.

Communities for Restorative Justice website, http://www.c4rj.com/index.php.

85- Work Closely with Neighboring Jurisdictions

Brandon Darnell, Sacramento Press, Attorney General addresses gang problem in Sacramento, April 19, 2011, http://www.sacramentopress.com/headline/49371/Attorney_General_addresses_gang_problem.

California Cities Gang Prevention Network, http://www.*CCGPN*.org/.

KTVU.com and *Bay City News*, OPD Hosts Summit to Fight Gang Violence, August 24, 2010, http://www.foxreno.com/news/24751333/detail.html.

FBI New York Field Office, http://www.fbi.gov/newyork/press-releases/2011/manhattan-u.s.-attorney-charges-members-of-newburgh-latin-kings-with-murder-and-racketeering-in-second-coordinated-multi-agency-law enforcement-strike.

Sunita Vijayan, The Californian, Five arrests part of *CalGRIP* state grant, August 14, 2010, http://www.thecalifornian.com.

86- Know At-Risk Kids by Name

City of Minneapolis, http://www.ci.minneapolis.mn.us/dhfs/yv.asp.

Valerie MacDonald, Ontario Northumberland Today, January 19, 2011, http://www.northumberlandtoday.com/ArticleDisplay.aspx?e=2935960.

Bernews (Bermuda Multimedia News), http://bernews.com/2010/12/ex-commissioner-on-gang-violence/.

87- Promote Your Initiatives Using Websites and Social Media

KREM 2 News, Police hope anti-gang website cracks down on crime. June 30, 2011 http://www.nwcn.com/home/?fId=124798209&fPath=/news/local&fDomain=10222.

Santa Monica Daily Press, http://www.smdp.com/Articles-c-2010-12-28-71007.113116-City-Hall-launches-youth-violence-prevention-website.html.

http://yakimacounty.saynotogangs.com/default.aspx.

Elaine Pittman, Government Technology, Solutions for State and Local Government http://govtech.com/public-safety/Houston-Website-Solicits-Anonymous 1/1/2011.

http://archive.constantcontact.com/fs077/1103540043517/archive/1104322333836.html.

Jackie Valley, Las Vegas Sun, New iPhone app aimed at getting help to troubled teens, November 22, 2010, http://www.lasvegassun.com/staff/jacquelyn-valley/.

88- Expand the Role of Police with *Community Policing*

U.S. Conference of Mayors' Best Practices of Community Policing 2006, http://www.usmayors.org/bestpractices/community_policing_2006/gangbp_2006.pdfMayor's.

89- Deploy Prosecutors in the Neighborhoods with *Community Prosecution*

http://www.courtinnovation.org/index.cfm?fuseaction=page.viewPage&pageID=510&documentTopicID=26.

http://www.suite101.com/content/creating-a-community-prosecution-program-a145128.

U.S. Department of Justice, Office of Justice Programs, Bureau of Justice Assistance, http://www.ncjrs.gov/pdffiles1/bja/192826.pdf.

Office of the Albany County District Attorney, http://www.albanycountyda.com/issues/comm_pros.html.

Philly.com, http://www.philly.com/dailynews/local/20101027_District_attorney_to_launch_community-prosecution_program.html.

90- Call for Injunctions Against Specific Gangs

http://zennie2005.blogspot.com/2010/12/john-russo-on-oakland-gang-injunction.html, December 15, 2010.

Ali Winston, Crosscurrents from KALW News, Oakland City Council votes to continue injunctions with limits, May 18, 2011, http://informant.kalwnews.org/2011/05/oakland-city-council-votes-to-continue-injunctions-with-limits/.

Visalia Times-Delta, Gang suppression had results in 2010, http://www.visaliatimesdelta.com/article/20101229/OPINION/12290.

Oakland Local, Oakland Public Safety Committee hearing becomes 'polarized', February 23, 2011, http://oaklandlocal.com/article/oakland-public-safety-committee-hearing-becomes-polarized-analysis.

Oakland Local, http://oaklandlocal.com/article/oakland-public-safety-committee-hearing-becomes-polarized-analysis.

91- Don't Let Gangs Take Over Your Shopping Mall

Patty Rhule, USA Weekend Magazine, She fought the mall, and the mall... compromised, http://159.54.226.237/97_issues/970504/970504teen_mall.

Opinionbug.com, http://www.opinionbug.com/2643/huge-gang-fight-closes-triangle-town-center-mall-in-raleigh.

Natalie Hayes, http://www.pioneerlocal.com/niles/news/3090962,niles-golfmill-030311-s1.article.

92- Check your State Gang Statutes –Prosecute Gang Recruitment

Tony Marrero, Tampabay.com, Two Spring Hill teens face burglary charges in gang recruiting, Wednesday, December 29, 2010, http://www.tampabay.com/news/publicsafety/crime/two-spring-hill-teens-face-burglary-charges-in-gang-recruiting/1142346.

Mike Carlie, Ph.D., Into the Abyss: A Personal Journey into the World of Street Gangs, http://people.missouristate.edu/MichaelCarlie/what_I_learned_about/legislation_2.htm.

93- Cultural Targeting of Parenting Classes Creates Support Groups

Atlanta: Centers for Disease Control and Prevention, National Center for Injury Prevention and Control, 2002.

TN Thornton, CA Craft, LL Dahlberg, BS Lynch, K. Baer, Best Practices of Youth Violence Prevention: A Sourcebook for Community Action (Rev.). Young children (10 years and under).

94- Consider the Judicial Innovation of Community Courts

Aubrey Fox, A Tale of Three Cities: Drugs, Courts and Community Justice-The Bureau of Justice Assistance and the Center for Court Innovation, http://www.ojp.usdoj.gov/BJA/pdf/CCI_Tale_3_Cities.pdf.

95- Attack Poverty's Impact on Young People with a Youth Enrichment Zone

Harlem Children's Zone website, http://www.hcz.org/home.

Cape Fear Community College News and Events http://cfcc.edu/blogs/news/2011/01/04/ppd-establishes-blue-ribbon-commission-scholarship-fund-at-cfcc.

96- Share, Communicate, Cooperate with Regional Gang Summits

250 News Monday, November 01, 2010 www.opinion250.com/blog/author/13/3/250+news. http://www.streetgangs.com/news/082310_law_enforcement_oakland_gang_summit.

97- Make Bold House Calls

Renat Kuenzi, swissinfo.ch (Adapted from German by Susan Vogel-Misicka) http://www.swissinfo.ch/eng/swiss_news/Youth_violence_becomes_a_table_topic_in_Zurich.html?cid=30417592.

98- Confront Gangs with a Trained Ministers Ride-along Campaign

National Criminal Justice Reference Service, http://www.ncjrs.gov/App/publications/Abstract.aspx?id=132214. http://www.chron.com/disp/story.mpl/metropolitan/5207949.html.

99- Walking School Bus Creates Safer Neighborhoods

Christchurch City Council, What is a walking school bus? http://www.ccc.govt.nz/cityleisure/gettingaround/saferroutestoschool/walkingschoolbus.aspx.

Dr. Angela Wolf, Jack Calhoun, Livier Gutierrez, David White, California Cities Gang Prevention Network Bulletin http://www.CCGPN.org/Publications/CA%20Cities%20Bulletin%2021.pdf.

100- Honor the Heroes - Create Peace Prize for Interventionists

Jerry Soifer, The Press-Enterprise, Moreno Valley: Man honored for work quelling gang violence, http://www.pe.com/localnews/morenovalley/stories/PE_News_Local_W_waquil20.270329f.html.

http://www.panzouproject.org/home.

Bibliography

Arthur, M. W., J. D. Hawkins, J. A. Pollard, R. F. Catalano, A. J. Baglioni, Jr. (2002), "Measuring Risk and Protective Factors for Substance Use, Delinquency, and Other Adolescent Problem Behaviors. The Communities That Care Survey," Evaluation Review, 26(6):575-601.

Bonderman, Judith. (2001). Working with Victims of Gun Violence. Washington, D.C.: U.S. Department of Justice, Office for Victims of Crime.

Braga, Anthony A., Kennedy, David M., Piehl, Anne M. (2001). Reducing Gun Violence: The Boston Gun Project's Operation Reducing Gun Violence, The Boston Gun Project's Operation CeaseFire, Developing and Implementing Operation CeaseFire, David M. Kennedy Anthony A. Braga Anne M. Piehl, Measuring the Impact of Operation CeaseFire, Anthony A. Braga, David M. Kennedy ,Anne M. Piehl, Elin J. Waring, September 2001 NCJ 188741.

Cahill, Meagan and Hayeslip, David, Findings From the Evaluation of OJJDP's Gang Reduction Program by Highlights U.S. Department of Justice, Office of Justice Programs, Office of Juvenile Justice and Delinquency Prevention, December 2010.

California Cities Gang Prevention Network, December 2009, Angela Wolf, Senior Researcher, National Council on Crime and Delinquency (NCCD), Hunter Smith, Research Associate, NCCD, Linh Vuong, Research Associate, NCCD, Vanessa Hisert, Administrative Assistant, NCCD, and Jack Calhoun, President, HopeMatters, Consultant, National League of Cities.

California Cities Gang Prevention Network, October 2009 white paper "Developing a Successful Street Outreach Program: Recommendations and Lessons Learned."

The California Cities Gang Prevention Network Strategy Paper "Implementing a Citywide Gang Violence Reduction Strategy, Three Promising Examples.

Catalano, R. F., J. D. Hawkins (1996), "The Social Development Model: A Theory of Antisocial Behavior." In J. D. Hawkins (ed.), Delinquency and Crime: Current Theories (pp. 149-197), New York: Cambridge University Press.

Clute, Sylvia, Beyond Vengeance, Beyond Duality — A Call for a Compassionate Revolution ISBN: 9781571746337 Book (Paperback) Hampton Roads Publishing Company.

Comprehensive Gang Model, A Guide to Assessing Your Community's Youth Gang Problem 2009, http://www.nationalgangcenter.gov/Content/Documents/Assessment-Guide/Assessment-Guide. pdf).

Flores, J. Robert, Best Practices to Address Community Gang Problems, OJJDP (2007).

Fox, Aubrey, Director of Special Projects Center for Court Innovation, A Tale of Three Cities: Drugs, Courts and Community Justice — The Bureau of Justice Assistance and the Center for Court Innovation have released this new publication that outlines how community courts in three locations — Brooklyn, the Bronx, and Orange County, Calif. — are combining elements of *Drug Courts* and community courts to respond to the needs of defendants and their communities.

Guo, J., J. D. Hawkins, K. G. Hill, R. D. Abbott (2001), "Childhood and Adolescent Predictors of Alcohol Abuse and Dependence in Young Adulthood," Journal of Studies on Alcohol, 62(6):754-762.

Harvard Civil Rights Project, Confronting the Graduation Rate Crisis in California. (2005)

Hawkins, J.D., Catalano, R.F., Miller, J.F. Risk and Protective Factors for alcohol and other drug problems in adolescence and early adulthood: Implications for substance abuse prevention. Psychological Bulletin 12 64-105, 1992.

Hawkins, J. D., R. F. Catalano, et al. (1992), Communities That Care, San Francisco: Jossey-Bass.

Hawkins, J. D., M. L. Van Horn, M. W. Arthur (2004), "Community Variation in Risk and Protective Factors and Substance Use Outcomes," Prevention Science, 5(4):213-220.

Houston, Charles Hamilton, No More Children Left Behind Bars: A Briefing on Youth Gang Violence and Juvenile Crime Prevention, Institute for Race and Justice, Harvard Law School, March 6, 2008.

Howell, James C., Juvenile Justice Bulletin, Gang Prevention: An Overview of Research and Programs, Highlights, December 2010 http://www.ojp.usdoj.gov/BJA/pdf/CCI_Tale_3_Cities.pdf. December 2010 Jeff Slowikowski, Acting Administrator Office of Juvenile Justice and Delinquency Prevention, http://www. ojjdp.gov.

Howell, J. C. (2003), Preventing and Reducing Juvenile Delinquency: A Comprehensive Framework, Thousand Oaks, California: Sage Publications.

Howell, J. C., A. Egley, Jr. (2005), "Moving Risk Factors Into Developmental Theories of Gang Membership," Youth Violence and Juvenile Justice: An Interdisciplinary Journal, 3(4):334-354.

Kegler, M. C., R. F. Oman, S. K. Vesely, K. R. McLeroy, C. B. Aspy, S. Rodine, L. Marshall (2005), "Relationships Among Youth Assets and Neighborhood and Community Resources," Health Education and Behavior, 32(3):380-397.

Kirby, L. D., M. W. Fraser (1997), "Risk and Resilience in Childhood." In M. W. Fraser (ed.), Risk and Resilience in Childhood (pp. 10-33), Washington, DC: National Association of Social Workers.

Mills, James. The Underground Empire: Where Crime and Governments Embrace. Garden City NY: Doubleday, 1986. 1165 pages.

National Institute of Justice (February 2005). Research Report: Reducing Gun Violence - Operation in Los Angeles, http://www.ncjrs.gov/pdffiles1/nij/192378.pdf.

National League of Cities toolkit, "Preventing Gang Violence and Building Communities Where Young People Thrive," is now available to municipal leaders and their community partners. Published by NLC's Institute for Youth, Education, and Families (YEF Institute), the toolkit draws upon lessons learned over the past three years from the California Cities Gang Prevention Network. The YEF Institute formed this 13-city network in 2007 in collaboration with the National Council on Crime and Delinquency, and with support from the California Endowment, California Wellness Foundation, Evelyn and Walter Haas Jr. Fund, Richmond Children's Fund and East Bay Community Foundation, to identify strategies for reducing gang violence and victimization.

Policing Gangs and Youth Violence, ed. Scott H. Decker, Belmont, CA: Wadsworth-Thomson Learning, 2003: 102–130.

Reducing Gun Violence: Results from an Intervention in East Los Angeles, by George Tita, K. Jack Riley, Greg Ridgeway, Clifford Grammich, Allan Abrahamse, and Peter W. Greenwood, Santa Monica, CA: RAND Corporation, 2003.

Province of Manitoba, Canada, Street Gang Awareness for Families and Communities, Third Edition, website:www.gov.mb.ca/justice/safe/gangproof/index.html resource line: 1-800-691-4264945-4264 (Winnipeg) Project Gang-Proof is the family handbook.

Stouthamer-Loeber, M., R. Loeber, E. Wei, D. P. Farrington, P. H. Wikstrom (2002), "Risk and Promotive Effects in the Explanation of Persistent Serious Delinquency in Boys," Journal of Consulting and Clinical Psychology, 70(1):111-123.

Stouthamer-Loeber, M., E. Wei, R. Loeber, A. S. Masten (2004), "Desistance From Persistent Serious Delinquency in the Transition to Adulthood," Development and Psychopathology, 16:897-918.

Tita, George, Riley, Jack and Greenwood, Peter "From Boston to Boyle Heights: The Process and Prospects of a 'Pulling Levers' Strategy in a Los Angeles Barrio,".

Thornton TN, Craft CA, Dahlberg LL, Lynch BS, Baer K. Best Practices of Youth Violence Prevention: A Sourcebook for Community Action (Rev.). Young children (10 years and under).

Urban Institute Justice Policy Center, Families Left Behind: The Hidden Costs of Incarceration and Re-entry, rev. 2005.

U.S. Department of Justice – Office of Justice Programs – Bureau of Justice Assistance http://www.ncjrs.gov/pdffiles1/bja/192826.pdf.

Virginia Governor Bob McDonnell Executive Order Number Twenty Eight (2010) The Commonwealth's Gang and Violent Crime Executive Committee Governor's office, Richmond, VA.

Deep Research

A number of federal repositories offer further information about current delinquency prevention programs that may help.

- National League of Cities, to download toolkit on preventing gang violence, visit www.nlc.org/iyef.

- FindYouthInfo.gov is the U.S. government website that helps you create, maintain, and strengthen effective youth programs. Included are youth facts, funding information, and tools to help you assess community assets, generate maps of local and federal resources, search for evidence-based youth programs, and keep up-to-date on the latest, youth-related news. Learn more about FindYouthInfo.gov.

- The Office of Juvenile Justice and Delinquency Prevention's Youth Gang Strategic Planning Tool: www.nationalgangcenter.gov/SPT.

- The Office of Juvenile Justice and Delinquency Prevention's Model Programs Guide: www2.dsgonline.com/mpg.

- Blueprints for Violence Prevention: www.colorado.edu/cspv/index.html.

- The National Registry of Evidence-Based Programs and Practices: http://nrepp.samhsa.gov.

- The Exemplary and Promising Safe, Disciplined and Drug-Free Schools Programs: www2.ed.gov/admins/lead/safety/exemplary01/index.html.

- The What Works Clearinghouse (on educational interventions, some of which address youth violence and substance abuse prevention): http://ies.ed.gov/ncee/wwc.

Source: Federal Repositories of Research-Based Delinquency Prevention Programs Juvenile Justice Bulletin 12

"We are passionate about prevention, intervention, enforcement and re-entry strategies. We are passionate about measurement. And even more passionate about helping children."

The National Center for the Prevention of Community Violence

Newport News, VA * San Jose, CA

Our Mission is to create new pathways for communities to react with passion to the wave of youth violence sweeping America and Canada, and to share what we have learned with every community we can engage in the crisis.

NCPCV principals bring over a hundred years of practitioner expertise in working in law enforcement, public affairs and Strategic planning. Our clients include cities, counties, state governments, progressive business leaders, civic groups, elected officials – all with an eye on sound business practices and inspiring community-wide action.

Our principals have been honored with the top award in the nation for crime prevention (International Association of Chiefs of Police 2008) and top international awards for public affairs (Public Relations Society of America, Silver Anvil for Public Affairs — 2010).

We are committed to helping communities make good decisions in responding to the crisis of gangs and youth violence, available to you to help create positive change by shaping your resources to build sustained capacity for success.

The National Center for the Prevention of Community Violence located in Eastern Virginia is a nonprofit 501c(3) organization that conducts research, training, and evaluation on violence prevention efforts around the United States. This organization offers project management and evaluation services with a goal of directing best practice resources toward tangible results.

A big part of our Mission is to help communities establish a Strategic Plan, and provide appropriate resources to deal with this crisis. And then spread the news about what measurable tactics that are working.

We welcome your inquiries regarding helping your community reduce youth violence and gangs. Send us an email at rjkandassociates@cox.net and let us know how we can help.

National Center for the Prevention of Community Violence

East Coast: PO Box 11083 Newport News, VA, 23601 757-327-0711

West Coast: 6580 Gardenoak Court, San Jose, CA 95120

About the Authors

Bobby Kipper is founder of the National Center for the Prevention of Community Violence. He is a battle-hardened ex-cop with a quarter century of *Community Policing* in one of America's toughest gang environments. Kipper organized one of the most effective crime prevention program ever developed by the Justice Department. He has consulted for the White House, for Congress, for governors and for communities across the nation.

Bobby is a national consultant, having assisted communities in twenty states with developing effective strategies for dealing with youth violence. He resides in coastal North Carolina and eastern Virginia. Bobby can be reached at rjkandassociates@cox.net.

Bud Ramey is the 2010 Public Affairs Silver Anvil Award winner of the Public Relations Society of America — the highest public affairs recognition in the world. Bud is a freelance public affairs consultant and author. His work in the areas of public policy, education, the electoral process, health care, fund raising and community development stretches over three decades. Bud resides in eastern Virginia and can be reached at budramey4@gmail.com.

Tom Emswiller is an amazingly versatile public affairs consultant and writer, having developed some of America's most effective public relations and advertising for over thirty years for national agencies in New York, Denver and California. On commission from the community of Newport News, VA, he immersed himself in San Jose, CA's gang prevention efforts for months, extracting the art and science beneath that City's laudable successes.

No COLORS Volume Two Is Underway –

Don't Let Us Leave Your Community's Progress Out!

If we have failed to include a great program your community has implemented, we can make up for that oversight in our *No COLORS* subsequent editions.

You can email your comments and your program results to us with our deep appreciation. While we cannot guarantee inclusion, we can promise we will review it carefully and thoughtfully, with an emphasis on measurements and programs with the right stuff.

We will be honored if you could email us at budramey4@gmail.com.

Send Copies of *No COLORS* to Your Colleagues

Take advantage of our discount for ten copies or more
Credit card orders are securely welcomed on our website.
Kindly visit http://www.solveviolence.com/

Order by mail with check or money order

BILLING ADDRESS

Your name _____

Organization _____

Address_____

Address Line 2 _____

City _____

State_____ Zip _____

Email _____

Telephone_____

SHIP TO:

BILLING ADDRESS

SHIPPING ADDRESS

Name _____

Organization _____

Address_____

Address Line 2 _____

City _____

State_____ Zip _____

10 copies of No COLORS or more @ $15.00 per copy _____copies x $15.00 = $ _____

Shipping (add $2.50 per book) $ _____

Virginia Residents add 5% sales tax $ _____

Check Enclosed $ _____

Send to: NCPCV PO Box 11083 Newport News, VA, 23601

Credit card orders are securely welcomed on our website.

Kindly visit http://www.solveviolence.com/

Questions? Please call us at 757-327-0711

SINGLE COPY ORDER

No COLORS $19.95

Shipping $ 6.00

Virginia Residents add 5% sales tax   ($1.25)

Total Enclosed   **$_____**

BUY A SHARE OF THE FUTURE IN YOUR COMMUNITY

These certificates make great holiday, graduation and birthday gifts that can be personalized with the recipient's name. The cost of one S.H.A.R.E. or one square foot is $54.17. The personalized certificate is suitable for framing and will state the number of shares purchased and the amount of each share, as well as the recipient's name. The home that you participate in "building" will last for many years and will continue to grow in value.

THIS CERTIFIES THAT

YOUR NAME HERE

HAS INVESTED IN A HOME FOR A DESERVING FAMILY

1985-2010

TWENTY-FIVE YEARS OF BUILDING FUTURES
IN OUR COMMUNITY ONE HOME AT A TIME

1200 SQUARE FOOT HOUSE @ $65,000 = $54.17 PER SQUARE FOOT
This certificate represents a tax deductible donation. It has no cash value.

Here is a sample SHARE certificate:

YES, I WOULD LIKE TO HELP!

I support the work that Habitat for Humanity does and I want to be part of the excitement! As a donor, I will receive periodic updates on your construction activities but, more importantly, I know my gift will help a family in our community realize the dream of homeownership. **I would like to SHARE in your efforts against substandard housing in my community!** *(Please print below)*

PLEASE SEND ME _____ SHARES at $54.17 EACH = $ $_____

In Honor Of: _____

Occasion: (Circle One)   *HOLIDAY*   *BIRTHDAY*   *ANNIVERSARY*

       OTHER: _____

Address of Recipient: _____

Gift From: _____ *Donor Address:* _____

Donor Email: _____

I AM ENCLOSING A CHECK FOR $ $_____ PAYABLE TO HABITAT FOR HUMANITY <u>OR</u> PLEASE CHARGE MY VISA OR MASTERCARD *(CIRCLE ONE)*

Card Number _____ Expiration Date: _____

Name as it appears on Credit Card _____ Charge Amount $ _____

Signature _____

Billing Address _____

Telephone # Day _____ Eve _____

PLEASE NOTE: Your contribution is tax-deductible to the fullest extent allowed by law.
Habitat for Humanity • P.O. Box 1443 • Newport News, VA 23601 • 757-596-5553
www.HelpHabitatforHumanity.org

CPSIA information can be obtained at www.ICGtesting.com
Printed in the USA
LVOW031736211111

255809LV00002B/1/P